THE AARP CRASH COURSE IN
FINDING THE WORK YOU LOVE

THE ESSENTIAL GUIDE TO REINVENTING YOUR LIFE

BY SAMUEL GREENGARD

AARP STERLING

New York / London
www.sterlingpublishing.com

To my mother, Marcia —S.G.

AARP Books publishes a wide range of titles on health, personal finance, lifestyle, and other subjects that promise to enrich the lives of older Americans. For more information, go to www.aarp.org/books. For information on changing careers, go to recareering-guide.com.

AARP, established in 1958, is a nonprofit organization with more than 39 million members age 50 and older.

The AARP name and logo are registered trademarks of AARP, used under license to Sterling Publishing Co., Inc.

The recommendations and opinions expressed herein are those of the author and do not necessarily reflect the views of AARP.

STERLING and the distinctive Sterling logo are registered trademarks of Sterling Publishing Co., Inc.

10 9 8 7 6 5 4 3 2 1

Published by Sterling Publishing Co., Inc.
387 Park Avenue South, New York, NY 10016
Distributed in Canada by Sterling Publishing
c/o Canadian Manda Group, 165 Dufferin Street
Toronto, Ontario, Canada M6K 3H6
Distributed in the United Kingdom by GMC Distribution Services
Castle Place, 166 High Street, Lewes, East Sussex, England BN7 1XU
Distributed in Australia by Capricorn Link (Australia) Pty. Ltd.
P.O. Box 704, Windsor, NSW 2756, Australia

Sterling ISBN 978-1-4027-5240-7

For information about custom editions, special sales, premium and corporate purchases, please contact Sterling Special Sales Department at 800-805-5489 or specialsales@sterlingpublishing.com.

CONTENTS

◆◆

◆◆◆

◆◆◆◆

SECTION IV:
PUTTING YOUR PLAN INTO ACTION

FOREWORD

ASK A CHILD what she wants to be when she grows up and you're likely to get an earful: anything and everything from doctor to toy maker, astronaut to veterinarian. That's because kids—and the parents, teachers, and family members who raise them—promote the concept of dreaming and exploring. Thankfully, these youthful minds haven't yet encountered the immobilizing gravity of "I can't do that!" or "What would my friends think?" There are no mental boundaries or limitations, only possibilities.

Fast-forward a couple of decades, and most of us find ourselves plowing through a heaping dose of reality. We need to support our families and ourselves. We want to show our parents, siblings, and friends that we are faring well. And we would dearly love to plan for a retirement period that becomes more elusive with each passing decade.

Having worked so hard to get where we are, making any sort of departure from that spot—even if it's to pursue our dreams—looms as a scary and uncertain proposition.

Not until middle age do many of us gain the perspective and wisdom needed to recognize, amid all that noise, the signals to which we are truly attuned. The professional path we "selected" (or were shunted into) at age

25, we realize, now differs radically from the one we would choose from scratch at 50. At this stage of life, however, with the clock inexorably ticking, achieving life goals and leaving a legacy assume a new sense of urgency.

Fortunately, it's also at this point that we're finally able to dream like children—while putting a lifetime of knowledge and experience to work. We're finally ready to reinvent ourselves. And we're in a position to enjoy the fruits of that redefinition more than at any other time in our past.

To be sure, summoning the courage and resources to change careers (or to embark on a new path in an existing career) demands fortitude, patience, and poise. Along the way, we may question our own thinking and desires. We may harbor misgivings about our ability to go back to school, learn new skills, and venture into an entirely new field. Worse yet, others may "encourage" us in the doubt department.

It may help to view such qualms as the occupational hazards of reinventing one's life. Faced with the enormity—and novelty—of switching careers, it's tempting to second-guess yourself: "Why am I tossing so much away? My education and training, my professional stature and hard-won salary, my office with a door—goodbye to all that?"

In actuality, the opportunity to recharge one's batteries can be a special gift. We're able to grow and put our talents to work. If we're fortunate, we can make a tangible impact on the world.

Finding the work you love needn't be an abstract undertaking. Whether you're 40 or 60—whether you've toiled in the trenches of bureaucracy or blazed an entrepreneurial trail—it's best to obey the recareering urge when it strikes. Growth, after all, is the one sure antidote to stagnation.

A first foray into career change. I feel fortunate to have learned this lesson relatively early in my life. In junior high school, a talented teacher named Mrs. Lewis helped bring my imagination to the surface in her creative-writing class. As I began churning out short stories, I discovered that I genuinely enjoyed the magic of putting thoughts into words, then arranging them in patterns that communicated messages. It was a special act that guided me through some difficult emotional times. I enjoyed writing for the pureness of doing something I truly loved. You may have experienced the same sensation sewing, cooking, or building model airplanes.

During high school and college, I worked part-time at an amusement park in Southern California. I started out as a busboy in the mid-1970s, earning less than $2 per hour. Over the next six years I steadily climbed the company ladder, working successively as a cashier, food preparer, cook, supervisor, restaurant manager, and finally area manager. In the end, I oversaw five restaurants with more than 100 employees and close to $5 million in annual revenues.

Not surprisingly, the business world beckoned.

So, after graduating from college in 1979, I accepted an offer to manage a restaurant. A year later, weary of the long hours, high turnover, and constant headaches, I landed a management position at one of the Baby Bells. I bought the compulsory suits, learned the ropes of the business, and found myself pulling down $80,000 a year. My parents told me how proud they were. My friends congratulated me on my success. I felt—and acted—as though I had arrived.

But a funny thing happened on the way to the golden handcuffs: I began waking up nights in a cold sweat. I had recurring nightmares of being confined in a space so small I couldn't even stand up and I could barely breathe. I quickly realized that my unconscious mind was trying to tell me something, namely this: The highly structured corporate world was boxing me in and killing my creative spirit.

So I walked. In 1981 I quit the "dream" job, collected what little severance was coming my way, and went home to figure out my next direction in life. All I knew was that I had to find work I could feel passionate about—something that would bring a sense of happiness and meaning to my life. Money was less important than salvaging my soul.

My father—a Depression-era baby—was sure I had lost my mind. For once there was generational solidarity between him and my friends: Most of them shared his view. I got tired of telling people what I had done, because the majority shook their heads in disbelief: How could a rational person toss away such a lucrative opportunity?

The dream that spurred me to explore new fields was a 180-degree turnabout from the claustrophobic nightmare that had prompted me to abandon telcom: I wanted to reconnect with my passion and become a professional writer. Never mind that neither a regular paycheck nor a pension was part of the deal. Disregard the fact that any future job security was out of the question. I was naïve enough to take a chance and give it a whirl. So I designed and embarked upon my own program of self-study, attending writers' conferences, proposing article ideas to magazine editors, and working diligently to polish my prose. Through it all, I approached my work with a sense of wide-eyed enthusiasm.

Within two years I was earning a solid income, and since that time I have never looked back. Today, ironically, I probably have more job security than most denizens of the corporate world. Most important, I'm doing something that makes me feel good and leaves a positive mark on the world. Even on my worst days, I wouldn't trade my work for any alternative.

Times change, of course, and so do industries. Over the years I've reinvented myself on several occasions—sometimes by choice, other times of necessity. A couple of years ago, for example, I decided to make the transition from writing magazine articles to authoring books. The title you hold in your hands thus constitutes something of a coming-out party for me—an exciting new phase in my life that's enabling me to grow personally and professionally.

Sometimes I have to remind myself to keep doors open, to take risks. So should you. Career change beckons because it permits us to experience new and worthwhile things. Done right, it creates a renewed sense of purpose—a feeling that we're doing something valuable, not only for ourselves but for others as well. We all have special talents that are unlike anyone else's. When we line up the tumblers and the lock finally springs opens, we gain entree to an inspirational space. We step into a world that's both familiar and alien, challenging yet rewarding.

The landscape ahead. As you turn the pages of this book, you will encounter inspirational stories as well as nuts-and-bolts information. You will learn how to use career counselors and therapists; understand your personality traits and how they manifest themselves in your recareering style; research career options and volunteer opportunities; make community-to-community comparisons; harness conventional and online job-search and networking tools; polish your résumé and interviewing skills; devise a financial plan; and sidestep potential pitfalls. You will hear from those who have taken the leap, confronted various challenges in mid-flight, and landed happily—though in a few cases resignedly—in new careers.

Switching careers at any age is a challenge, yet older workers typically have more to overcome than their younger counterparts. They must master new trends and technologies. They must cope with ground-shaking lifestyle changes, such as the likelihood of a lower income or the reality of "parachuting" into an unfamiliar social circle. They must confront—and learn how to evade or vanquish—the very real peril of age discrimination. And, finally, they must accept the basic truth that landing a rewarding position will never be a panacea for life's problems.

For all that, the destination justifies the journey. If you're a member of a generation that reinvented society, it's the next logical step in the progression to reinvent yourself as well. This crash course can help you do just that by deconstructing the career-change process and helping you build a workable plan. For those willing to pursue their dream, the possibilities for regeneration and renewal are practically limitless.

—SAMUEL GREENGARD

◆

SECTION I
MAKING SENSE OF TODAY'S WORKING WORLD

1

A New Attitude

The search for more fulfilling work often follows pathways to a more meaningful life

A BOARD GAME MAY SEEM FAR REMOVED from the vagaries of life—unless that board game happens to be called *Life*. Almost every child in America has played Milton Bradley's famous game at one time or another—and virtually every parent and grandparent has gotten into the act as well. One thing that makes the game so compelling is the inexhaustible opportunity it offers—the chance to choose a path through life and see where it leads. You can attend college and become a doctor or accountant. You can choose to work as a salesperson, an artist, a police officer, a teacher, an entertainer. You can become an athlete or a computer consultant.

Somewhere between giving the spinner a whirl to see how many spaces you advance and turning over tiles and cards to determine your paycheck and expenses, there are the predictable milestones of life: getting married, buying a house, having kids, buying a larger house, and eventually retiring. (There's even a midlife crisis: Land on this space and you must trade in your current career for a new one.) In the end, the winner of the game retires to Millionaire Estates to enjoy his or her fortune.

Best of all, if you don't do well in *Life*, you simply play another game. If only course corrections were that simple in real life! In reality, if you've invested a couple of hundred thousand dollars to attend medical school and become a physician, you are a physician. If you've spent two years at technical school to learn computer repair, you are a computer-repair specialist. For most of us, changing course means tossing away the time, money, and effort that went into earning the degree—or the years spent mastering the job.

Beyond being impractical, it's frightening to ponder a career change. There is no guarantee of success, there are substantial financial and practical risks, and most of us define our lives by our colleagues, associates, and friends. We spend time with them at dinner parties, going to baseball games, shopping, playing sports. Opting for a new job—let alone a brand-new career—can mean leaving friends and a satisfying social life behind. It's not something you decide to do on a whim.

Or is it? When Milton Bradley invented the original version of *Life* in 1860, it was out of ingenuity, yes, but also out of necessity. Bradley, a lithographer whose claim to fame was a portrait of a clean-shaven Abraham Lincoln, found sales lagging—and his wallet sagging—after the nation's 16th President unexpectedly grew a beard. So Bradley sat down and devised *The Checkered Game of Life*—the predecessor of today's version. The career-oriented variation on classic checkers sold a whopping 45,000 copies by the end of the first year and grew into a perennial favorite. Bradley, who also invented the paper cutter, was set for, well, life.

Bradley probably didn't view his move as a career tactic. It was equal doses adventure, good business sense, and a powerful will to succeed. The irony, of course, is that things aren't much different in the game of *Life* than they are in its real-world analogue. The money spent and the time passed cannot be retrieved. For the wise, life is about periodically reinventing ourselves—by choice or by circumstance—to reflect our evolving thinking and our changing physical condition. What sparked our professional passion at 20 or 30 may not light our fires at 50 or 60.

Bradley recognized this fact throughout his life. Although *The Checkered*

Game of Life and its subsequent iterations made him a wealthy man, board games were something of a trivial pursuit for Bradley. He spent most of his later years promoting and funding scientific and educational causes, including the idea that children should be taught as children— a then-revolutionary concept known as kindergarten. Bradley also published two magazines, *Kindergarten News* and *Work and Play*. These remained his No. 1 interest until he died in 1911.

Understanding the New Order

For a generation that redefined society with social protests and sexual experimentation, recareering may represent the final frontier of personal reinvention. Yes, a few brave souls have historically changed career paths in midlife. After selling paper cups and milk-shake machines for more than a decade, Ray Kroc started McDonald's at age 53. Anna Mary Robertson Moses, better known as Grandma Moses, began painting in her 70s when arthritis crippled her embroidery career. Her works are now deemed folk art; those not hanging in major museums sell for tens of thousands of dollars. And Ronald Reagan and Arnold Schwarzenegger both jumped from acting to politics later in life.

But what was once only a trickle has lately become a torrent. Some in-dividuals, faced with downsizings, outsourcings, offshorings, "rightsizings," or other thinly disguised dismissals, find themselves forced to adapt to a new job or career. Others who might prefer to retire feel squeezed by eco-nomic realities, such as the impossibility of stretching a fixed income to cover soaring health-care costs. Still others seek a more subtle change— perhaps a lateral move within their present organization, or a similar posi-tion but with greater growth opportunities at another company.

In short, the number of people reinventing themselves at age 45 and beyond is growing into nothing less than a tidal surge. They may return to college (or enter it for the first time) to earn a new degree; they may invest their savings in something they have always dreamed of—growing coffee in Kona, perhaps, or becoming a primary school teacher; or they may join a social-service organization out of a deep-rooted desire to give back to society and add significance to their lives.

The reasons for changing careers—mapped out in this book—are as varied as each individual's personality. The common thread is that achieving happiness and success requires a tremendous amount of thinking, planning, and action. Recareering may represent a fresh start, but it does not automatically deliver a new beginning. Those who leap impulsively from one career to another may find themselves in a new profession, but with the same set of personal problems. Without a thorough self-analysis, they may exchange their pipe wrench for a camera but find their lives still out of focus. They may wake up one morning and ask: *Why did I ever switch? What could I have been thinking?*

Career-Change Checklist

Switching from one career to another doesn't happen overnight. Success revolves around preparation, planning, and constant adjustment and adaptation. Use these guidelines to keep your career moving forward at all times:

Know what you want. What ignites you on a cold winter morning? Take time to think through what makes you happy and what gives you satisfaction. Ponder your attitudes and values. To focus your thinking and sharpen your approach, I strongly suggest you consider using a career counselor. A good place to start your search is the National Career Development Association: www.ncda.org; 866-367-6232.

Maintain high career standards and expectations. The idea of working only for money and neglecting happiness is a surefire ticket to boredom, poor performance, and cynicism. Expect— better yet, demand—the most from yourself and your career: You will find yourself achieving more and complaining less.

Confront your fears. Venturing beyond your comfort zone requires ongoing effort. Yes, it's possible that you might fail in a new position or career. Your family might think you're insane. But if you've stayed true to your interests and aptitudes, and you've communicated with those near and dear, your biggest fear is likely to be a simple dread of the unknown.

Take smart risks. For many, avoiding risk means clinging to the status quo. Yet risk avoidance can sometimes equate to greater risk. Stagnation and predictability often lead to underperformance and low achievement—a cycle that creates genuinely forlorn people. Calculated risk, by contrast, can pay big dividends. What if Henry Ford or Bill Gates had not bothered to pursue their dreams?

Stay focused. Transforming a dream into reality is hard work. It requires planning, adjusting to changing conditions, and dealing with setbacks. A career transition is not easy. It may require overcoming financial and emotional hurdles. But if you're committed to making it work and you can furnish yourself with the skills to succeed (see next guideline), the odds are in your favor.

Upgrade your skills. In today's knowledge-based economy, yesterday's red-hot job is tomorrow's pink slip. Those looking to recareer must therefore commit to learn new skills and gain new knowledge. It's crucial to keep up with the latest literature, attend courses and workshops, and return to school for specific courses or an advanced degree.

Understand trade-offs. There's an upside and downside to almost everything. A new career may offer new opportunities and challenges. It may ignite a spark—a raging inferno, perhaps—of emotions that have lain dormant for years. Yet the same situation may entail financial problems, an unfamiliar social circle, perhaps even marital strife. What's more, a new career is no panacea: It won't transform the life of someone who is fundamentally unhappy.

On the other hand, a well-conceived plan—which I hope this book will help you devise and implement—ups the odds of discovering your true purpose. New life challenges can yield rewards beyond anything you may have imagined. Not surprisingly, this newfound passion often ripples outward, improving interpersonal relationships and boosting health, energy, and creativity. Indeed, when it serves as the springboard to the creation of new products or services, or to the solution of a social problem, the right career change can even make the world a better place.

What Is Recareering?

Don't go looking for a dictionary definition of recareering. Although the word is now widely used in magazine articles and career workshops, Wikipedia, Dictionary.com, Merriam-Webster, and other guardians of the English language have not yet included the word in their databases or reference books. Nevertheless, it isn't difficult to figure out that the term relates to a person shifting gears from one career to another. What's less clear is whether a person who changes jobs at the same company and takes on different duties is recareering. Or, say, someone who stays in the same field but tackles an entirely different set of challenges.

This book embraces a broad definition of recareering as *a deliberate transition to a new position with entirely different responsibilities*. An architect who takes courses in management and is then promoted to project manager is changing careers—even if he works at the same company. So is a nurse who becomes a hospital administrator—even if the process occurred with no premeditated planning. A graphic designer who leaves a company to become a Web designer is also recareering. (If that designer were promoted to head her department but kept the same basic duties as before, she would simply be handling a larger aspect of the same job.)

Despite recareering's somewhat amorphous nature, the goal of the undertaking is unmistakable: to find greater clarity in your work, and thereby in your life. Changing careers may be as simple as meeting someone at a networking event who follows up with a job offer: One day you're a marketing specialist, the next you're a venture capitalist. Or it can be as complex as spending weeks in career counseling, going back to school, earning a degree, and passing an exam: One year you're an electrician, the next you're a Certified Financial Planner®.

Recareering therefore knows only the bounds we impose on ourselves.

Find Your Work Style

Stereotyping boomers: big mistake! Even though the news, film, and music industries are fond of painting the boomer generation with broad brushstrokes, a mind-bending level of diversity—and diverse thinking—pervades this demographic group. Statistics cannot tell each individual's story. Michael Smyer, Director of the Center on Aging & Work/Workplace Flexibility at Boston College, puts it this way: "What do Dolly Parton, George Bush, and Carlos Santana have in common?" The answer: "They're all boomers." You get the point.

When AARP examined why workers 45 and older stay in the labor force, it found four key motivations:

Sustainers. These individuals, who constitute the largest segment (36 percent) of the 45+ workforce, say they "work to live." The majority, approximately 70 percent, enjoy working, while 91 percent report that money is a major factor in their decision to work. Noneconomic factors—enjoyment, personal fulfillment, personal connections—drive Sustainers' thinking less than that of the three other groups.

Providers. It's not unusual for this group to balance multiple caregiver roles while holding down demanding jobs. Providers—usually in their 40s and 50s—often find themselves sandwiched between raising children and caring for their parents. Most view time as a premium. As a result, many of these individuals are in search of greater work-life balance. Working is generally important to their self-esteem because it allows them to fulfill their roles as providers and caregivers. Men and Hispanics are more likely to belong to this group. One-quarter (25 percent) of 50+ workers fall into the Provider category.

Connectors. Stability is an important consideration for this group, which spends more years with a single employer and is more likely to stay there until full retirement. Connectors, as the name implies, are likely to enjoy the social aspects of work. Many forge strong relationships with co-workers. In general, they prefer a collegial atmosphere. However, this group also values health and retirement benefits, which often accrue after long years of dedicated service. Connectors are the smallest group of older workers at 16 percent.

Contributors. The "live to work" philosophy is a core part of this group's identity. More educated and affluent—many work in executive or professional jobs—Contributors are likely to be deeply engaged in their work (and genuinely satisfied by it as well). Feeling useful and making a contribution to society eclipses this group's desire for money, perhaps because many of its members have already lived long and prospered. Contributors often include retirees who reenter the workforce after experiencing isolation in retirement. They plan to postpone full retirement as long as possible. Contributors make up 22 percent of the 45+ workforce.

The common theme among boomers is a desire to finish out their careers in different roles and on different terms than those that defined the first half of their lives. The AARP survey that uncovered the existence of these four groups also established that more than one-third of respondents plan to work on a part-time basis "for interest and enjoyment." Nine out of 10 hope to learn something new, while three-quarters want to pursue something they have always wanted to do. Many are willing to take "bridge jobs"—short-term employment that pays the bills and helps them transition from a past career to a future one. They are likewise amenable to testing out other, as-yet-unidentified strategies that promise to create greater job flexibility.

Longer Lives = Richer Careers

A primary factor driving mid- and late-life recareering is longer life spans. For most of history, changing jobs in middle age or working into older age just wasn't possible. At the beginning of the 20th century, the average American man lived to the age of 48. The average woman made it to 51. Contrast this to 2004, when expectancies had soared to 76 and 81, respectively. But as people live longer, they need more money. Four out of five older workers anticipate working beyond age 65. What's more, says the Center on Aging & Work at Boston College, only 10 percent of boomers anticipate a traditional retirement.

Boomers are motivated to work for personal reasons beyond earning money: identity, social status, social connections, remaining active and healthy, and experiencing a sense of accomplishment. A 2005 Harris Interactive survey found that 59 percent of older workers (defined as 55+) agreed or strongly agreed that "A good deal of my pride comes from my work and career." Among 35- to 54-year-olds, that figure was 48 percent, but among 18- to 34-year-olds it was only 37 percent.

It's also clear that boomers view aging through a skewed, if not flawed, lens. When polling firm Yankelovich Partners asked members of the 76 million–strong Baby Boom Generation to define when old age begins, the average response *exceeded* the life expectancy of the average American by three years! Such optimism—perhaps "foolhardiness" is the more apt term—is leading boomers down a path of lifelong work. Combined with advances in health care and potential gains in genomics (the science of understanding genetics and human DNA in order to create new treatments and medicines), many individuals believe they will work well into their 90s.

The Workforce Redefined

The concept is not so far-fetched. In November 2007, *Inc.* magazine ran a story entitled "Forget Bingo! 80 Is the New 30." It highlighted 106-year-old Jack Weil, who runs Rockmount Ranch Wear, a clothing company based in Denver, Colorado. It also featured Bob Galvin, the 85-year-old former CEO for Motorola, who now heads two venture-capital firms, and 84-year-old Phyllis Apple, CEO of the Apple Organization, a public-relations firm in North Miami Beach, Florida.

Major corporations are starting to get the message. Drugstore chain CVS, with 6,200 stores across the United States, began recruiting older workers in the early 1990s—partially to stave off labor shortages, partially to mirror the demographics of its clientele. Since then, CVS has watched its workforce gray—and its strategy pay. The chain deploys its older workers as managers in pharmacies, greeting-card departments, and warehouses. As of 2007, it employed 19,507 people in their 50s, 8,266 in their 60s, 2,140 in their 70s, 244 in their 80s, and 6 in their 90s. At the time, the company's workforce totaled 173,283, making 50+ workers nearly one-fifth of its labor complement (most retailers fall below 10 percent)—and more than double the percentage 10 years before. In the future, says Steven Wing, a senior executive at CVS, "I fully expect to see people in their 100s holding down a job. It's only a matter of time."

For CVS, hiring older workers is about both dollars and sense. Although older workers face certain unique challenges, the chain has found that they often require less training—particularly in areas such as customer service and prioritizing tasks. What's more, they don't miss work for dates, dances, or other social events. Their absenteeism rate is lower. And when they are at work, they're better able to stay on task.

Karen Tuttle can relate to the concept. In 1999, she retired after more than 30 years of teaching first through fourth grade. The Springfield, Ohio resident was dismayed by recent developments in the classroom—government-mandated standardized testing, highly structured curricula, inflexible teaching plans—so a retirement package had its attractions. She worked as a substitute teacher for a time, but wearied of that as well.

After only three weeks of traditional retirement, however, Tuttle grew

Generations at Work

Today's workplace spans four generations, each with its own approach and characteristics. Here's a brief overview of these groups (keep in mind that you may vary from these general characteristics and attitudes):

Traditionalists (*Born before 1946*): This group is known for its dedication and willingness to sacrifice. There's a strong undercurrent of conformity, along with deep respect for rules and authority. Traditionalists put work before pleasure and approach their jobs with discipline and fortitude.

Baby boomers (*1946–1964*): Personal gratification, a live-to-work attitude, and devoting long hours to the job in order to advance are hallmarks of boomers, some 76 million strong. This outsize generational cohort also tends to be team-oriented and displays an optimistic outlook toward work and life.

Generation X (*1965–1980*): Gen Xers are self-reliant, skeptical, and view work as a necessity they must endure to support their lifestyles. Heavily focused on results rather than processes, they adapt easily to changing conditions.

Generation Y (*1981–1995*): This group, also referred to as Millennials or Echo Boomers, challenges authority and demands work-life balance. Gen Yers have a disproportionately large need to feel valued. The cohort is comfortable using technology and working in teams.

restless. She began to weigh other career options. "The one thing I knew," she reflects, "is that I wanted to do something completely different." For a year and a half, Tuttle worked as a salesperson at an antiques mall. Then, still looking for a stable career that would allow her to learn new things and stay socially and mentally engaged, she applied at a local CVS store.

The drugstore chain hired the 56-year-old Tuttle as a pharmacy technician, a 40-hour-a-week job that she has now held since May 2003. Tuttle finds the work enjoyable and stimulating. She and her husband aren't desperate for the income she earns from the job. Instead, says Tuttle, "It's a way to stay mentally and physically active. Staying at home is not for me. Right now, I can see myself working for another 20 years, at least."

For boomers, embracing a new career may simply be the latest new adventure. That game-board goal of retiring to Millionaire Estates is steadily being eclipsed by a more balanced approach to work—and to life.

Stepping Back
to Move Forward
Achieving a greater sense of purpose in your life needn't be an abstraction. When Barbara Moses, president of BBM Human Resource Consultants Inc., steps into a company and asks, "Does your work make you happy?," 70 percent of managers and professionals typically say "No" or "Not particularly." The reasons vary—some hate their boss or clash with their co-workers, others feel overworked or lack the flexibility they desire—but the most common problem is a mismatch in values. The unavoidable result? A lack of fulfillment. Workers have not been given the opportunity to display their unique talents.

Too many individuals remain in a job or career they don't particularly like, Moses says. They may not be certain what they really want; they may see money and happiness as mutually exclusive; they may fear making a change; they may lack skills or education; or they may simply be tolerating an uninspiring position. Fear of making a change leaves many individuals coping with big frustrations: overdemanding bosses, underperforming colleagues, and irrational or unrealistic customers.

Not only does a new career represent a fresh start, it offers a greater sense of purpose—precisely what 57 percent of Americans ages 50 to 70 say they want in a job, according to the 2005 MetLife Foundation/Civic Ventures New Face of Work Survey. Half of the survey respondents desired jobs that contribute to the greater good of society—not just in retirement, but in the here and now. This suggests that today's older workers are unwilling to wait for a retirement that may be 10 to 20 years off. Instead, they want to put a positive spin on their productive years. In many cases, they hope to leave a legacy.

Rita Bennett knows all about stepping out of a comfort zone. For six years, she and her husband, Martin, ran a successful intercultural training business, helping multinational companies prepare workers for the rigors of overseas assignments. After selling the company in 1996, Bennett continued to run the business for another five years—before opting to retire. At age 59, she envisioned a life of leisure—visiting family and friends, gardening, traveling to exotic locales.

But a funny thing happened on the way to Social Security: Within a year, Bennett began to feel a calling. "I couldn't rest at night knowing that I had a lot of energy and vitality left and wasn't putting it to good use," she explains. "I still had something to contribute to society."

So at age 60, Rita Bennett embarked on a new career.

Bennett went to work for CARE USA, a nonprofit humanitarian outreach organization that battles global poverty. She served as director of development for CARE for two years, then returned to the corporate arena as an executive at a consulting firm that helps companies mobilize and train workers. "Moving from the private sector to a not-for-profit was a difficult transition," Bennett recalls. "Not-for-profit organizations move at a different speed than the private sector, so it felt like I was being held back." Now she's weighing returning to school for an MBA.

"There's something else I want to do and *need* to do," Bennett explains. "I don't know what it is yet, but I'm hoping to do something that makes a profound difference. It's important to leverage my past experience, do something I enjoy, and continue to make a contribution. I'm not ready to throw in the towel. I can't conceive of retiring anytime soon. I was put on Earth for a purpose, and sitting on the beach isn't it."

Whatever she does next—whether it's working for a company or independent consulting—Bennett believes it will revolve around corporate social responsibility. "I'm probably a year away from making my next move," Bennett explains. But already she has begun pressuring her current employer, Aperian Global, to embrace a more socially conscious business approach.

A New Mindset
Takes Hold
That our thinking and values change over time is a given—and it is one that continues to intrigue Boston College's Michael Smyer. Over the past half-century or so, Smyer notes, individuals followed a fairly predictable career trajectory: They received an education early in life, worked through midlife and into early old age, then pursued a leisure-filled retirement. This scenario unfolded in an orderly fashion, as did other rites of passage such as getting married, having children, and buying a house.

In the last two decades, however, it's as if someone rearranged the cards in the deck. Increasingly, life events occur in an almost random order, according to however the deck is shuffled. Some people marry and have children in their 50s. Others go back to school and earn a degree. Still others approach career issues as if they were twentysomethings out to conquer the world. Today, a majority of older workers in the United States retire incrementally rather than abruptly, gradually working their way toward retirement in a series of what Smyer refers to as "stages" or "bridge jobs." In many cases, they're working less than full-time. Sociologists and demographers have dubbed this trend a "redistribution of work" across the human life span.

The implications are profound. The notion of a single career is steadily disappearing. Some individuals are partaking in two, three, even six careers during their lifetime. This approach, sometimes termed "serial careering," means that one person may become a doctor at age 30 and a teacher at age 50, whereas another follows just the opposite path. Still another person may "retire" from a corporate position as a manager of information technology at age 62 precisely in order to start her own consulting firm. The rules and mores that once guided society—or that once restricted it, some might say—are rapidly fading.

Myths Be Damned!

A few scant decades ago, the idea of someone working into older age seemed downright frightening. However, growing evidence suggests that changing careers and remaining active in the workforce pays dividends both physical and mental. Social ties, intellectual engagement, and moderate physical activity can help ward off disease and other health problems. They can also keep a person enthusiastic about life. Those who don't work are more prone to depression and boredom—and a spate of

---

Key Questions

What is my motivation for working at this stage of my life? For many, there's an ongoing need to earn money. For others, there's an overarching desire to give back to society. Whatever your reason for working—and changing careers—be honest with yourself up front. It can save headaches and heartaches later on.

What will I do in my later years? Mandatory retirement is on the brink of extinction. As people live longer, healthier lives, they will want to stay productive and engage in meaningful activities. It's never too early to think about how you will live into your 70s, 80s, 90s, and beyond.

Am I prepared for coming social changes regarding work and old age? Once upon a time, lives and careers followed a predictable path that led to a gold watch at age 65. Today you are likely to retire incrementally—through a series of career changes or new jobs. It's important to understand work options as well as the growing demand for older workers.

physical ailments, too. They are also less likely to see themselves as productive members of society.

Statistics bear this out. A study conducted at Cornell University from 1994 through 1999 found that married men aged 50 to 74 who had retired—and whose wives were still working—displayed a higher level of marital stress than did newly retired men whose wives did not work. Those who had retired but returned to work reported the highest morale and the lowest rates of depression. Among women, entering retirement posed a risk of depression, especially if their husbands were still working.

Another study—this one in the *British Medical Journal* in 2005—found that U.S. workers who retired early at 55 and who were still alive at 65 had a significantly higher mortality than those who retired at 65. Mortality was also significantly higher for individuals in the first 10 years after retirement at 55 compared with those who continued working during that decade. By remaining active and engaged, it appears, it's often possible to sidestep the anxiety and depression that can lead to a premature death.

Part of the problem is that society clings to outmoded notions of what it means to be an older worker. Many believe that workers in their 50s, 60s, or 70s lack the physical stamina to keep up; that they're woefully out of touch with technology, business practices, or social trends; or that they're looking for work only on a short-term basis. In reality, older workers offer many advantages: Lower absenteeism. Higher productivity. An increased willingness to upgrade skills through training and formal education. Better social skills. Deep reservoirs of experience and knowledge.

What's more, according to consulting firm Towers Perrin, organizations that replace an experienced worker of any age may find themselves forced to shell out 50 percent or more of the displaced worker's annual salary in turnover-related costs. Jobs requiring specialized skills, advanced training, extensive experience, and layered knowledge—qualities typically possessed by workers above age 50—push costs up even higher. In other words, smart employers understand that older workers make good business sense.

Books

The Age Advantage: Making the Most of Your Mid-life Career Transition, by Jean Erickson Walker, Berkley Trade, 2000. Sorts through the myriad issues that factor into a midlife career change.

One Person / Multiple Careers: A New Model for Work / Life Success, by Marci Alboher, Business Plus, 2007. The profiles in this collection focus on finding more meaningful work and a more satisfying life.

Portfolio Life: The New Path to Work, Purpose, and Passion After 50, by David Corbett with Richard Higgins, Jossey-Bass, 2007. A look at how longer life expectancies and changing attitudes are altering our perception of work.

Thinking About Tomorrow: Reinventing Yourself at Midlife, by Susan Crandall, Wellness Central, 2007. Guides readers through the process of ongoing growth and change.

What Should I Do with My Life? The True Story of People Who Answered the Ultimate Question, by Po Bronson, Ballantine Books, 2005. Offers compelling insights into the minds of people who have reexamined their life—and their life's work.

More Resources

AARP
In the Middle: A Report on Multi-cultural Boomers Coping with Family and Aging Issues
http://aarp.org/inthemiddle

Looks at boomers' emerging role as caregivers for both parents and children, and how this affects their family, work, and career decisions.

Staying Ahead of the Curve: The AARP Work and Career Study
http://research.aarp.org/econ/multiwork.html

Examines demographic trends and changes in attitude and behavior among boomers and other older workers.

Center on Aging & Work
http://agingandwork.bc.edu/template_index

This leading research center, located at Boston College, offers news, research, facts, statistics, and more.

Change Rangers
www.changerangers.com/

This site offers news, information, and insights into various factors affecting career longevity. It includes archives dating back to 2004.

**Harvard School of Public Health–
MetLife Foundation
Reinventing Aging: Baby Boomers
and Civic Engagement**
www.hsph.harvard.edu/chc/
reinventingaging/read_report.html

This report looks at how boomers
are redefining aging, work, and
other life activities.

**National Academy
on an Aging Society**
www.agingsociety.org/agingsociety/
links/links_older%20workers.htm

You can peruse a wide range of articles and information on topics ranging from management attitudes to
retirement trends, from boomer
work values to the opportunities
and challenges of working later
in life.

NAVIGATING THE WORLD OF WORK

How today's rapidly evolving work environment affects boomers and other older workers

THROUGHOUT MUCH OF THE 20TH CENTURY, the typical career trajectory followed a fairly predictable path. High school and college graduates entered the working world and punched the clock to the tune of 40 or 50 hours each week. They marched in and out of an office or factory 50 weeks per annum for close to 45 years. Those who were fortunate climbed the career ladder, followed the rainbow, and reached retirement—traditionally at age 65—with a gold watch and a comfortable pension. The hubbub of the workplace then faded into quiet afternoons knitting or playing golf.

Retirement was the American dream. In his 1949 book, *How to Retire—and Enjoy It*, author Ray Giles sketched out the sort of attitude and approach he saw as key to ensuring a golden retirement: Individuals should focus on hobbies, avocations, and developing their untapped talents, Giles suggested. With the right planning, a lifetime worker should be able to retire before age 65—even in his or her 50s. As for the boredom that was apt to ensue, Giles warned, people would have to work that out on their own.

Fast-forward half a century, and it's safe to say that the world and the workplace have changed dramatically. For the typical boomer, the notion

Set Your Sites on Making a Change

Here are a few independent career websites that can help you understand today's labor environment and find out which qualities employers are seeking in workers:

CareerJournal.com www.careerjournal.com

The Wall Street Journal's "Executive Career Site" provides in-depth articles and news about current work and business trends. It also features career-management tools, job-hunting advice, and salary and hiring information.

Forbes magazine www.forbes.com

Although the focus is on business, there's plenty of career information, financial-planning advice, details about business opportunities, and special reports that retirees, near-retirees, and career shifters can use to their advantage. The magazine's "Best Places for Retirees" offers detailed information about desirable places for boomers and others to live.

Money magazine http://money.cnn.com/magazines/moneymag/bestjobs/2007

The "Best Jobs" site offers a mélange of stories and resources on finding dream jobs and adjusting to work after 50. There are also career strategies and an assortment of tools and resources.

Society for Human Resource Management www.shrm.org

Although this organization caters to HR directors and others within companies (a membership costs $160 annually), it's also a valuable resource for "civilians," with news, articles, and knowledge bases about current workforce trends.

Workforce Management magazine www.workforce.com

The award-winning magazine provides a mix of news, stories, and directories that cover all aspects of the workplace and workforce. Much of the content is free; you may need to register for archived articles or reports.

of sitting around the house waiting for the clock to strike midnight is beyond fathoming. Indeed, the very concept of work—how it defines lives, how it molds relationships—has undergone a radical transformation. No longer is it unusual for individuals to change careers several times during their lives, periodically sailing into uncharted waters in search of new challenges and opportunities.

According to a 2005 study conducted by Merrill Lynch, 76 percent of boomers intend to "retire" but keep right on working and earning—most of them after launching a new career. Driving the change for some is burnout from an existing job or the desire to tackle new challenges. For others, it's about connecting to longtime interests or a lifelong passion. Still others have change thrust upon them: They are fired or downsized, or they get out while the getting's good by accepting a buyout package. That doesn't mean they're ready to hang around the house or head out to pasture. They're willing to confront potential age discrimination and, in many instances, turn their expertise into an advantage.

What all these people share is a desire to rethink their options. Civic Ventures president Marc Freedman, whose San Francisco think tank addresses issues of social service and aging, snaps the concept into focus: "Many people in their 50s want to make a difference and feel as though they're not just passing through life," says the author of *Prime Time: How Baby Boomers Will Revolutionize Retirement and Transform America*. "They want to put the productive years they have remaining to good use."

This evolution has not occurred by accident. Boomers—whose sheer numbers have guaranteed their outsize role in society—are now colliding with an array of demographic, financial, and practical forces. As Thomas Friedman observed in his landmark book, *The World Is Flat*, the Internet and modern communications have flattened the world, creating global competition for labor—notably highly skilled labor. Meanwhile, many countries, among them the United States, have watched their economies grow as their labor pools have shrunk.

Now add to all this the startling reality that many boomers *must* work: The erosion of defined-benefit pensions, compounded by unrelenting consumerism, has depressed savings rates to record lows. (Fortunately, older individuals are healthier and more engaged than ever before, and many of them are able to work well into their 70s and 80s.) At the same time, organizations are grappling with an exodus of people and knowledge as older workers retire and others start their own businesses. As a result, they have had to reexamine their attitudes, approaches, and overall thinking.

Simply put, as society's values change, employers are being pulled along. In the words of Tamara Erickson, co-author of *Workforce Crisis: How to Beat the Coming Shortage of Skills and Talent*, "Only now are people waking up to the fact that business as usual isn't good enough. They're beginning to understand that they must make changes. We're approaching an entirely different workplace and work environment."

Retirement
Redefined
As early as World War II, a few progressive thinkers had begun to question the notion of pushing older workers out the door at an arbitrary age. In 1946, Louise Fitch—a social researcher and former dean of women at Cornell University—argued that older workers should be encouraged to continue leading productive lives independent of pensions. "You are happy and well occupied in your work," she lamented, "and then one day the calendar says you have a birthday and must retire."

Although job-hopping has always existed to some degree—and middle age has always been a time of angst and change—there's no question that society's outlook about work has undergone a remarkable transformation. In the late 1980s—by which time layoffs, downsizings, and "rightsizings" had become unpleasant facts of working life—early-retirement programs grew commonplace. Often they were transparent ploys to purge higher-paid, older workers. In some cases, companies trimmed their workforce with no advance notice and no post-pink slip benefits.

America's Fastest-Growing Occupations

As boomers age, the demand for many jobs and careers—particularly in the healthcare and personal-services arena—will skyrocket.

RANK	OCCUPATION	2006 EMPLOYMENT	2016 EMPLOYMENT	PERCENT CHANGE	EARNINGS	TRAINING & EDUCATION REQUIRED
1	Network systems and data communications analysts	261,800	401,600	53%	More than $43,600	Bachelor's degree
2	Personal and home care aides	767,300	1,155,800	51%	Less than $20,180	Short-term on-the-job training
3	Home health aides	787,300	1,170,900	49%	Less than $20,180	Short-term on-the-job training
4	Computer software engineers, applications	506,800	732,500	45%	More than $43,600	Bachelor's degree
5	Veterinary technologists and technicians	71,200	100,400	41%	$20,190 - $28,570	Associate degree
6	Personal financial advisors	176,200	248,400	41%	More than $43,600	Bachelor's degree
7	Makeup artists, theatrical and performance	2,100	3,000	40%	$28,580 - $43,590	Post-secondary vocational award
8	Medical assistants	416,900	564,600	35%	$20,190 - $28,570	Moderate-term on-the-job training
9	Veterinarians	62,200	84,000	35%	More than $43,600	First professional degree
10	Substance abuse and behavioral disorder counselors	83,300	112,000	34%	$28,580 - $43,590	Bachelor's degree

Source: CareerOnestop (www.careerinfonet.org)

These cost-cutting measures may have cheered shareholders, but they left the workers themselves feeling vulnerable and betrayed. Those who wound up in the unemployment line—particularly employees who had served a single employer for 10, 20, or 30 years—realized their loyalty had gotten them precisely nowhere. The workplace survivors they left behind, meanwhile, couldn't help wondering when their own numbers would come up.

Today, global competition is an unavoidable reality. Information and capital both flow across international boundaries with the force of a tsunami, washing away jobs and depositing them on distant shores. Companies construct elaborate alliances, only to see them disintegrate in the blink of an eye. Today's leading-edge business concept is tomorrow's dusty

Boost Your KQ

KQ stands for "Knowledge Quotient," a key factor in becoming a hot prospect these days. Here's what you can do to maximize your own KQ:

Go back to school and earn another degree. In addition to bolstering your résumé and ramping up your recareering effort, a deeper education will better prepare you to enter the field of your choice.

Take job-targeted classes at a university extension program, community college, or private organization. Try to earn certifications that show you've achieved a certain level of knowledge.

Attend seminars, workshops, and conferences. Even if you can't shoehorn these into a résumé, they'll make you more knowledgeable and better prepared for job interviews and future work.

Create a regular reading list. This should include magazines, trade publications, and online sites. Use services such as Google Alerts (www.google.com/alerts) and Yahoo! Alerts (http://help.yahoo.com/l/us/yahoo/alerts/) to have word of relevant articles sent directly to your e-mail inbox. At Google Alerts, for instance, you type in your search terms, then designate what content you want the service to search (news, blogs, video, Web, Groups, or all) and how often you wish to receive an alert. Any time Google finds content matching your criteria, you'll automatically receive an e-mail notice.

Network with colleagues and spend time "talking shop." Consider using social networking services such as LinkedIn, Facebook, and others. (See Chapter 11 for more information about these services.)

Attend training courses your employer offers. Although it's often difficult to break away from day-to-day responsibilities, these sessions can equip you with the knowledge and skills to excel—at your present employer and a future one.

Negotiate tuition reimbursements before accepting a job. A substantial allowance can go a long way toward making learning affordable.

relic. For the vast majority of workers at the start of the 21st century, the notion of job security has gone the way of the Beta videotape. Individuals increasingly understand that they must manage their careers, enhance their skills and knowledge, and remain forever on the prowl for the next great opportunity.

Working for Life
Harleys and hippies, miniskirts and mantras; over the last half-century, boomers have left an indelible stamp on society. Approximately 76 million Americans were born from 1946 to 1964, and today that cohort accounts for 39 percent of the U.S. population over the age of 18. The sheer number of boomers, with their relative affluence, has altered the face of politics, religion, sports marketing, education,

entertainment . . . and work. They've shaped and molded society more than any generation before them.

That's not about to change. It's no coincidence that society views retirement utterly otherwise than it did only a generation ago. Today, many boomers plan to work until they simply no longer can. In 1985, only 18 percent of Americans aged 65 to 69 held a job. By 2006, that number had climbed to 30 percent. "Boomers view their work as a more integrated part of their life," observes Rick Beal, a consultant for Watson Wyatt Worldwide. "They hate being bored, and they're constantly looking for new ways to apply their experience and knowledge."

That may be so. But it's also true that Americans have a tough time cutting the cord from work. Joe Robinson, a work-life balance coach and author of *Work to Live*, says that Americans "create the self through their job." In a highly mobile society, where people change houses and friends with disarming alacrity, work becomes a constant identity—even if it's an artificial one.

The proof is in the numbers. In the United States, paid vacation days and holidays mandated by the government total precisely 0. By contrast, Denmark boasts 25 and 9, respectively, Germany 24 and 10, Australia 20 and 7, Spain 22 and 12, Canada 10 and 8, and Japan 10 and 0. Even at domestic companies that offer paid vacation time (the U.S. average is about 14 days), many workers skip all or part of their mandated days off, and when they do manage to avail themselves of a company-proffered respite, they typically stay connected via notebook computer, cell phone, or PDA. In 2006, 23 percent of U.S. workers reported checking their e-mail or voice mail on vacation. That was up from 16 percent the previous year.

Boomers in Demand
It's a good thing boomers are willing to redefine work and retirement. Dire predictions about future labor shortages may be overdone, some analysts say, casting doubt on the more extreme projections

that the United States will be short 35 million workers by 2030. Yet there's little question that a tighter job market is emerging—particularly in key areas such as healthcare, science, engineering, information technology, and systems programming and development. According to consulting firm Ernst & Young, just under 40 percent of employers cited their No. 1 concern as a shortage of talent over the next five years.

Ponder a few projections: The National Restaurant Association predicts a shortage of 1.5 million restaurant workers by 2014. The American Hospital Association reports that hospitals were short 118,000 registered nurses as of 2005. That's an 8.5 percent vacancy rate. By 2020, the supply of nurses in America will fall shy of the demand by more than one million.

Even those aspects of the infrastructure we take for granted are apt to suffer: Electric and water utilities are faced with the prospect of losing up to 60 percent of their top management and other key workers to retirement by 2010. The Ernst & Young survey reported that more than 6 out of 10 respondents believe retirements over the next five years will trigger a major brain drain in at least some business functions.

As the workforce ages, paradoxically, society grows more dependent on older workers. The U.S. Bureau of Labor Statistics reports that the workforce of 16- to 54-year-olds (excluding those in the military or in jail) will grow by a mere six million people from 2002 to 2012. The number of workers in the 55 and older bracket, by contrast, will expand by 18 million during that time. In late 2006 the number of workers 55 and older hit 24.6 million—the highest level ever recorded. Nearly one-quarter of them were 65 or older.

John A. Challenger, chief executive at Challenger, Gray & Christmas, a Chicago-based outplacement-consulting firm, believes this situation bodes well for older workers. "It has become increasingly apparent that the workplace can ill afford to lose these individuals. Fortunately, we have come to realize that an artificial retirement age, somewhere in the 60s, doesn't make sense for most people. There's a tremendous amount of

STILL FLYING HIGH

CURT MOORE, *from Air Force colonel to teacher*

I'M 81 YEARS OLD and still going strong. I've always found meaning in my work. I was in the Air Force for 21 years. During that period I spent time in Vietnam, Germany, and Japan. Later I spent four years teaching for the ROTC program at the University of Colorado. Then I worked at AARP, managing issues and problems for 32 million members. When I left there in 2006, I wasn't ready to retire—I can't sit around and play golf every day. Instead, I wanted to continue to do something meaningful with my life. So I applied as a substitute teacher in Calvert County, Maryland, and they accepted me. I attended an orientation and began teaching at age 79.

Since then I've worked with all age ranges, from kindergarten to high school. I get up at 5 a.m. and check to see if I have an assignment. If I do, I drive 8 to 35 minutes to reach the school where I'm teaching that day. Fortunately, I still feel like I'm in my 40s. I have a lot of energy and I rarely get ill. I walk the dog every day; I golf and swim; I go to parties and plays.

Working as a substitute teacher is enjoyable and fulfilling. I feel like I put all my life experiences to work. I don't find the experience the least bit intimidating—perhaps because of my past experience in the military. I've learned how to deal with a wide range of people, and I can usually defuse any situation. One time, for example, three boys from the wrestling team were making a lot of noise. I asked one of them what weight class he wrestled in, and when he answered I let him know that I had wrestled in high school too. We established a rapport, and I never had any problem again. I'm proud to say it's not very often that I have to have a school administrator remove a disruptive kid from the classroom.

As you can see, the job is more than teaching—sometimes it's counseling. Some of these kids come from disadvantaged households and don't get their needs met. Sometimes it's a matter of just listening to them.

Several friends and neighbors are teachers, so we have a lot in common. But I also make it a point to stay in touch with my friends from before, who have been very supportive. They say, "I don't know if I could do it, but I admire you for what you're doing." I hope I can keep doing this for a number of years.

knowledge and productivity left in older workers. Companies are beginning to recognize that they have to tap into this labor source or risk losing their competitive edge."

It's increasingly likely that those who continue working into older age will enjoy greater leverage over employment terms and working conditions. In fact, you could say that silver represents a gold mine: In many instances, boomers will be able to dictate how and when they work—and many will find themselves courted by organizations that once would have considered them over the hill. This new work order will bring greater career options and the ability to put skills, experience, and knowledge to use in ways unimaginable just a few years ago. Some individuals will recareer; others will reinvent themselves. Some will do both.

The concept hasn't escaped James Parch. The 67-year-old resident of Phoenix worked as an electrical engineer at Motorola for 32 years. Nearly a decade ago, he decided a major career change was in order. "It was work, work, work," he says. "The company's costs were fixed because engineers were salaried, so they got as much out of us as possible." Parch soured on 45-hour workweeks that included handling tasks on weekends. "Working extra hours and weekends determined whether you were going to get a promotion and a raise," he states.

Reassessing his career, Parch came to the realization that he wanted to be a nurse. It was a perfect opportunity to solve problems, work with people, and do something that matters. So he attended night school for six years while working full-time as an engineer, then took early retirement from Motorola and entered nursing school at Scottsdale Community College. After completing the four semesters required for an RN degree, he graduated in May 2000, passed the required nursing exams in July, and accepted a position the following January.

Since 2001, Parch has worked on staff and then on contract at two different facilities; he now works approximately 20 weeks each year and travels with his wife between stints. He puts in 12-hour days two days each week and takes the other three days off. "When I'm on contract, I'm working hard," he explains. "But when I'm between contracts, I can enjoy other activities. It's a great balance. I keep myself mentally and physically sharp without overextending myself."

His life is now more balanced and complete, Parch says, than at any time in the past. "I'm able to positively impact people's lives, I leave work at the end of the day and I'm done, and I'm able to call the shots about when I work and who I work for. I feel far more in control of my life than I ever did in the corporate world."

Where Gray Matters

Social philosopher and business guru Peter Drucker coined the term "knowledge worker" in his 1959 book, *Landmarks of Tomorrow*. Now, as the 21st century unfolds, information and knowledge are prized far above equipment and products. So rapid is the pace of change that a success story today is often but a footnote tomorrow. Consequently, employers must find ways to retain knowledge and expertise. And with the labor pool receding, the emphasis is increasingly on gray matter.

Although some companies have discovered that gray does indeed matter, other organizations continue to follow the path of least resistance, offering entry-level positions to highly qualified individuals or ignoring the problem altogether. In the view of David W. DeLong, author of *Lost Knowledge: Confronting the Threat of an Aging Workforce*, too many companies have cultures that "drive older workers out": At some point they no longer value their contributions, and this neglect marginalizes their expertise. Many also look askance at employees unwilling to put in 50+ hours a week or remain tethered to the job via mobile phone or PDA.

Age bias and discrimination are nothing new. Some firms, however—John Deere, Michelin North America, Vanguard, and BlueCross BlueShield, to name a few—are starting to understand that business as usual just won't cut it anymore. To attract and retain older workers, they are turning to more innovative approaches, notably special programs designed to attract and retain older talent. A 2005 AARP study found that 58 percent of HR managers consider it more difficult today than five years ago to locate qualified job applicants. And more than half of these managers believe their firms are likely to face a labor shortage within the next five years.

As the tipping point approaches and older workers gain leverage, companies will be forced to rethink the gamut of human resource activities:

 **Key Questions**

Do I understand how changing demographics are working to the advantage of older workers? A shrinking labor pool, a backlash against traditional retirement, and a growing shortage of skills and knowledge are moving boomers toward the center of the labor universe. Older individuals are living longer, more active lives, making them ideal candidates for work later in life.

What are my personal objectives and requirements? It's essential to distinguish between the desirable and the doable. Those in a position to retire may opt to step away from paid work and volunteer instead, either part-time or full-time. Others may find it best to juggle work and other activities. Still others may require an income or some of the intangibles—such as a social network— that stem from a job. If you have inventoried your objectives and your needs, you can make a smarter decision.

Is volunteerism part of the picture? According to the MetLife Foundation/Civic Ventures 2005 New Face of Work study, more and more boomers seek "work that is not only personally meaningful but that means something important in service to the wider community." Experiment with a few volunteer stints; you many find that these help you to both broaden and narrow your subsequent career decisions.

hiring, training, benefits, and retention policies. Enlightened organizations, rather than viewing older workers as the labor force of last resort, will find ways to weave them into the strategic fabric.

Take, for example, the Federal Bureau of Investigation (FBI). After 9/11, the agency recognized that it lacked the manpower to conduct a thorough worldwide investigation. Many of its most knowledgeable and experienced agents had retired. More than 40 percent of its workforce had less than five years' experience. Rather than wait out a recruiting drive—a process that could consume months or years—the agency appealed to retired agents to fill the void. What's more, the FBI hired the agents on a temporary basis in order not to disrupt their pension benefits. Although these agents do not carry weapons and aren't chasing down embezzlers, fraudsters, or terrorists in the field, they provide valuable expertise and acumen that managers can tap for investigations.

Other organizations also understand this value proposition. They are confronting the brain drain head on—and honing their competitive edge—through a more progressive approach. John Deere, honored as one of AARP's Best Employers for Workers Over 50, uses senior placement agencies, offers flexible work hours, sponsors learning and development programs geared to older workers, and makes available an array of other perks and benefits. Thirty-six percent of the company's employees are age 50+. The average on-the-job tenure of this cohort is 24.6 years. Such loyalty is rare in today's slash-and-burn corporate world.

Though there's no single formula for recareering success, it's wise to check out best-employer lists—as well as organizations with an expressed desire to hire older workers and tap their knowledge and experience. As demographics shift and demand grows for older workers, those who have prepared will be in a position to excel. The next chapter explores the mindset and attitudes likeliest to engender a successful career change.

Books

Leap!: What Will We Do with the Rest of Our Lives?, by Sara Davidson, Random House, 2007. The insights and interviews here focus on how older individuals can find work that expresses one's purpose, locate a community in which it's natural to age in place, and discover a spiritual path.

The Leisure Economy: How Changing Demographics, Economics, and Generational Attitudes Will Reshape Our Lives and Our Industries, by Linda Nazareth, Wiley, 2007. Examines economic changes in North America due to both the retirement of baby boomers and the attitudes of ascendant generations X and Y

The New American Workplace, by James O'Toole and Edward E. Lawler, Palgrave Macmillan, 2006. Discusses how globalization, technology, and other forces have shaped today's workplace and changed the outlook of individuals.

Prime Time: How Baby Boomers Will Revolutionize Retirement And Transform America, by Marc Freedman, PublicAffairs, 2002. Discusses how boomers will turn their golden years into an intense time of social activism, volunteerism, and lifelong learning.

The World Is Flat: A Brief History of the 21st Century, by Thomas Friedman. This bestseller looks at the myriad ways in which technology and globalization are changing work—and creating a global workplace.

More Resources

AARP
http://assets.aarp.org/rgcenter/econ/workers_fifty_plus.pdf

Examines the business case for workers 50+, dispelling stubborn myths about older members of society.

Administration on Aging
www.aoa.gov

This agency, part of the U.S. Department of Health and Human Services, serves as a clearinghouse for information about aging, including community-based care and caregiving.

Centers for Disease Control and Prevention
www.cdc.gov

The report entitled *The State of Aging and Health in America 2007* offers insights into work and life trends in the United States.

Ernst & Young
2007 Aging U.S. Workforce Survey: Challenges and Responses—An Ongoing Review
http://www.ey.com/global/content.
nsf/US/Human_Capital_-
_Aging_Workforce_Survey

This survey shows how Fortune 1000 HR executives view today's corporate attitudes about an aging workforce and emerging strategies for dealing with a potential "brain drain."

International Longevity Center-U.S.
http://www.ilcusa.org

Bills itself as "the first nonprofit, nonpartisan, international... organization formed to educate individuals on how to live longer and better, and advise society on how to maximize the benefits of today's age boom."

Merrill Lynch
www.ml.com/index.asp?id=7695_769
6_8149_46028_46503_46635

The New Retirement Survey examines and analyzes trends in both work and retirement.

North Carolina Center for Creative Retirement
www.unca.edu/ncccr/index.htm

UNC/Asheville serves as a clearinghouse for retirement-related information, events, and services. It also includes a college for seniors: the Center for Creative Retirement.

The Population Resource Center: The Aging of America
http://www.prcdc.org/300million/
The_Aging_of_America

Offers news, statistics, research, and insights into how older Americans are impacting work and life in the U.S. Also links to numerous other Web sites that provide information about aging.

TammyErickson.com
http://www.tammyerickson.com/

The consultant and author, a thought leader in workforce issues, offers news, information, and resources for those looking to understand today's workplace and navigate change. She also offers a widely read blog at: http://discussionleader.hbsp.com/erickson/

University of North Carolina Institute of Aging
www.aging.unc.edu/research/
index.html

Offers news, information, and reports on various aspects of aging and work.

U.S. National Institutes of Health - National Institute on Aging
http://www.nia.nih.gov

This federal government site links to new, events, publications, and other information relevant to older individuals.

3

ARE YOU READY TO CHANGE CAREERS?

*Understanding what it takes to make
the right decision and move forward*

EMBARKING ON A RECAREERING INITIATIVE is not for the faint of heart. It can entail difficult and potentially life-altering decisions that prompt an overhaul of your lifestyle or living standard. It can affect family members and friends. It can bring radically different hours and demands, including travel and social obligations.

What's more, a new career may generate a great deal of internal stress—particularly in the early going. Many older workers find they miss the seniority and respect they had built up at a previous job. They may suddenly have younger managers telling them what to do—and how to do it.

Those seeking to switch horses in midlife must confront a variety of other issues as well. For one, it's crucial to recognize that dissatisfaction may result from a bad job or a stressful work environment rather than the wrong career; in that case a lateral move, or a shift to job sharing or flex-time, might solve the problem. For another, a career change later in life may lead to financial problems. Taking a 10 percent cut in salary at age 30 is vastly different than taking a 50 percent cut at age 50. It's essential to face these issues up front and devise a plan to deal with them—by saving, downsizing, or adopting another strategy.

The question of whether to change careers frequently requires deep introspection and family discussion. For many, career counseling or therapy may enter the picture (both can provide a potent jumpstart). More than anything else, it's critical to explore your *motivation* for making a change—and understand what's likely to result from it. "There is a lot of fear and anxiety associated with making a career switch," explains Helen Harkness, president of Career Design Associates, a Texas counseling firm.

This chapter examines the tools, tactics, and mindset needed to embrace change and gain momentum in the search for a new and satisfying career. It also spotlights how age affects thinking, and identifies some of the common traps career switchers fall into while pursuing change. There are no easy answers, but one thing is clear: A glance inward goes a long way toward achieving success.

Motive: To See the Big Picture

Here's a key question every recareering candidate should ask: Am I running toward one thing or away from another? Although the distinction isn't always easy to draw, running away incorporates a desire to break free from inordinate pain, anxiety, or stress. The trigger may be an abusive boss, the sense that your current employer is exploitive or unfair, a feeling of boredom or burnout, or simply a mismatch between individual talent and organizational needs.

Sometimes dissatisfaction with a job results from *passion drift*. Let's say a nurse who excels in that role receives a promotion, then perhaps another. One day she wakes up to find she's no longer healing the sick—her original passion—but instead managing other nurse's schedules and drowning beneath piles of paperwork. Or a traffic engineer who always relished troubleshooting problems in the field wakes up to discover he is a desk jockey mired in project management.

Running *toward* something, by contrast, is all about striving to reach a defined goal—whether it's going back to school to earn a master's degree

Putting Career Matters into Perspective

You can't have a vision if you don't have a view. To snap things into focus if you're a career-change candidate, ask yourself the three questions explored below. These can help you get a handle on your career ambitions and develop a personal road map:

What do I hope to accomplish? Figure out why you are working (or why you *began* working) in a certain career in the first place—or why you're interested in a particular field. These reasons should transcend compensation. Do you feel a sense of satisfaction when you help others? Do you enjoy solving problems? Do you want to influence the social fabric or change a public policy? Leave a legacy? Or is it simply enough to have fun at work and enjoy the interaction with your co-workers?

What are my core attitudes and values? Each of us has internalized a unique set of values that shape how we feel about work and career issues. These typically center on traits such as independence, creativity, responsibility, security, and honesty.

Is there alignment between my living and my life? When our objectives and core values are out of sync with a job or career, we're likely to feel discouraged, disaffected, and perhaps even depressed. When the two accord, by contrast, we are able to raise our performance to a higher level and achieve a sense of satisfaction and fulfillment. It may be unreasonable to expect an individual who treasures creativity and independence to thrive in a large corporate environment. Conversely, a person who depends on constant validation from a boss is most likely a poor candidate for a home-based business.

and become a teacher or saving the money required to open a boxing gym. You may feel that you no longer want to hoe the row you're in but remain uncertain about which new field of endeavor you want to cultivate.

Unfortunately, if you jump too soon you may find that you've simply shuffled jobs or moved to a new career but feel just as unhappy as you did before. Without some genuine introspection and a commitment to change, you're apt to follow the same patterns (or make the same fundamental choices) over and over again. The scenery may have changed, but the feeling of déjà vu lives on. The upshot? It is crucial to know what (if anything) you're running from now and where you want to wind up next.

Career counseling (explored in greater depth in Chapter 5) is ideal because it lets you try on alternative guises and learn about yourself. By the same token, a good psychotherapist can help you explore the behaviors, both conscious and unconscious, that may hinder your personal and career progress. You're likely to leave a series of sessions knowing which qualities make you edgy and which others bring you happiness, fulfillment, and the career edge you're seeking. It's tough work, and it demands brutal honesty from you in order to be effectivve. Much of the process must take place

Dealing with Depression

There's mounting evidence that middle age and depression are inextricably intertwined. A group of British and American researchers reported in January 2008 that happiness often follows a U-shaped curve, with the average person bottoming out at age 48. The wealthy, the poor, and all races and demographic groups were afflicted by downward mood swings in midlife. Most pulled out and regained a sense of happiness by their mid-50s. Researchers posited that middle age was the time when many of these people realized that they would not achieve certain aspirations, and that they have limited time left to accomplish the things they desire.

Depression's invisible tentacles reach into the workplace—and into career issues. Most obvious is the fact that holding onto an undesirable job until retirement age breeds despair. But the problem doesn't stop there. For many older workers, epochal life events such as divorce, disease, or the death of a spouse can wreak havoc. "A lot of women wind up recareering in midlife because of divorce," states Robin Ryan, a Seattle, Washington career counselor. "They're angry and depressed because they don't like their life circumstances."

Ryan says it's crucial to monitor the situation—and, if necessary, to seek counseling. "We always hear about how work can be therapy for those facing a difficult life situation," she says. "What we don't hear about is that your personal life affects work. If you're dealing with personal problems and depression, you're probably not going to make the best decisions or find satisfaction in whatever you're doing."

internally: You must be willing to confront your interior dreams *and* demons. You'll also have to identify the abilities, aptitudes, interests, strengths, weaknesses, and conflict points that are uniquely your own.

Chasing the latest hot job or career is an almost foolproof formula for disaster. Nonetheless, career counselors witness a seemingly endless parade of people skewing their aptitudes in order to make a change. Oftentimes, these individuals—the recent recipients of pink slips—face the prospect of pounding the pavement in search of work. "People turn themselves inside out to fit into positions that are a fundamental awful match with their skills, interests, and values because they are so terrified of being without a job," writes career counselor Barbara Moses in *Career Intelligence: The 12 New Rules for Work and Life Success.* "They make career choices on the basis of, 'It will look good on my résumé.'"

A better approach: Move deliberately. Take as much time as you can afford to understand yourself and where you want to go. Those who undergo the difficult, often painful process of self-analysis are far better situated to make good choices—or at least move in the right direction.

Career Tracks

Individuals in midlife (and later) reassess their careers and make changes for all sorts of reasons. Perhaps most significantly, as the number of years remaining in one's life dwindles, the desire to spend the remaining time wisely and productively grows more urgent. In many cases, the end result is a yearning to engage in activities—including work—that imbue a life with greater meaning. There's often a strong desire to leave a legacy and effect positive change in the world. In addition, some individuals come to realize they've somehow drifted away from the things that ignite their passion or tap into their talents. Finally, some people are looking for new challenges, opportunities, or adventure. After decades of reviewing insurance claims or installing telephone systems, they crave a fresh experience.

Gene Retske, who had ascended to the higher rungs of the corporate ladder by the late 1980s, finally decided that running the treadmill faster and faster wasn't getting him any further ahead. The South Carolina resident, now 61, had earned a bachelor's degree in broadcast journalism in 1969. He worked for a couple of newspapers and television stations after graduation, earning $8,500 to $11,000 annually. Four years later, he accepted a position as a marketing executive at Southern Bell, which was then a division of AT&T. "The pay was much better," he recalls. "The hours were more agreeable. And with a wife and young children, it was the responsible thing to do. 'How boring can it be?' I thought."

Over the next two decades, Retske found out. Although he received regular promotions and his salary topped $200,000 a year, Retske ultimately realized he was "bored silly." By the early 1990s, "My job was to get rid of people—either find them jobs within AT&T or get them to

A Mental Makeover

Changing careers demands a sizable shift in mindset. As Beverly Hills psychologist and family therapist Alisa Ruby puts it, "It's extremely easy to fall into old habits and become distracted by all the things going on in life." Too often, people magnify their daily obligations or the steps required to recareer. These include therapy or career counseling, returning to school, creating a leaner budget, and heading out on job interviews. At some point, these tasks become barriers to change. Rather than confront their fears, people mask them with excuses. It's enough to defuse any self-reinvention program before it has a chance to leave the ground.

Those who succeed in changing careers usually follow a fairly consistent path:

They allow themselves to dream. Imagining that a complex event or action is taking place is often the first step toward achieving success. Just as elite athletes visualize a winning performance, you can benefit by conjuring in your mind what it will be like to work in your new career. There's no charge for spinning out various "what if" scenarios.

They explore possibilities and opportunities. It's easier than ever today to gather information about a new line of work. Online searches yield a wealth of information about jobs and professions. Sites such as Monster.com, CareerBuilder.com, and Yahoo! Hotjobs are especially rich resources; many career sites also sponsor job fairs in cities across the U.S. Meanwhile, other organizations and communities offer senior job fairs that are tailored to job seekers 50 and older.

They create a plan and goals. Trying to migrate from one career to another without some sort of blueprint makes as much sense as driving from New York to L.A. without a road map or a GPS. To skirt the mental gridlock that might otherwise result, create a list of long-term goals—including the type of career and job you want. Next, draft some medium-range goals, such as the training or education you believe will be required to land the job. Finally, draw up short-term goals—immediate next steps you will need to set your career transition in motion.

They embrace risk and confront failure. Rather than viewing missteps as derailments, those who successfully recareer dust themselves off and move on. In the wake of the inevitable setback, they reassess the situation and make whatever adjustments they deem necessary. As Paul and Sarah Edwards point out in *Changing Directions without Losing Your Way,* a toddler doesn't stop trying to walk simply because she falls down. A young child doesn't give up trying to learn to tie a shoelace merely because he can't master it at first. True failure, they point out, is an endpoint—not a stage in a journey.

They maintain their focus. Many worthwhile accomplishments in life require sacrifice and hard work. In a society where "instant gratification takes too long," it's crucial to realize that things don't always happen overnight. It takes patience and persistence to change careers. As a result, it's wise to build on small accomplishments and celebrate important milestones. Accept the fact that your own personal journey may play out on meandering country roads, not superhighways.

accept severance packages." Then, in 1992, Retske suddenly became a target of elimination himself: Downsized but with a generous severance package in hand, he elected to strike out on his own. Since then he has started and sold a company, written two books about telecommunications, served as an expert witness in legal cases, and become co-owner and editor of an industry newsletter, *Pre-Paid Press*, which tracks developments in the prepaid-card industry.

A 50-year-old thinks very differently, of course, than a young college graduate. In many cases, says Sarah Edwards, a licensed clinical social worker and co-author (with her husband Paul) of *Changing Directions without Losing Your Way*, individuals entering the workaday world are merely looking to establish themselves or prove their worth. They often pursue a career path based on their academic major or their parents' attitudes and opinions.

In the beginning, says Edwards, "The thinking is, 'How great, I got the job. I can break away from the influence of my parents and support myself.' Then the person gets married, has children, and winds up on a career track. It becomes more difficult to make a career move because it entails a certain amount of risk. In addition, many workers are so busy climbing the corporate ladder and chasing job titles and status that they don't take the time to think about career issues in any real depth."

Then, according to Edwards, around midlife the person winds up thinking, *Gee, how did I get here? Is this really where I want to be? I'm not sure I would have taken this position if I'd known then what I know now.* "They wind up wearing a set of golden handcuffs," Edwards points out. "They've got a job with a great salary, and that's tough to walk away from. They have a social circle and a community they're engaged in." Making a change seems like a radical step. At that point, a person has to be willing to accept *significant* changes—chief among them less seniority, diminished clout, lower pay.

Not everyone follows a predictable career trajectory, of course. A layoff or a failing business may forcibly steer an individual down the path of re-discovery and recareering. What's more, a career sometimes isn't what it seems to be up front. A person might love the study of law but hate the grittier tasks of managing clients, wading through paperwork, or arguing cases. An interior designer might reach a state of bliss choosing paints, fabrics, and furniture for a house or office, only to bridle at the interactions—and compromise—customarily required to please a client.

In some cases, the solution might be as straightforward as teaching law rather than practicing it. In other cases, a career change might mean leveraging one's expertise in law to move into a new field such as medicine or public policy. Or it could mean abandoning the field altogether in pursuit of something more fulfilling. No matter which approach a person takes, coping with change is unavoidable. Understanding all the various options—as well as attempting to foresee all the various pitfalls—is essential. One thing you'll want to factor in is time: It frequently takes a person up to six years, Edwards has found, to make a career transition.

Fighting the Resistance

Whereas some individuals thrive on change, many of us—perhaps most of us—find it a frightening proposition. Sometimes we resist recognizing that the world around us has moved forward but we have not kept up. We live in a state of denial and disbelief. At other times it's difficult to acknowledge that we've slowly migrated away from work that makes us content. This process may occur so incrementally as to be imperceptible. Sometimes a traumatic life event—a layoff, a divorce, a death—

Are You Ready to Change Careers?

Here are 10 strategies for getting a fix on recareering and making it relevant to your current stage of life:

Determine why you want to change careers. Is it to work in a new field? To earn necessary or supplemental income? For intellectual or physical stimulation? Or do you simply wish to stay connected with others?

Acknowledge your ideal scenario—as well as the likely reality. Do you hope to work full-time, part-time, seasonally, or cyclically? Because you're apt to land on a lower rung of your new career ladder—at least initially—many career changes require a high level of commitment.

Consider using an interest, hobby, or passion as a platform for a new career. What we gravitate toward is usually what we like to do. More than a few successful businesses—and careers—have grown out of a consuming hobby with no immediately apparent real-world application.

Inventory the skills you have and those you want to use. Just because you possess a certain skill doesn't mean you *must* use it in your next job—or that doing so will guarantee success. It's critical to examine your attitudes and values, and decide how they relate to a particular career. Being highly organized does not necessarily mean you long to manage an office—or that you will flourish in that undertaking.

Conduct the necessary research. Spend time learning about your targeted next career. If possible, visit a work environment where you can witness the job being performed firsthand. Job fairs, career sites, and career counselors can all provide a wealth of information.

Understand that you may need to invest time, money, and energy to obtain the proper credentials. Securing a mandatory degree or certification can affect other aspects of your life, including your relationship with a spouse, family, and friends.

Expand your horizons. Develop a resource list of people, places, and things to help you investigate new work choices.

Broaden your network. Stay in touch with people of all ages and across all professional boundaries. Consider registering for a social-networking site such as LinkedIn or FaceBook (Chapters 7 & 11).

Manage your expectations. A career change is typically a protracted process in which results don't occur overnight. As you consider your definition of success, make sure it's realistic and achievable.

Follow your head and your heart. Resist conforming to the expectations (or succumbing to the doubt) of others. Instead, blaze your own path and take ownership of your career and life plans.

abruptly triggers questions about how best to spend the rest of one's life. Other times, an individual may grapple for years with feelings of uncertainty, drifting toward significant change in almost desultory fashion.

The common denominator is that every person seeking change must confront the unknown. And, in the end, those who do not master their fears are likely to become enslaved by them. They're apt to feel paralyzed and powerless—if not depressed—while they watch their career stagnate or their self-worth erode. An individual is left with the feeling that something is wrong but can't pinpoint the cause or the solution. This sense of discontent builds until it reaches crisis proportions.

According to author Michael Shermer, who has written extensively about how human behavior evinces itself in economics and other "complex adaptive systems," the "symptoms of depression—restlessness, agitation, loss of appetite, disturbed sleep, impaired concentration, and loss of motivation"—are often mistaken as signs of a physical illness. In *The Mind of the Market: Compassionate Apes, Competitive Humans, and Other Tales from Evolutionary Economics*, Shermer observes that such physical manifestations of depression "may represent an adaptive response to prod you into doing something different in your life…. Depression serves as a wakeup call, prodding people to abandon dead-end jobs…. Moving the out-of-balance system back to homeostasis feels good."

The irony, says Bill Treasurer, a career consultant and former member of the U.S. High Diving Team, is that the *perceived* risk of making a change is often out of whack with reality. "There's risk associated with action, granted," he explains, "but there's also risk in inaction. Sitting on the sidelines can result in obsolescence and a slow psychological death." The most common roadblocks, he notes, revolve around money, a fear of making the wrong choice, and a fear of failure.

Few decisions in life are irreversible, Treasurer points out, so a career change that doesn't work out is not necessarily a mistake: It can be used as a learning experience that fine-tunes your future decision-making.

Living proof of that concept is Terry Nicholetti. After graduating from high school in Puerto Rico, she decided to become a Roman Catholic nun. She spent five years living out her vows and teaching at a Catholic elementary school. Then, finding the convent too restrictive, she opted to leave it. In the years since then, Nicholetti has worked as a theater director, a sales manager, a book author, and a seminar host. "All along," she says, "I've been moving in the direction of performing and artistic expression. But I couldn't see it until a few years ago."

Early on in life, Nicholetti suffered from debilitating anxiety attacks that sabotaged her career. "I would get to a certain point where I was achieving real success," she relates, "and then I would just fall apart." Much of the problem stemmed from childhood sexual abuse and an alcoholic father, says Nicholetti, but today, at age 62, she is realizing her dreams. Nicholetti, who now lives in Washington, D.C., stages business-skills workshops for companies, one-woman shows, and stand-up comedy routines. She used a home-equity line of credit to launch this latest chapter in her life. "All the things that have happened, good and bad, have made me who I am today," she explains. "I am living my heart's desire. I have learned that desire is not evil—it's how the universe lets us know what our purpose is and what we've been called to do."

Out of Sight, Out of Mind

The transition to a new career can be extra tough for those who have been out of the workforce, by default or design, for years or even decades. The cause for their absences can be diverse—the death of a spouse, a prolonged illness, the need to care for a family member, a divorce, or raising toddlers to teens—but the result is almost always the same: a pent-up need for more money, more meaning, or both. According to a study conducted by the University of Pennsylvania and the Forte Foundation, approximately half of those trying to reenter the workforce become discouraged in the course of securing full-time employment.

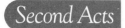
Second Acts

THE INGREDIENTS OF CHANGE
HENRY M. STEWART, *from public-relations agency owner to chef*

I GRADUATED FROM THE UNIVERSITY of South Carolina with a degree in journalism and English in 1971. I worked as a reporter at newspapers for four years, then moved into public relations. I spent approximately 15 years in the field before opening my own public relations agency in 1990. At first it seemed exciting and challenging, but after several years I realized I wasn't having fun anymore. I was losing clients to mergers and acquisitions. Things didn't feel right.

For years, I had fantasized about becoming a chef. I bought cookbooks, watched cooking shows, put together elaborate meals for family and friends. Two or three times I tried to go to cooking school, but I had too many bills and obligations. Then, after my brother died from cancer and I spent the last eight weeks of his life with him, it struck me: I had to make a change.

I spent more than three months undergoing career counseling and testing; I did a lot of self-evaluation and self-analysis.

One day I told my wife, Randi, that I wanted to go to cooking school. She said, "Please do." I applied and was accepted at LeNotre Culinary Institute in Houston. I spent $20,000 and participated in a 30-week program where we would cook from 8:30 a.m. until 2:00 p.m., then plate it up and serve it to faculty and other students. It was very high-end French cuisine.

What I found appealing is that the top person in the class would receive an internship to work at a premier restaurant in France. I was one of 17 students in the class and I was definitely the oldest. I managed to graduate number one and received the internship. So I went to the Alsace region of France for two months and received a realistic dose of what it's like to prepare outstanding food in an outstanding restaurant. When I came back, I began prospecting for jobs. I interviewed at the Renaissance Worthington Hotel in Fort Worth in 2006 and was hired in their fine-dining kitchen, Kalamatas. Today I create pasta dishes, salads, dressings, and a variety of other dishes. We're now migrating from Mediterranean cuisine to New South Cuisine.

The tough thing about restaurant work, especially in a hotel, is that it is continuous. Everything goes 24/7. There is a lot of prep work, especially for Sunday brunches. But I love being out there on the front lines, cooking in front of customers, interacting with them.

I was extremely fortunate. The executive chef was happy to have me come work for him because he has found career changers to be highly motivated and dependable people. He also didn't have a problem with my age—I was 58 when he hired me—because he has also found that older workers are more flexible. I don't have dates to go out on or parties to attend. I don't mind working holidays. And I never leave until my work is done.

The work is physically demanding, but I'm in reasonably good shape and I can handle it well. Really, after putting in 15-hour days in France, an eight-hour shift is a breeze. I didn't worry about age discrimination because I figured that if I had worked the long hours in France every day it was pretty clear that I could handle shorter workdays here in the U.S.

My only regret is that I didn't make the change years ago. I never realized that my love for cooking could translate into a full-time career. I figure I'll have a 15-year run at this. I'm hoping to gain experience and become a sous-chef at a top restaurant within the next few years. I want to cook first-class food, whether it's French, Vietnamese, or Middle Eastern. I love learning and growing. I'm having the time of my life.

Unable to find new jobs equivalent to the ones they left behind, many settle for downgrades.

Even though subtle and not-so-subtle age discrimination exists, the best antidote, career counselor Helen Harkness maintains, is to purge yourself of (often unrecognized) internal biases or feelings of inadequacy. "I have seen many talented women feel completely inadequate and lose confidence in themselves once they are out of the workforce for an extended period," Harkness explains. She relates the story of a senior engineer at a prominent company who left the job temporarily to raise her children. When the engineer informed people at social events that she was now a full-time mother, they routinely failed to ask her any follow-up questions, making her feel like she was a "second-class citizen."

Shattering the glass wall—or ceiling—can therefore be an act of sheer will. "It's important to have confidence and be able to communicate what you're good at so that you don't come across as second-rate," Harkness says. It's also wise to develop a plan for managing gaps in employment; to maintain social and professional networks; to renew licenses and professional accreditations; to take refresher courses; to expand knowledge; and to consider staying active through occasional contract work or part-time volunteering—even if it's at your child's classroom or a local homeowner's board.

Human nature being what it is, there's probably no way to immunize yourself from every condescending remark directed your way. Yet a healthy dose of confidence and ability can provide a powerful inoculation. One woman, a prominent fashion model who had worked in Paris and New York for two decades, silenced the dismissive voices by opening her own clothing store near Detroit, Michigan. Another woman, previously an actuary at an insurance company, went back to school after nearly a decade's absence from the workforce, then landed a job in the finance department of a major corporation as a 45-year-old newly minted CPA.

An Age-Old Problem
Another challenge is outright age discrimination. In 2005, the U.S. Supreme Court blazed a trail for greater age equality in the workplace by expanding laws that protect workers against discrimination by sex, race, and age. Another high-court ruling in June 2008 strengthened such protections further. Between those statutes and reality, however, yawns a chasm full of entrenched biases and practices. "Ageism," as one social critic observed, "is the final refuge of the prejudiced mind."

Far too many employers cling to the discredited notion that 50+ workers are too old, lack the energy or commitment to do the job, demand too much money, or are merely biding their time until retirement. Never mind all manner of studies showing that older workers require one-third less job

Have You Faced Age Discrimination?

In 2006, the U.S. Equal Employment Opportunity Commission (EEOC) recorded 13,569 complaints of age discrimination and recovered $51.5 million in monetary benefits (not including awards resulting from litigation). You can obtain information about age discrimination and learn how to file a claim at the EEOC website (www.eeoc.gov) or at any EEOC office (a complete list is available online). Here are some things to know in advance:

The Age Discrimination in Employment Act (ADEA) protects people age 40 and over from employment discrimination based on age. The law says that an employer may not fire, refuse to hire, or treat you differently than other employees because of your age. The terms of the ADEA dictate that individuals in only three categories—police and firefighters, certain federal jobs such as air-traffic controllers, and tenured university faculty—are exempt.

If you believe you're a victim of age discrimination, talk to your potential employer or current employer and try to resolve the matter. If that proves impossible, consider filing a charge with the EEOC. You often have to file within 180 days of the perceived infraction, but some states have laws in place that extend the deadline to 365 days.

A charge can be filed by an individual or by an organization or agency on behalf of another person (in order to protect the aggrieved person's identity).

Antidiscrimination laws apply to organizations with 20 or more employees, including state and local governments. The laws also apply to employment agencies, labor organizations, and the federal government.

ADEA protections include apprenticeships, job notices and advertisements, preemployment inquiries, and benefits. With few exceptions, employers cannot force employees to retire at a certain age.

The ADEA does not specifically prohibit an employer from asking an applicant's age or date of birth. However, because such inquiries may deter older workers from applying for employment or may otherwise indicate possible intent to discriminate based on age, the ADEA closely scrutinizes all requests for age information.

State laws usually apply to employers with fewer than 20 employees. As a result, employers often must comply with state laws even when a federal law has no sway over them.

training, are absent infrequently, and stay in their jobs longer because they're less intent on climbing the corporate ladder. (On top of all that, they are also more productive.)

A 2005 report issued by Boston College's Center for Retirement Research found that age discrimination is real—and rife. Although Americans are capable of working longer—several studies suggest that today's 70-year-olds are comparable in health and mental function to 65-year-olds from 30 years ago—many employers have yet to catch up with this change. The center conducted an audit study in which it sent out 4,000 fictitious résumés for job applicants of differing ages, then gauged the response rates. For older workers, the results were chilling: A younger worker (defined as less than 50 years old) is 40 percent more likely to be called in for an interview than an older worker.

Regrettably, no battle-tested tactic has yet emerged for combating age discrimination. "The primary thing a person can do," consultant Bill Treasurer says, "is prevent your own obsolescence." That means going beyond maintaining your current skill set by acquiring new knowledge and new talents. It means transcending habit and routine, and learning new ways to work. Hardly a profession or job today has not been touched by the Internet, information technology, or new ways of doing things. "It's not enough to be competent," says Treasurer. "It's important to stand out. Some older workers are in great demand because they are clearly the most qualified candidate for the job. They have the attitude and skills to succeed in many different environments."

If you believe you've been a victim of age discrimination and decide to pursue a claim, keep detailed notes of the episode in question, including dates, statements made by the offending person, and any other evidence. To strengthen the case, mail yourself a letter with the information inside, but do not open the letter when it arrives at your home; the postmark on the envelope can be used to substantiate the date. You can also send yourself a message by e-mail and print it out; if your employer is the offending party, use a private e-mail account not monitored by the employer. (Note, however, that altering e-mail dates is not difficult, so a court may give an electronic message less legal weight than a postmarked letter.) A growing number of attorneys specialize in age-discrimination cases. You can usually find a qualified attorney through your local or state bar association, or through the National Employment Lawyers Association (www.nela.org). Or log onto aarp.org and go to the section Age Discrimination at Work (www.aarp.org/money/careers/jobloss/a2004-04-28-agediscrimination.html).

The good news is that employers are coming around. In 2006, former recruiter Steven Greenberg created Jobs 4.0, a website devoted to workers 40 and older (he founded the company at age 46 after undergoing his own recareering journey). Availing themselves of Jobs 4.0, Vanguard, Macy's, Starbucks, New York Life, Allstate, Alexion Pharmaceuticals, and many others have begun actively seeking older workers in fields as diverse as accounting, advertising, architecture, biotechnology, engineering, finance, graphic design, information technology, retail, and publishing. The site now boasts thousands of listings.

Some individuals, too, are breaking through barriers that would have seemed impenetrable only a few years ago. Richard Thomson, a resident of Auburn, New York, who had worked as a chef and truck driver for much of his adult life, decided to leap into law enforcement at age 51. He took a civil service exam for Cayuga County in New York State, passed the test, and was hired by the Cayuga Sheriff's Department to work as a corrections deputy in the country jail. Thomson has held the job since 2003, managing approximately 40 inmates at any given moment. "With a wife and two stepdaughters," he says, "I'm very happy that I switched careers. It has given me stable work, health insurance, and a good pension."

All in the Family

The ripple effect from a career change can affect friends, family, and significant others. It can entail a change in pay and benefits, a new social circle or peer group, and perhaps a move to another neighborhood—or coast. It can also unravel your carefully constructed networks of childcare or eldercare. Given such profound implications, it's wise to consult with family members and elicit their support before embarking on a career odyssey. "Changing careers is not easy and it is not a casual decision," Harkness observes. "A person is essentially changing identities. There comes a point when you have to lose your old identity, but you don't yet know what your new identity is! Without adequate support, the change cannot happen successfully."

Not every partner is likely to go along with the new plan. Nor is every friend guaranteed to show support. That was the case for an investment banker, who left a lucrative career on Wall Street to become a minister. Not long after, his wife divorced him. Her explanation: "I married an investment banker, and that's what I want." There are also plenty of instances of children, friends, and aging parents reluctantly coming to the conclusion that the career changer has flipped his lid when he cashes in a 401(k) to open a collectibles store.

Communication is key. During any career transition, it's important to keep a partner and close family members apprised of the situation but also elicit their input. Discuss the full spectrum of concerns, problems,

Worksheet: **Gauge Your Goals**

The exercise below can help you get a fix on your current career goals in order to see how well they mesh with today's work environment.

Which careers sound most interesting to you?

_____

_____

What specific aspects of these careers appeal to you the most?

_____

_____

What skills, education, and knowledge will you need to work in these fields? Which of these might you have to add to your repertoire?

_____

_____

What types of organizations—companies, government agencies, or non-profits—offer jobs in these careers?

_____

_____

What sort of work environment is typical for these careers?

_____

_____

Do you feel you're a match for the composition or demographics of the workforce?

_____

Once you complete this worksheet, use it to assess career possibilities in relation to market conditions, potential employers, and your own values. You might decide to work in software development, for example, only to discover that employers in the industry expect 50+ hour weeks. Or perhaps you are so set on becoming a museum curator that you're willing to put in the years of study and training required to land such a position.

practicalities, and financial issues, then try to work out a solution everyone can agree on. Some unexpected advantages of this approach: Family and friends may have sound ideas for streamlining the transition and finding a great job. Or they may be able to provide professional networking opportunities and job leads. Pam Fischer, a former motor-vehicle-safety advocate who now works for the State of New Jersey, knows all about the need to communicate. In February 2007, the 47-year-old—previously a vice president of public affairs for the New Jersey chapter of the AAA—accepted an appointment from New Jersey governor Jon S. Corzine to direcct the state's Division of Highway Traffic Safety. But it wasn't without long and involved discussions with her husband and son. "I wanted to bring them into the loop," she explains, "because it's a huge commitment to the family."

Fischer's new job, she realized, would not exactly be Security Central: A political appointment, it meant she would be serving at the whim of

---

Key Questions

Am I truly interested in changing careers? We have all bad days; sometimes we have bad months. When a boss is berating you or a co-worker can't seem to get things right and it forces you to pick up the slack, it's tempting to dream about ditching a job and finding something less stressful. If you're not careful, however, you may simply trade one set of stresses for another: You may wind up running just as fast, only on a different treadmill. It's important to differentiate whether you dislike the job, the employer, or the career.

Do I understand where I am in life and what's important? No person is the same at 50 as at 20. In order to switch careers successfully, it is important to establish exactly what you hope to achieve, what sort of legacy you wish to leave, and how much time and energy you can devote to a job.

Have I put risk in the proper perspective? It's easy to see the potential downside to changing careers: You might wind up making less money or working in a field you don't like. That would mean a return to the starting line and a redo of the entire recareering process. But there's a downside to avoiding risk as well: Deliberately not making a long-term change is tantamount to courting on-the-job stagnation, unhappiness, or even depression.

Am I willing to confront age bias or discrimination? There's no lack of hard evidence that age bias is rife in our society. Nor is it difficult to find plenty of people who buck that trend and succeed wildly in new careers after 50. You can't control the world. You can, however, control your thoughts, feelings, and the attitude you project to others. A positive and confident outlook goes a long way toward redefining yourself.

Am I ready to field ignorant comments—perhaps even sacrifice a friendship or two? Family, friends, and colleagues may wholeheartedly support your move. Conversely, significant others may disapprove. Many a marriage has foundered on the shoals of career change. Then there's the likelihood that a new job or career will parachute you into the middle of an unfamiliar social circle. While some existing friends may fade into the background, others will move to the forefront.

the governor—a drastic turnaround from her previous post at the AAA, where she enjoyed almost complete job security. On top of the unaccustomed instability, her new routine would reshape family dynamics. "I told my family I wouldn't be around the house as much as before." Indeed, longer work hours and a three-hour commute (versus 20 minutes for the previous job) affected grocery shopping, meal preparation, ferrying their son to hs sports practices, and a tangle of other household chores.

In the past, Fischer had made it a point to leave her work issues at the office. "I have always tried to avoid coming home and 'dumping' on my husband," she says. The new job, however, required more emotional support—and thus a good listener to help her work through new challenges, issues, and frustrations. "There has been a significant adjustment for everyone in the family," Fischer reflects. "It's a good thing we discussed everything up front and worked together before I made the change. Otherwise there could have been considerable ill will and problems."

The family continues to discuss her career change, reports Fischer, including how it has affected her role as a mother. Although her son understands his mother's passion and need to work, "At the end of the day there's still the question, 'Where is my mom?' It's a constant juggling act."

Acclimating to a Geographic Move

In some cases, a new career might necessitate a geographic move. It's essential to know up front whether you're willing to relocate and what type of living environment is acceptable. If the hurly-burly of urban life sends you over the edge, even a dream job will wear thin in short order. On the other hand, if the prospect of shoveling snow or sweating through hot summers paralyzes you with dread, it's probably best to look for an opportunity in some other location—or reconsider your career choice altogether.

Living conditions and climate aren't the only factors guiding a decision, of course. There's also the practical and emotional adjustment of moving away from friends and family—or, if you're fortunate, closer to them; the cost and turmoil associated with a major move; and differences in housing prices and the cost of living from one region to another. As a result, significant salary and expense differentials exist in areas and cities across the country. Inhabitants of New York City, for example, spend an average of $4,161 per month on rent. The typical household in Santa Fe, New Mexico shells out $1,245.

In many cities, a chamber of commerce or local real estate company can provide the data you need to make a cost-of-living comparison. A growing number of cities also provide online calculators (a Google search for "cost of living" should bring them up). Another source of detailed and reliable data is the ACCRA Cost of Living Index. It covers more than 300 cities and is available from the Council for Community and Economic Research (www.coli.org/compare.asp). Reports for two communities cost $7.95, while each additional city using the same origination point (you can include up to five in a single report) costs $4.95. The data is updated quarterly. Other valuable resources include epodunk.com, the *Places Rated Almanac* by David Savageau, and AARP's own "Location Scout" feature (http://web02.bestplaces.net/aarp/ls/).

If you're serious about making a move, visit the community a couple of times. Bring your partner or other family members. A spouse may want to check out the local job market as well, plus take a look at shopping, recreational opportunities, police and fire protection, hospitals and medical facilities, and other lifestyle amenities. The more you know, the less likely you are to go into shock when the moving van drives away.

Dreams & Realities
At this point in the recareering process, it's wise to think big and keep your mind open to possibilities. Yet it's equally important to temper those dreams with reality. Perhaps you've always hungered to be an actor. Don't quit your day job—but *do* join a community theater and live out your passion part-time or on a volunteer basis. Then, if your acting career takes off, you can make the adjustments needed to reach the next level. Or maybe at 45 you harbor the wish to become a doctor. If you know what's involved in attending medical school, serving internships and residencies, and landing a staff position, give yourself the green light.

Just as important, however, is the ability to think realistically and recognize when the time has come to move on. Do you want to spend a decade becoming a doctor and enter the profession at age 55? Will you have the energy, enthusiasm, and drive to succeed at that age? If you sense that the window of opportunity has closed on your M.D. dreams, you may still be able to find a niche in the medical field—as an occupational therapist, perhaps, or a radiology technician—that does not demand quite so much education, training, and development.

Once you understand your income needs and your definition of meaningful work, you will be free to explore a mind-bending array of options and opportunities—and make smart decisions along the way. Now all you need is a plan. The next chapter helps you devise one.

Books

Career Intelligence: The 12 New Rules for Work and Life Success, by Barbara Moses, Ph.D., Berrett-Koehler Publishers, 1998. Moses provides focused advice on how to become a "career activist" and achieve ongoing career success.

Changing Directions without Losing Your Way: Managing the Six Stages of Change at Work and in Life, Paul and Sarah Edwards, Tarcher Putnam, 2001. Provides concrete suggestions for navigating career changes, downsizings, and other disruptive events resulting from today's work landscape.

If You Don't Know Where You're Going, You'll Probably End Up Somewhere Else, David P. Campbell, Sorin Books, 2007. Offers information, tips, and advice on how to manage career and life change.

The Complete Idiot's Guide to Dream Jobs, by Brian O'Connell, Alpha, 2005. Offers insights and glimpses into an array of jobs and professions, from mystery shopper to crossword-puzzle creator to organic farmer.

Your Rights in the Workplace, by Barbara Kate Repa, Nolo Press, 2007. Discusses an array of legal topics, including how to deal with various forms of discrimination.

More Resources

AARP
Age Discrimination at Work
www.aarp.org/money/careers/jobloss/a2004-04-28-age discrimination.html

Offers examples of age discrimination and provides counsel if you believe you have been a target.

Nolo
Asserting Your Rights in the Workplace
www.nolo.com

Provides information about age discrimination and possible claims.

Reinvention Institute
http://reinventioninstitute.com/

This Miami-based organization bills itself as a partner in growth, change, and reinvention. It offers in-person and virtual classes and workshops, online tests and analysis, and books on how to get started and navigate career issues. 800-928-1874.

◆◆

SECTION II
FINDING
YOUR RAINBOW

CHAPTER

4 What Is Your Recareering Style?

Some strategies for finding happiness and comfort—beyond your comfort zone

CHANGING CAREERS HAS A WELLSPRING of diverse origins. For some, job burnout or the desire to face new challenges drives the change. For others, it's about connecting to longtime interests or a soul-satisfying passion. Still others have change thrust upon them—they are fired, downsized, or accept a tempting buyout. Some individuals, particularly women, may have spent the last few decades raising children or supporting a partner's career. Now they're once again looking to expand their possibilities. Or life circumstances—including the death of a spouse or a divorce—may create entirely new demands.

What all these individuals share is a desire or need to rethink their options. As life events unfold, the comfort and stability of the past fades into the background with every new risk, opportunity, or reward that enters the picture. Expectations change. Relationships evolve. Life may acquire new meaning and purpose.

Making a career switch can rank among life's most stressful events. It can force a person to conduct a deep self-examination of his or her values, needs, and desires. And it can bring about positive changes, negative changes, or simply unanticipated changes.

Recareering assumes numerous guises. However, those undergoing a career transformation typically fall into one of the following six categories: Adapters, Opportunists, Change Agents, Reinventors, Active Retirees, and Fantasy Seekers.

This chapter examines each of these recareering styles in turn. Not surprisingly, your personality will dictate how you conduct your own decision-making process. It will also play a role in guiding you toward particular careers and jobs. No matter what career you ultimately choose to pursue, understanding your psychological outlook—and biases—can help you focus on making the right decision. After you have read this chapter, I hope you will be ready to embark on a process of self-analysis that will point you in the right direction.

Now let's take a look at these varied styles of recasting one's professional existence.

Adapters

Adapters Layoffs have become an inescapable facet of modern worklife. As companies seek to cut costs, the quickest and most obvious target is often the workforce. In some cases, the rationale is a downturn in business; in other instances, a merger or acquisition may legitimately create redundancies and overlapping positions. Regardless of the specific reason, a pink slip can wreak emotional and financial havoc. It can lead to a painful reexamination of priorities—particularly among older workers, often at the higher end of the income scale. It's no news flash that a new job often entails lower pay and diminished stature.

The more fortunate may receive a severance or early-retirement package. The cash and benefits are welcome, but frequently it's the extra time that proves most valuable—time that a person can put to good use by researching and learning about other careers. Meanwhile, those at lower education and income levels may feel the pain more directly—especially if they lack savings and health benefits. These individuals may find their options limited and their decisions restricted.

Traits of an Adapter

Resourceful when necessary.

Prefers stability to excitement.

Personal and professional growth are not always top priorities.

Rarely changes careers unless forced to.

May find, by contrast, that a forced career change was the "best thing that ever happened."

They may be forced to take the first job that comes their way in order to right the ship and stay afloat.

As the name implies, Adapters must rely on their existing skills and knowledge to find work. Most have never actively considered a career change, nor have they made plans to return to school to earn a degree. Instead, they usually find themselves adjusting on the fly to the circumstances at hand.

Most of us have been in this category at one time in our lives: Adapters are likely to scan online job boards and newspaper classifieds for openings at similar firms, or sound out colleagues and friends for job leads. Depending on the industry and its current labor demand, these individuals may wind up in the unemployment line for days or months on end.

Yet Adapters aren't entirely without resources when it comes to making a career change. A sudden and traumatic event at a long-held job can serve as the perfect opportunity to reevaluate life and make a break from routine. It can provide an unanticipated chance for professional development. "Too many people find themselves in a rut," observes Helen Harkness, president of Career Design Associates. "They choose predictability and stability over happiness and personal growth." If you wind up holding a pink slip, inventory your work attitudes and interests, looking hard for ways to better align your work goals with your life objectives. Career counseling and coaching should both become top priorities on any Adapter's task list.

A shifting workscape—and a crumbling career foundation—ignited Adapter Linda Reardon's passion for sewing and embroidery. For more than 14 years, she worked as a project manager in the information-technology department of Birmingham, Alabama-based SouthTrust Bank. When SouthTrust merged with Wachovia Bank in 2004, however, Reardon was suddenly jobless. Just 56 at the time, she wasn't yet ready to call it a career. "I wanted to stay active and involved and do something I really loved," she says. "I wanted to do something on my own, for myself."

Sewing had always been a part of Reardon's life. As a young girl growing up in West Middlesex, Pennsylvania, she had learned the ropes— or threads—on her grandmother's sewing machine, then competed as a member of her local 4H Club. Later Reardon married, had two children (now in their mid-30s), and began to stitch clothes for her family.

After leaving the bank with a bonus for "staying until the bitter end," Reardon plunked down $20,000 for a 15-needle Toyota commercial-grade embroidering machine and set up shop as "Letters by Linda," embroidering jackets, caps, and other items for local firms. She is now looking to add a direct-to-garment computer-based printing system that will allow her to produce photo T-shirts and other items quickly, without using a traditional screening method. "I feel like I am putting my talents to work and having a lot of fun," she says.

Opportunists
Many a detour branches off the road to happiness. Some individuals drift into a profession in their 20s, then continue in that line of work for the next few decades; others find that what enthralled them at age 25 merely has them in thralldom at 50.

Regardless of the underlying reason, more and more boomers want to make a change. Many of them seek work that's more meaningful—and beneficial for society. Some have contemplated the change for years or harbored a dream of doing something truly different since childhood. They've come to see a major shift as a now-or-never proposition.

Opportunists take stock of their situation and consciously plan to make a change. They read, go back to school, or attend conferences to gain the skills and knowledge required to thrive in a new field. Once they're in a position—financially and practically—to make the switch to a new career, they send out résumés, tap into their professional network, or ferret out opportunities to make the transition. In most cases, Opportunists know what they want, then make it happen. They're generally confident—or at least they don't let their misgivings stop them—and they're usually fairly persistent. In the mind of an Opportunist, adventure is a good thing and change is requisite.

Traits of an Opportunist

Highly motivated to make a career change.

Willing to invest money and time in recareering.

Often more affluent.

Looking for greater meaning in work in particular and in life in general.

Wants to contribute to society.

Take Ivonne Guerra. The 38-year-old West Linn, Oregon woman had taught Spanish at Milwaukie High School in the North Clackamas School District since 1997. But several years ago the native of Colombia—who came to the U.S at age eight—realized she had higher aspirations. "I am a person who thrives on change," she says. "I like being challenged."

So Guerra, who had already earned a master's degree in education in 2001, decided to go back to school so that she could recareer within the education field. "I wanted to find a way to help more kids and make an

Key Questions

Do I understand my recareering style? Understanding your reasons for recareering and your motivation for doing so can help you make wise decisions. Take the time to analyze your situation. Then consciously decide if you want to go with the current or swim in a different direction.

Does my recareering style make sense for me? If your recareering style does not match your current life situation or you feel that something just isn't right, seek out career counseling. At the very least, explore other options and possibilities. It's always better to sort out issues up front than attempt to reverse course once you've invested time and money in a career change.

Am I clear on my goals? It's easy to get excited by a new business or career opportunity. The idea of moving to Vermont and starting a B&B or opening a sports memorabilia shop on a fashionable boulevard may get your pulse racing. But it's vital to understand your life situation and take into account finances, family and friends, childcare and eldercare issues, and a spate of other issues. There's no one-size-fits-all decision.

Am I willing to undergo significant change? Gaining understanding is one thing; acting on it is another. Unless you're willing to venture beyond your comfort zone, you may not achieve the kind of growth and self-actualization you're after. As a result of this particular phase of self-scrutiny, you may decide to stick with your natural career style or embrace a different one.

Have I explored all my options? Whether you decide to do the research yourself or work with a career counselor, it's vital to understand the ramifications of a move: You'll want to make sure you investigate the myriad ways in which a career change is likely to affect every aspect of your life. Each new option or opportunity you discover will only amplify your career-change flexibility.

What is my motivation for working at this stage of my life? For many, there's an ongoing need to earn money. For others, there's an overarching desire to give back to society. Whatever your reason for working—and changing careers—be honest with yourself up front. It can save headaches and heartaches later on.

What will I do in my later years? Mandatory retirement is on the brink of extinction. As people live longer, healthier lives, they will want to stay productive and remain engaged in meaningful pursuits. It's never too early to think about how you will live into your 70s, 80s, 90s, and beyond.

Am I prepared for coming social changes regarding work and old age? Once upon a time, lives and careers followed a predictable path that led to a gold watch at age 65. Today you are likely to retire incrementally— through a series of career changes or new jobs. It's important to understand work options as well as the growing demand for older workers.

even greater impact," she explains. That meant becoming an administrator. A divorced mother with two children in tow, she had to juggle 50-hour workweeks with 10 to 20 hours of study. She also had to live with her mother to make ends meet and manage childcare responsibilities.

"There were times when I felt overwhelmed by fear of the unknown," Guerra confesses. "I really wondered if I had bitten off more than I could chew." Despite those bouts of self-doubt, Guerra—an Opportunist and Reinventor—has made the grade. In May 2008, she landed a job as vice principal at Estacada Web Academy, a charter school in the North Clackamas School District.

In retrospect, the career change of Ivonne Guerra was not exclusively about money. "I learned at an early age to follow my heart and my goals," she reflects. "I never thought about going into a field just for the money.

I think that if you do what you want to do—if you like it and you are good at it—the money will come."

Change Agents

Some career moves involve a distinct leap from one profession to another but hinge on using the same basic skills. The people who make these sharp breaks are Change Agents, and they like to put their existing skills to work in new, more fulfilling ways. An elementary school teacher, for example, may decide to open a day-care center. Or a corporate executive might decide to lend her leadership and management skills to a nonprofit organization.

Even as Change Agents sniff out new opportunities and challenges for themselves, they look for ways to make a positive impact on society. They view their transition as part of an organic evolution. Like Opportunists, Change Agents don't hesitate to chase rainbows. They're willing to invest in themselves—by going back to school, perhaps, or by sinking savings into a new business. And they're willing to vault obstacles (including the human variety, in the form of naysayers and skeptics) to achieve their objectives. "Some people feel a profound sense of direction or destiny at a certain point in their lives," observes career counselor Helen Harkness. "They feel they can put their abilities and skills to better use in a different job or profession."

Traits of a Change Agent

Applies skills and knowledge in new ways in a new career.

Feels a sense of purpose and mission.

Often gravitates to a profession that aids others.

Is motivated to make a change and willing to confront challenges in order to find fulfillment.

Often feels a sense of destiny.

Susan Musser is a Change Agent. After working as a nurse in the early 1970s, earning a master's degree in the field, and spending time in hospitals for more than 20 years, she found the field increasingly taxing, both physically and mentally. To remedy her ennui, the resident of Lakeland, Florida went to work for an attorney who specializes in medical malpractice cases—a job that also allowed her to spend more time with her then five-year-old son. "It was a way to do chart review but not be in the hospital every day," she says.

Then, after dealing with a divorce, Musser decided she wanted a career that would give her greater independence and autonomy while still permitting her to use her interpersonal skills to help others. "The divorce was one of those life-changing events that opened my eyes to new possibilities and opportunities," Musser explains. "I was sitting in my financial planner's office one day and the lightbulb went off: I could help others, particularly women, get a handle on their financial lives." She applied at Smith Barney, took a battery of tests, and found herself face-to-face with an attractive job offer. She accepted.

Now, eight years later, Musser feels she has finally found her true calling. "Eighty percent of my day is spent managing my relationships," she reports. "I get to use the same skills I did in nursing, but in a way that's better suited to my interests and personality. There's a financial crisis in this country—people don't adequately plan, save, or invest—and I feel like I am helping people address that issue."

For Musser, transitioning from nurse to financial advisor was "a leap of faith," but it's important "to be a risk taker to the extent that we do what's important for us and what motivates us in life."

Another Change Agent is 61-year-old Joyce Roché, the former CEO of Carson Products, a leading hair-products firm. Roché, ranked one of the country's 40 most powerful black executives by *Black Enterprise* magazine in 1991 and 1994, began her odyssey toward self-actualization in the late '90s while living in Savannah, Georgia. After volunteering at a local church and for the American Diabetes Association out of a desire to give something back to society, Roché ventured into the nonprofit world full-time in 2000. "I felt that my business skills could be used to make a greater impact," she says. "I wanted to do something more meaningful and make a difference."

Some friends and business associates questioned her sanity: Why, they asked, would one of the most successful and highly paid businesswomen in America toss away fame and fortune for a relatively obscure job? But Roché knew where to look to find her guiding light. When she heard about an opening for president at Girls, Inc.—a New York-based civic and educational organization that was known as Girls Clubs of America until 1990—she applied and quickly landed the job. Today, she balances her time managing day-to-day operations and dropping in on local facilities to connect with girls from poor and high-risk neighborhoods.

The result? Roché has shifted gears into a more comfortable, more rewarding career. Despite earning 25 percent less than in the corporate world, she says, "I'm happier, more stimulated and challenged. I used to go on vacation to feel rejuvenated and reenergized. Now I feel that way every day. When I step into a local office and interact with the girls, I can see and feel the enormous positive impact."

Reinventors A yearning for variety and new challenges keeps Reinventors humming. Constantly building on their skills and knowledge and using them to stay fresh, Reinventors spin their careers tightly around a central theme or core capability. Rather than switching careers outright, as Change Agents do, Reinventors continuously rethink and recalibrate an existing career—sometimes in new jobs that focus on the same goals. A freelance magazine illustrator, for example, might expand into books. A paralegal might go back to school and reemerge as an attorney. A software developer might forsake a corporate job in order to start his own software company.

Traits of a Reinventor

Loves the career but needs new wrinkles, challenges, and accomplishments.

Is willing to work hard to reapply skills and knowledge in a new way.

Often thinks in creative and entrepreneurial ways.

Is flexible.

Takes risks.

Pam Fischer, first introduced on pages 58-60, is one such Reinventor. Having long ago established herself as a leading advocate on traffic-safety issues, including child-passenger safety and graduated driver's-licensing laws, Fischer believed that working for New Jersey governor Jon S. Corzine and developing state programs would put her skills to better use—without necessitating that she switch careers altogether. "My focus for all these years has been on trying to make a difference—to save lives," she reflects. "I'm ready to roll up my sleeves and work to reduce injuries and fatalities on our roadways."

With the change came challenges. "It's easy to get comfortable and stay where you are," notes Fischer. "You know the people, you know the politics, you don't have to prove yourself. Making a change is hard work. You have to think about what you really want to do and what you really want to accomplish."

"I wasn't unhappy, but I knew that I needed to grow. I took the position even though it's a political appointment. I could be here today and gone tomorrow. And just in case that happens, I carry this little piece of paper everywhere I go. It reminds me of an organization I may create someday. It's also my mission statement. It says, 'The Advocacy Group —providing services to the nonprofit and business community and individuals in need.' I keep it in my wallet to remind me that things are transitory. When my term ends at this job, I plan to take this passion to a whole new level. I may focus on advocacy for nonprofits, small businesses, and individuals in need.

The little piece of paper is a reminder that this job is part of an evolution—an ongoing process of changing and reinventing myself so that I can always put my talents to maximum use."

Active Retirees Many older workers have said good-bye to the long hours and responsibility attached to a career, but they're not ready to leave the workforce entirely. Some have lower financial demands— both the kids and the house payment are gone—yet they still need a paycheck. Still others may view retirement as an opportunity to stay active, maintain a social network, or give back to society through volunteerism. (Older individuals, reported the Harvard School of Public Health in 2004, are more likely to view volunteering as part of their "duty as a citizen." Chapter 10 has more on volunteer options.)

Active Retirees aren't the types who sit around playing bridge or solving sudoku puzzles all day—though they may find these activities enjoyable and make them part of their daily routine. As the name implies, they are people who put their hobbies, interests, and passions to work in either a part-time or full-time capacity—almost always after exiting a

Traits of an Active Retiree

Wants to stay engaged and busy but is not necessarily interested in demanding, full-time work.

Often seeking new and fun experiences.

May seek social interaction.

Often gravitates toward hobbies and long-time interests.

Frequently attracted to volunteerism.

previous career and initially welcoming retirement. Some take up painting. Others open a pet-sitting service. Still others run businesses trading
in sports collectibles or antiques.

When Dick Bere retired as president and chief operating officer of
the Cincinnati-based supermarket chain Kroger in 1995, he knew that
he couldn't sit around the rest of his life. The 63-year-old volunteered
at a local food bank for a year before joining another nonprofit organization that was just getting off the ground. Its founders called it "Crayons
to Computers," and by establishing it they hoped to create a free supply
store for less-affluent teachers. To spare teachers in particularly needy
Cincinnati-area schools from having to shell out as much as $3,000 a
year to provision their students with pencils, notebooks, art supplies,
and other basic items, Crayons to Computers would distribute overstock
and donations.

The organization proved to be a success, and Bere has deepened and
formalized his involvement by becoming its chief operating officer. "I
can't imagine someone playing golf every day and not contributing back
to the community," he muses. "This really makes me feel good. In fact,
sometimes I feel guilty because I'm having so much fun."

Bere works about 50 hours per week, all on a volunteer basis. He runs
the business, helps unload trucks, and handles any other tasks that require
attention. He is now working to expand Crayons to Computers to 50 cities.
"I'm hoping I can work with this organization for another 20 years," he says.

Another Active Retiree is Shelley Seyfried-Bourg. The Tucson resident worked as a legal assistant and paralegal for more than 30 years. "I
was enamored by the field," she says. "At one point I considered becoming
a lawyer myself." But she eventually grew tired of the work and, at age 62,
decided to move on. She took Social Security and began to think about
what else she could do with her life. "I'm a Type A personality. Sitting
around the house? Not an option!"

As Seyfried-Bourg mentally catalogued her interests in life, her love of animals kept bubbling to the top. As a child she had dogs, cats, ducks, and other pets, and she had toyed with the idea of becoming a veterinarian. But a so-called aptitude test at age 14 stopped her cold. The school counselor who interpreted the results told Seyfried-Bourg she was not suited for the work and probably would not succeed at it. "Nobody was there to say, 'You can do whatever you want,' " she recalls. " 'If you're willing to work at it, you can make it happen.' "

This time around, however, Seyfried-Bourg had age and wisdom on her side. She knew she had to follow her heart. She contacted an associate who operated a pet-sitting service and went to work for her.

Inspired by that experience, five months later Seyfried-Bourg decided to open a pet-sitting business of her own. She was aware she would face competition, including her past employer, but she was confident that she could make it work. So Seyfried-Bourg withdrew seed money of $2,000 from an IRA and opened Meow, Woof & Tweet. "My motivation was to make some money and enjoy my life," Seyfried-Bourg explains.

She has succeeded on both counts. "I absolutely love animals," she remarks, "and I am definitely a people person. I like being active, and the work provides a good deal of flexibility." Meanwhile, Seyfried-Bourg has grown her client list to 85, necessitating the addition of two employees. She typically visits five or six houses per day and occasionally puts in an overnight stay. "I am incredibly happy," she concludes. "I see myself doing pet sitting until I am physically incapable of it."

Fantasy Seekers
Almost everyone has at some time or another dreamed of working in a fantasy career. For some, the allure of becoming a tour guide or starting a chocolate company is the ticket to happiness and inner peace. For others, it's about opening B&B or growing coffee beans in Kona. Many Fantasy Seekers have worked in the corporate world, raised a family, and saved some money. Now they're ready to play—but they don't want to relinquish the pay. They may rediscover

Traits of a Fantasy Seeker

Wants to connect career to a desired lifestyle.

Is frequently entrepreneurial.

Is willing to take risks, including moving to a faraway place.

Often in a start-up business that involves a spouse, a partner, or another family member.

May also fall into the categories of Active Retiree, Opportunist, or Change Agent.

a hobby, as do Active Retirees, or they may dive into something exotic and learn as they go. Some start their own businesses; others buy an existing business or franchise.

Fantasy Seekers are usually risk takers. They're willing to sink their life savings—or retirement fund—into an endeavor for which there's no guarantee of success. Typical attributes of a Fantasy Seeker include a high level of education, a high degree of confidence, and a willingness to work long hours. Whereas some Fantasy Seekers become entrepreneurs, others look for dream jobs, such as leading tours to remote regions of the world. Ultimately, their work and lifestyles intertwine—and the new career offers a deep sense of identity. That's a good thing, for Fantasy Seekers are likely to put in long hours to build up the business.

Several years ago, 55-year-old Milwaukee residents Jim and Marion Hook began looking for something that would allow them to step out of the daily grind and spend time together. Marion had worked with the U.S. State Department and as a consultant for nonprofit organizations. Jim had carved out a successful career in sales for Keane, an information-technology firm. What they had always dreamed of, however, was running a B&B.

In 2003 the Hooks purchased the Adobe Rose, a six-bedroom B&B nestled in the historic Sam Hughes neighborhood of central Tucson.

They sank more than half a million dollars of their savings into the enterprise, including a large portion of their 401(k) accounts.

The Hooks' gamble paid off. They are living the lifestyle of their dreams and are happier than at any time before.

Running the B&B fulfilled "a desire to entertain people and engage in interesting discussions," Jim says. For Marion, it was about spending time in the kitchen and preparing meals for guests. "Cooking has been a passion of mine since I was 12 years old," she explains. "Some of our friends thought we were absolutely insane, but we are having a marvelously good time and making ends meet.

"There was a risk associated with buying the inn," Marion adds, "but there was also a risk associated with staying in the business world, where there's no job security and no assurance of happiness. This is the perfect bridge between a traditional work environment and retirement."

Dave and Trudy Bateman are likewise living a life that many would envy. For nearly 40 years, he worked as an attorney and she worked as a nurse. Eventually the couple wound up in Olympia, Washington. In early 2005, when Dave was 59 years old, a friend questioned why he was working such long hours. "He told me, 'You're killing yourself, Dave.' I realized he was right." The friend invited them to visit him in Hawaii. When they arrived, the Batemans visited a coffee farm, fell in love with the coffee, and decided to buy that very property.

In October 2005, the Batemans paid $2 million for a 35-year lease to Heavenly Hawaiian Farms, a 37.5-acre coffee farm about 10 miles from Kona. "We had to learn how to grow coffee, work in the fields, and manage the business," Dave recalls. "There is still stress—it takes a lot of knowledge and work to care for the trees—but it isn't the destructive type of stress that comes with constant confrontations, long hours, and courtroom trials.

"I'd say the move has probably added 15 years to my life. I love what I'm doing and have no intention of returning to law. It's like living out a dream. We are living in paradise."

Trudy, for her part, was initially less enamored of the idea. She wanted to stay closer to friends and family, including her two children and two grandchildren. At age 57, she went to Hawaii reluctantly—only after the couple agreed that she would have free rein to visit family members back in Olympia and Denver whenever she desired. That works out to a few weeks every six months or so.

Today, Trudy is reconciling herself to the change—and beginning to enjoy it. "We had talked about getting a place in Hawaii for some time," she says. "But my idea was initially to get a condo or a time-share. At first I thought Dave was joking. But when I realized this is something he really wanted to do and that he couldn't keep working the way he was, we discussed it and found a way to make it work for both of us."

Over the last few years, the couple has made new friends through church and an informal professional network. In addition, Trudy volunteers part-time at a local hospice. "It's a very special place to live," she says. "Today, I have Washington State, Colorado, and Hawaii. It's really the best of all worlds."

Recareering with Style

Like most things in life, recareering is filled with ambiguity and confusion. It's messy around the edges and can easily generate more questions than answers. Some individuals fit neatly into one category; others straddle two or even three different groups. Additionally, some people find that that their style morphs with them as they grow older.

Equally important, no law says a person must stick with his or her initial recareering style. Venturing beyond the boundaries of comfort can be difficult—it may require coaching or counseling—but never underestimate the human capacity for change. Once you understand which group (or groups) you fall into—or which you want to join—you can approach recareering in a more intelligent and organized manner.

Worksheet: Discovering Your Style, Step 1

Understanding your recareering style can go a long way toward demystifying the process. Rate how strongly you agree with the following statements. (There are no right or wrong answers.) Indicate 2 for a Yes answer, 0 for a No, and 1 for a Neutral. Then total each subset of numbers on the appropriate "Factor" line provided below.

	YES	NEUTRAL	NO
I enjoy new experiences and challenges at work.	2	0	1
You're never too old to go back to school.	2	0	1
Life is too short to do all the things I dream about doing.	2	0	1
Feeling stimulated and enthusiastic in a job is more important than the pay.	2	0	1
I prefer to be my own boss.	2	0	1

TOTAL RISK FACTOR _____

	YES	NEUTRAL	NO
I easily get bored and restless.	2	0	1
I am comfortable and confident in unfamiliar situations.	2	0	1
I always seem to land on my feet.	2	0	1
I wouldn't want to stay in the same career for life.	2	0	1
I reject the philosophy, "If it isn't broken, don't fix it." There are always new and innovative ways to get things done.	2	0	1

TOTAL CHANGE-TOLERANCE FACTOR _____

Discovering Your Style, Step 2

Now, find your place in the following chart by locating the intersection of your Risk Factor and your Change-Tolerance Factor. This will give you a fairly accurate idea of what category you naturally fall into.

	LOW > HIGH CHANGE-TOLERANCE		
HIGH RISK	**0-3**	**4-7**	**8-10**
8-10		Opportunist	Fantasy Seeker
4-7		Change Agent	Active Retiree
LOW **0-3**	Adapter	Reinventor	

Discovering Your Style, Step 3

Use the results of this worksheet to help guide your career decisions. You can compare your recareering style and its associated qualities to a particular line of work (or to the educational, training, and financial paths that lead to that career) and what's required to make the change.

If you're an Adapter, for example, you belong to a group with a limited appetite for risk and a low tolerance for change. Forking over several hundred thousand dollars for a fast-food franchise or becoming an entrepreneur is therefore probably not going to be in your cards. Starting your own home-based business in an area where you already have expertise, on the other hand, may make perfect sense.

Just as an aptitude test can never fully capture your true inclinations, this gauge of your recareering style does not return definitive answers. It's up to you to survey the landscape and discover how your needs, goals, and passions jibe with real-world careers.

Differing motivations, attitudes, and aptitudes all shape the process of changing careers—which, in the end, remains an intensely personal decision. So take a deep breath—and do some deep thinking about what you intend to accomplish—before you take the leap.

It's disconcertingly easy to be buffeted about by the latest career vogue or the opinions of others. But if you prefer the quiet introspection of driving a truck cross-country to the emotional turmoil of interacting with a classroom full of rambunctious fourth graders, you can be confident you're about to shift into the right career gear.

Books

Career Match: Connecting Who You Are with What You'll Love to Do, by Shoya Zichy and Ann Bidou, AMACOM, 2007. Delves into passions, personalities, and possibilities. Offers in-depth chapters on different personality types and making the right job and career match.

Careers for Nonconformists: A Practical Guide to Finding and Developing a Career Outside the Mainstream, by Sandra Gurvis, Marlowe & Company, 1999. Offers a glimpse into career success other than that defined by the traditional treadmills.

Do What You Are: Discover the Perfect Career for You through the Secrets of Personality Type, by Paul D. Tieger and Barbara Barron, Little, Brown and Company, 2007. Aims to help you find the job that best suits your personality through asessments and other tools.

Don't Waste Your Talent: The 8 Critical Steps To Discovering What You Do Best, by Bob McDonald and Don E. Hutcheson, The Highlands Company, 2005. Provides insight into matching interests and passions with a career.

I Don't Know What I Want, But I Know It's Not This: A Step-by-Step Guide to Finding Gratifying Work, by Julie Jansen, Penguin, 2003. Explores how to overcome boredom and dissatisfaction in the work you do.

The Renaissance Soul: Life Design for People with Too Many Passions to Pick Just One, by Margaret Lobenstine, Broadway, 2006. Examines how to transform your passion into a career—and, conversely, how to make your career passionate.

More Resources

About.com Career Planning
http://careerplanning.about.com/

Serves as a hub for all sorts of information about career changes and work, including self-assessments, exploring occupations, and how to choose a career.

The Career Key
http://careerkey.org/

Offers in-depth assessments, analysis, and self-evaluation surveys that can guide you though a career switch.

CareerPlanner.com
www.careerplanner.com/

Provides career tests, career counseling, and job-search tools.

National Career Development Association
www.ncda.org/

Promotes the career development of all people over their lifespan. Sells booklets and provides resources for career development, choosing a vocation, and more.

Princeton Review Career Quiz
www.princetonreview.com/careers-after-college.aspx?uidbadge=

Although the focus is on preparing for college, this highly respected organization can pay dividends for anyone looking for new ideas and perspectives on careers.

Self-Directed Search
www.self-directed-search.com

Offers resources focused on career change, as well as a low-cost personalized assessment.

DISCOVERING YOUR IDEAL CAREER

Tests & assessments, counselors & coaches can all help bring your interests—and opportunities—into focus

WHATEVER YOUR MOTIVATION for making a career change, it's crucial to identify your goals as early in the process as possible. In an ideal world, a new career should tap into your strengths, challenge you, provide meaning and value, fit your personality and values, and help guide you to the life you long to create.

If you read Chapter 4, you now have a clearer sense of your recareering style. That doesn't mean you can't test-drive a different style, of course, or approach recareering in your own idiosyncratic way. There's no single path to happiness and success. It's up to you to use a combination of logic and intuition to find your unique direction. It's likewise up to you to recognize when fears or insecurities threaten to cloud your thinking—and lead you down the wrong path or undermine your efforts.

At least one part of the process is incontrovertible: There's no substitute for self-analysis. Spending the time and energy to identify your passions, dislikes, skills, and values—then finding a match with careers you find interesting and attractive—is a worthwhile investment. At this point, the main goal is to find career matches that you can turn into real-world opportunities.

Career & Personality Tests

One of the oldest and most trusted methods for identifying interests and understanding career possibilities is the traditional aptitude test. Stretching back to the 1940s, corporations, universities, the military, and others used aptitude tests—including the well-known Myers-Briggs Test and the Strong Vocational Interest Blank—to help determine who had the right personality for a job or who was best suited (on paper, at least) for promotion.

In a quest to provide better guidance about which jobs and careers might fit graduates, school counselors began administering these questionnaires to students in the mid-1960s. The tests identified personality traits—introversion versus extroversion, for example, or a preference for structure over independence—and then offered a list of jobs that seemed to fit each test-taker's individual profile.

Understanding personality, however, is a complex endeavor. Even the most detailed tests are prone to errors, miscalculations, or misinterpretation. In many instances, it was still necessary for a counselor to examine the results, interact with the person tested, and sift through other information. Even then, the career matches produced by the test results were often hit-or-miss at best. Moreover, they sometimes yielded contradictory results upon retesting.

The good news is that the methodologies undergirding aptitude tests have improved dynamically since the 1960s, says David P. Campbell, a leading expert on career testing and career development. "When testing is combined with someone who has knowledge and expertise in administering a test," Campbell observes, "it can provide plenty of useful information." A low score in a specific test area does not necessarily mean a person can't succeed in that arena. Nor does a high score ensure outstanding achievement in any given field. Rather, "a test simply tells you what jobs are typical and atypical for a certain personality type."

Consider the Strong-Campbell Interest Inventory (SCII), which

Campbell co-created. Individuals are asked whether they like, dislike, or feel indifferent to 325 factors representing a wide variety of subjects, occupations, activities, and types of people. They also choose favorites from among listed pairs of activities and indicate which of 14 selected characteristics apply to them. The SCII test indicates a person's suitability for 162 separate occupational scales. It also factors in six general occupational

How to Gauge Your Interests Online

Dozens of sites now offer assessments based on personality, aptitudes, and career interests. Here are some of the more robust sites:

ANSIR http://personal.ansir.com/

This three-part, 168-question, self-perception test offers insights into your style of thinking, working, and emoting. It is easy to use but requires approximately 30 minutes to complete. You receive a fairly comprehensive analysis and can obtain more detailed results for a fee.

Campbell Interest and Skill Survey (CISS)
www.profiler.com/cgi-bin/ciss/
moreform.pl?client=ncs&page=intro

This is the online version of the widely used and highly respected assessment. CISS, which costs $18, features 320 multiple-choice questions focusing on skills and interests. It's simple to use but requires 30 to 45 minutes to fill out. You receive detailed results covering 60 occupations, as well as a comprehensive career planner that helps you interpret the results and map out a new career.

CareerPlanner.com www.careerplanner.com/

This site offers a detailed personality-and-interest inventory for $19.95 and up (depending on how fast you want the results). The 20-minute survey—which includes 180 True/False questions—guides you toward 30 to 100 compatible careers.

It is especially suited for those eyeing recareering in midlife. You'll receive an 8- to 11-page report focused on interests, values, and skill sets.

Job Assets and Strengths Profiler (JASPER)

http://my.monster.com/JobStrengthProfile/Intro.aspx.

Based on the Myers-Briggs survey, this 70-question assessment guides you to eight different job-related and career dimensions. It also offers a useful graphical interface that makes it easy to understand the results. The analysis requires 20 to 30 minutes; whereas the basic results are free, you'll have to shell out $59.95 for a more detailed report.

LiveCareer www.livecareer.com/

This free 100-question assessment helps you identify career interests and lets you know which jobs offer a match. The survey takes less than 30 minutes to fill in. For more detailed information about your career inclinations, there's a more in-depth test, but it requires a $24.95 fee.

Princeton Review Career Quiz http://www.princetonreview.com/careers-after-college.aspx?uidbadge=

The free 24-question survey measures your interests and work style. It takes less than 10 minutes to complete and presents the results in color-coded categories. Register at the site and you'll also receive a list of careers that match your interests and aptitudes. You can click on these career options to read detailed information about what it's like to work in any field and what sort of education and experience are required to land a job in each one.

What's the Right Job for You?

http://assessment.usatests.com/jobtest/?v

This $6.95 survey serves up 50 questions designed to identify the jobs that best match your temperament, lifestyle, and attitudes. It requires about 15 minutes to complete and provides a 20-page personalized report outlining your qualities and traits—along with a list of compatible potential jobs.

themes—realistic, investigative, artistic, social, enterprising, or conventional. In addition to the SCII, aptitude tests that have gained widespread acceptance today include the Guilford-Zimmerman Interest Inventory, the G-S-Z Interest Survey, the California Occupational Preference Survey, the Jackson Vocational Interest Survey, and the Ohio Vocational Interest Survey. These tests can help individuals familiarize themselves with career options and become aware of their vocational interests.

Career Counseling
Comes of Age
More and more individuals considering a career change are turning to professional career counselors. It's easy to understand why: Sorting through all the possibilities and options can seem overwhelming. It's also difficult to objectively view our own situation—notably, to discern which personal issues we may have cleverly disguised as roadblocks. A career counselor can add perspective and help guide a person down the appropriate trail.

Although there's no single approach to career counseling, the process usually follows a fairly predictable arc. The first step is an interview and an evaluation process that helps pinpoint the reason for dissatisfaction, explains Helen Harkness, whose Texas firm, Career Design Associates, has helped thousands of people find new careers. First and foremost, Harkness challenges clients to question the very necessity of abandoning their current vocation. "If the problem revolves around the company or a certain job," Harkness points out, "a career counselor can help you avoid the pain of recareering needlessly. There are many instances where a person thinks it's necessary to recareer when a realignment is all that's needed."

If an individual looks like a candidate for recareering, a career counselor will usually administer tests designed to assess one's personality, values, and career aptitudes. The counselor then conducts an interview to gauge how the tests stack up to real-world behavior and attitudes. Harkness, for example, uses a set of questions to identify whether personal issues are clouding

the professional picture. These might include a divorce, an addiction, a
midlife crisis, a death in the family, or any other traumatic life event. This
helps frame the recareering process and, in the case of an addiction, forces
an individual to confront the problem before moving forward.

Some career counselors work with individuals one-on-one. Others
place those hoping to recareer in a group setting where they may spend
30 to 40 hours (usually in one- or two-hour sessions a couple of times
each week) discussing interests, goals, and values while receiving feedback from other participants. The career counselor usually guides a class
through the self-discovery process, providing practical advice along the
way on how to segue from one career to the next.

Harkness also asks participants to create a list of "success criteria."
She directs each individual to divide his or her recareering issues into
two categories: glass balls, which cannot drop; and rubber balls, which
can. The glass balls contain life and work factors that a person deems
essential to achieving a sense of purpose. The rubber balls, by contrast,
hold motivational issues (such as pay or the desire to effect positive
social change) or lifestyle issues (such as the desire to work from home,
avoid travel, or attain a better work/life balance). So while rubber balls
are important, they are not a make-or-break issue: You can always
bounce back if one of them gets dropped or rolls out of the picture.

A career counselor is also likely to conduct a detailed skills assessment,
which typically takes the form of written tests and analysis through
questions and answers. The counselor then overlays the results of this
inventory with data about the participant's personality, interests, dislikes,
and values, derived through other written and verbal analysis. Although
this process hinges on looking inward, it's equally important to gaze
outward, constantly monitoring job trends, changing industry conditions,
the current employment picture, and what different careers entail. Done
right, the counseling process enables a person to see how various careers
measure up to a list of benchmarks that define professional success.

Is Counseling for You?

A career counselor can guide you to the work you love by performing any or all of several vital services. He or she might conduct an evaluation that sheds light on your work values, interests, and skills—some of them previously undetected. A counselor can also assess your experience and abilities to identify promising career paths; draft a career-development plan that includes projections of professional growth; help with résumé writing, job-interview skills, and networking; and offer unbiased—and unvarnished—career counseling.

Try these steps to find a qualified career counselor:

Inquire through colleagues or a professional network.

Seek low-cost (even free) counseling for qualifying individuals from selected cities, counties, and not-for-profit organizations. To locate such a program, search the Internet (keyword: career counselor) or the Yellow Pages, or inquire with local government officials.

Evaluate the counselor's previous employment history. How many years has he or she worked with other career changers? Has she taken courses or earned certifications?

Learn what degrees and certifications a career counselor has. Someone with a graduate degree in psychology or sociology will have a better knowledge base than a high school graduate. Still, knowledge and experience *can* substitute for a degree: Ask the counselor whether she holds a recognized certification, such as the National Career Development Association's National Certified Career Counselor, Master Career Counselor, or Master Career Development Professional.

Ask for references. Follow up by contacting each individual the counselor lists as a reference, asking the reference detailed questions such as: What specific problems did she guide you through? What challenges did he help you overcome? What are her strengths? His weaknesses?

Career counseling can also involve watching videos about different careers and professions, listening to motivational speakers, and using interactive software programs. A job counselor may be able to help you with general financial planning tasks; if not, he or she may recommend a qualified financial planner.

Nor are job counselors bereft of practical, tactical skills: Once you finally target a new career, the counselor can direct you to the required training and education, help fashion a strong résumé, chase down job leads, and role-play job-interview scenarios.

Depending on whether you participate in group sessions or one-on-one exchanges, private counseling can cost anywhere from hundreds of dollars to tens of thousands of dollars. Some not-for-profit organizations, among them Jewish Family Services, offer free or low-cost counseling to those who qualify.

What About
Online Counseling?
Like so many activities in the Internet age, career counseling has gone online. Dozens of worthwhile sites offer job tips, information, and personality assessments (see "How to Gauge Your Interests Online," pages 91-92). Although they cannot match the level of interaction and feedback provided by a well-qualified professional, these sites can help you winnow down options and possibilities. Many offer solid counsel about careers and career issues, and their interactive assessments can be a valuable point of departure for a recareering journey. Some of these services are free; others charge a fee as high as $80.

Does Your Employer
Offer Counseling?
A few large companies have established their own career-counseling and retirement-planning programs, which they offer to employees as a benefit. The paper-products giant Weyerhaeuser, for example, features a two-and-a-half day seminar that helps

employees and their spouses plan their retirement. It also offers a one-day course that's designed to help workers find their passion in retirement— or beyond their current position at the company. An outside instructor helps Weyerhaeuser employees sort through the tangle of issues—the role of money, personal values, and finding meaning, for starters—that confront workers in their 50s or 60s. Sally Hass, the benefits-education manager at Weyerhaeuser who leads the program, refers to it as "a midlife career checkup" or "midlife timeout."

Inevitably, perhaps, a few Weyerhaeuser workers out of every group that participates in the program discover they're ready for a career

---

Key Questions

Am I willing to spend the time required to identify my true passions and needs? There are the rare few who always seem to know what they want and when they want it. For the rest of us, self-discovery is an ongoing process— and one that requires not only introspection but also some welcome external guidance. Take in-person or online personality tests and do whatever self-analysis you can to know yourself better.

Would I benefit from career counseling? A professional counselor or coach can help you focus on what really appeals to you and nudge you toward your goals. He or she can keep you going when your recareering effort is running on fumes. However, counseling comes at a cost, both of money and of time; it can require weeks or months of meetings and sessions.

Is honesty my policy? It's easy to succumb to peer pressure or make decisions based on what a parent, spouse, or other key figure in your life might desire. Sure, it's important to consider the opinions of others—particularly immediate family members. Just make sure the voice in your head is your own.

change. Most, however, stay put but use the session to map out their futures. "We want what's best for each individual," says Hass. "If someone decides to leave, that's the right answer for us as well."

Does a Career Coach Make Sense for You?

A variation on the career counselor is the career coach. Since coming into vogue in the 1970s, this discipline has become wildly popular, if not trendy, particularly among executives and professionals. A career coach serves as a combination professional consultant, cheerleader, and personal trainer.

A career-coaching arrangement works something like this: Once you hire a person to serve as your coach, that individual guides you through the process of analyzing your needs and desires, setting attainable goals, and finding suitable work. A good coach will stick with you until the completion of the process, providing ongoing feedback, tips, strategies, and tactics. A coaching relationship may last for weeks, months, or years.

Transforming Skills into an Occupation

A fun way to assess your abilities and sync them up with various occupations is the O*NET® Online Skills Search. You check off boxes that describe your range of skills—basic, complex problem solving, resource management, social, systems, and technical—then view jobs that match. You can click on any of the resulting positions to view what's needed for the job and how closely your skills may be suited to it. You can also view the technology and tools used in the occupation, what type of knowledge it requires, and what "flavor" of work it entails, including the use of teams, face-to-face discussions, and the proportion of structured to unstructured work. The free site is available at: http://online.onetcenter.org/skills/. You can also use the O*NET® Career Exploration Tools at http://www.onetcenter.org/tools.html.

Friends and colleagues are usually a good source for finding a qualified coach. You might also consider contacting a coach who appears at a workshop, conference, or job fair, or get in touch with a professional organization such as internationalcoachfederation.com. It offers a database that invites you to search by specialty, professional experience, or geographic location. Although rates vary, most career coaches charge a fee of $75 to $150 for a 60- to 90-minute session.

Coaching Qualifications

Anyone—regrettably—can attach the title "career counselor," "consultant," or "coach" to his name. And when the unscrupulous break out the shears, the unsuspecting get fleeced.

So how do you find someone with the knowledge, experience, and professional skills to guide you to a new career? Before you plunk down a single dollar for counseling services, do your homework. Check references and ask questions. Find out which professional organizations have the strictest standards. The National Career Development Association (NCDA), for example, certifies professionals as National Certified Career Counselors. That means these individuals have earned a graduate degree in counseling or a related field from an accredited institution; that they have completed a supervised internship; and that they have at least three years' experience in career development. Another NCDA certification, the Master Career Development Professional (MCDP), is awarded to those with a master's degree or higher in counseling or a related field. An MCDP has at least three years of post-master's career-development experience in training, teaching, program development, or materials development.

Organizations that recognize and certify career counselors include the National Career Development Association (www.ncda.org), the National Board for Certified Counselors (www.nbcc.org), the American Counseling Association (www.counseling.org), and the American Psychological Association (www.apa.org).

OF BLUEPRINTS & BEDPANS

REBECCA ARMSTRONG, *from architect to nurse*

IN 1973, I GRADUATED from Oberlin College in Oberlin, Ohio, with a degree in music. I spent a couple of years singing professionally and working in libraries, but then I thought I'd better find a way to make a living. I had always dreamed about becoming a doctor. But I thought I was too old to go to medical school when I was 25—which only shows you how young and immature I really was. Deciding to go back to school and do something useful, I took an aptitude test that suggested I become an architect. And that's exactly what I did.

It seemed to be a good fit initially. I worked at several firms and eventually earned my license. I helped design schools, libraries, fire stations, and other buildings. Some of my credits include the Bronx Zoo, the library at West Point Military Academy, and the Women's Rights Historical Park in upstate New York.

But I always found architecture tough. It encompasses a lot of financial responsibility. The field also involves hours and hours of overtime. So the entire time I was working as an architect, I never once stopped wishing that I had gone the medical route. I wanted to do something that mattered more in the moment.

Some people seem blessed with the ability to figure things out when they are still at a fairly young age; others take a while to find the right path. I guess I fall into the latter category. I never thought I could make a change, because I got married and had two kids: We had a mortgage and a lot of expenses. I couldn't stop working for a month, let alone go to school for months on end and pay my tuition.

Fortunately, several years ago we happened to buy an apartment in New York City. At first it dropped in value, and we worried that we had made a huge mistake. But prices have shot up over the last five to seven years, giving us a good deal of equity.

I had a calling for more meaningful work. I finally decided that I would go back to school and earn a nursing degree. At age 55, medical school, an internship, and a residency are a long path. At that particular point in my life,

I decided, I could probably be more productive as a nurse. The more I researched the profession, the more excited I got. My older daughter had already transferred to a different college in order to pursue a nursing degree; as the two of us began to "talk shop," my enthusiasm snowballed. I decided to make the switch.

I applied to four colleges all told, including Columbia University and NYU [New York University]. Columbia was my first choice, but it was also the most expensive. The only way I could make it work would be to rent a small apartment near campus, stay there during the week, and take the subway back and forth to our home in Brooklyn on weekends. So that's what I did. It's about a 90-minute ride each way. I was accepted at Columbia in 2006 and started there in May. In terms of schedule and lifestyle, it was a big adjustment.

I received my bachelor of science degree through a one-year accelerated Bachelor of Science, Nursing degree program in May 2007. You could go on the fast track if you had taken certain prerequisites, including anatomy and physiology, microbiology, statistics, chemistry, developmental psychology, and nutrition. It's a solid 12-month program that was fast but grueling. Before I started the program, I worked three days a week for a year while satisfying the prerequisites.

I took the licensing exam at the end of July, and began working in the neonatal intensive care unit at Maimonides Infants and Children's Hospital in Brooklyn. I'll continue to work there while I'm studying in the master's program at Columbia.

By January 2010, I should have my master of science degree in nursing and my certification as a neonatal nurse practitioner. At that point I will be a 58-year-old practitioner, much like the attending physicians in the hospital, with treatment and prescribing authority.

I'm spending over $100,000 for these nursing programs. The good news is that my starting salary is not much less than the one I left behind in architecture, which took 25 years to work up to! But money has never been a primary issue. I'm very excited about this change; not for a moment have I looked back with regret—or looked back at all. I feel like I am finally on the right course in life.

Self-Assessment
Can Trigger Change

In addition to using a career counselor or coach, you can conduct your own career analysis. The self-assessment process, detailed below, centers on six key steps:

Step 1: Identify your passions. It's important to know what excites you and motivates you. Do you love to travel? Do you have an intense passion for environmental issues? Do you enjoy using computers and the latest gadgets? Does human behavior fascinate you? Does an artistic activity, such as writing, art, or music, make your soul sing? Does cooking warm the cockles of your heart? Do you enjoy being around animals?

Keep in mind that at this point we're not ready to make any binding career decisions. We're simply trying to find a starting point—without having to determine whether or not any given passion translates into a viable career. So avoid the judgment process and just let your ideas roll out onto paper. Rather than thinking, "There's no way this ridiculous idea could ever become a real career!," try to work your way to the point where you discover, "Aha! So *that's* what I've always wanted to pursue!"

Step 2: Discover your dislikes. It's entirely possible to change careers and wind up in the same job (or at least a job that seems the same). Imagine that an office manager grows weary of constantly surveiling people, schedules, and reports. In response, she accomplishes her lifelong dream: opening a sandwich shop. Ultimately, however, she finds herself confronting many of the same tasks, for the life of a small-business owner invariably entails dealing with the vagaries of staffing needs, budget projections, and reviews of sales reports.

Knowing what you don't like and what you don't want to do can therefore be almost as critical as pinpointing your passions. You might find writing reports to be the seventh circle of hell. You might dread cold-calling potential clients or harbor a pathological aversion to keeping detailed records. You might resolve never to get stuck behind a desk all day or be forced to work rigid schedule hours. However simple or

Worksheet #1: **Self-Assessment**

My passions include:

_____

_____

_____

My dislikes include:

_____

_____

_____

My skills include:

_____

_____

_____

My values include:

_____

_____

_____

Desirable careers include:

_____

_____

_____

_____

_____

involved your list of dislikes turns out to be, cataloguing your "non-nego-tiable items" should help steer you away from undesirable career choices.

Step 3: Sort your skills. Once you've listed your passions and your dislikes, it's time to take the next step and tot up the various skills you possess. Although it's not advisable to choose a career based solely on skills—in fact, it's a really bad idea—this inventory can help you under-stand whether you have the foundation in place to make the transition to a particular career.

Are you a good verbal communicator? Are you an excellent problem-solver? Do you have solid leadership skills? Are you good with numbers or writing? Do you have an entrepreneurial mentality? Now it's time to list these skills. You can combine your own self-appraisal with any unsus-pected aptitudes that a personality or career test may have disclosed.

Step 4: Inventory your values. One of the primary considerations for making a career switch is how well (and, ideally, how much better) it will mesh with your value system. Even if you find a career that taps into your passions, minimizes your dislikes, and harnesses your skills, you may ulti-mately discover that it isn't a good match for your personal ethos.

Let's say you realize that you love the idea of working in marketing or public relations. You have great communication skills, but you don't want to wind up pitching another meaningless consumer product to the masses. This might lead you to a not-for-profit organization that addresses key social concerns, such as homelessness or healthcare.

Values fall into two categories: extrinsic, which usually revolve around pay and the working environment; and intrinsic, which relate to the spe-cific work and how it improves or exploits society. If extrinsic values matter to you most, you may place a premium on earning a high salary and being granted an impressive job title. If intrinsic values drive you more, on the other hand, you may feel it's paramount to contribute something to society.

In some cases, values encompass an entire career. In other instances they cover only a specific job within a particular organization. Consider:

A person may love working in advertising but loathe the idea of promoting a tobacco product. Or an individual may want to focus his advertising talents on advancing the agenda of a political party or social cause.

Finding a Career
You Admire
Let's pause here to identify a few likely career possibilities. At this interim point in the process, any reasonable idea will afford acceptable traction. Your ideal may be as lofty as becoming an airline pilot or as grounded as working as a gardener at a botanical garden. Think "blue sky" and let your fantasies fly. (Save the practical concerns for later; we'll sort through them shortly, when we develop a basic career map.)

You might want to consider your list of passions (see Worksheet #1, page 103) and think about careers that build on them. For example, a love of travel might translate into working as a tour guide, working in a travel bookstore, becoming a travel agent, or finding a job that allows you to travel and see various parts of the world. Similarly, a passion for working with children along with good communication skills might translate into working as a teacher or supervising a private or municipal youth program.

Step 5: Find a career match. Now we're at the point where you're going to put all the pieces together and discover some real-world possibilities (see Worksheet #2, page 106). By taking each career possibility and rating each of your responses in four categories—passions, dislikes, skills, and values—you will gain a keener insight about which career choices are viable and which others you can safely exclude from the mix.

Step 6: Transform numbers into action. You can use this method to experiment with additional career possibilities, if you like. In general, the higher your category scores in a particular career or job, the more likely you are to find it compatible (with the notable exception of the "dislikes" category, where a higher score is a warning).

This system cannot provide a definitive answer, of course, about whether any particular career is a perfect match for you; rather, it furnishes

Worksheet #2: **Assessing Careers**

Using the following charts, write down each answer from Worksheet #1 (page 103) and assign it a number from 1 (low value) to 10 (high value), based on how important that answer is in the context of the career you're considering. Then total the ratings and divide each column total by 4 (or however many qualities you were able to identify) to give you the average for each category.

Career Possibility #1:

PASSIONS		DISLIKES		SKILLS		VALUES	
TOTAL		TOTAL		TOTAL		TOTAL	
AVERAGE		AVERAGE		AVERAGE		AVERAGE	

Career Possibility #2:

PASSIONS		DISLIKES		SKILLS		VALUES	
TOTAL		TOTAL		TOTAL		TOTAL	
AVERAGE		AVERAGE		AVERAGE		AVERAGE	

Career Possibility #3:

PASSIONS		DISLIKES		SKILLS		VALUES	
TOTAL		TOTAL		TOTAL		TOTAL	
AVERAGE		AVERAGE		AVERAGE		AVERAGE	

some useful general insights into how different careers may stack up against your attitudes, desires, abilities, and needs. You can also use this system to evaluate specific jobs within a certain organization.

Now let's take a look at your overall results (see Worksheet #3, below). Although it is difficult to forcibly change your passions, dislikes, and values (unless you're willing to compromise on the latter—usually a ticket to unhappiness later on), the one factor you *can* directly control is your skills. If you lack the knowledge or skills required for a particular career, you might be able to address the shortfall by going back to school, attending a training session, or accepting an entry-level position and then working your way up the organizational ladder.

Worksheet #3: Pulling It All Together

	PASSIONS	DISLIKES	SKILLS	VALUES
Career Possibility #1				
Career Possibility #2				
Career Possibility #3				

If you feel that you have a knowledge or skill gap for a specific career (if your rating is 5 or lower, this is something you need to consider), note below how you might address it.

SKILL/KNOWLEDGE GAP	SOLUTION

Focus on
the Future
Once you've spent time mulling your possibilities—and which of them might represent opportunities—it's time to begin planning your career change in earnest. You're about to enter the world of résumés, online job boards, job fairs, adult education, and a dizzying array of personal and professional changes and challenges. Hope, adjustment, excitement—they're all mile markers on the road to reinventing your life.

Books

Career Match: Connecting Who You Are with What You'll Love to Do, by Shoya Zichy and Ann Bidou, AMACOM, 2007. Offers extensive self-testing in order to guide you to positive career choices.

How to Find the Work You Love, by Laurence G. Boldt, Penguin, 2004. Offers information, tips, and exercises for connecting to work that represents your calling in life.

Life's a Bitch and Then You Change Careers: 9 Steps to Get Out of Your Funk & On to Your Future, by Andrea Kay, STC Paperbacks, 2006. Walks you through the process of changing careers.

Passion at Work: How to Find Work You Love and Live the Time of Your Life, by Lawler Kang and Mark Albion, Prentice Hall, 2005. Helps guide you through the process of finding the job of your dreams.

More Resources

Association of Career Professionals International
www.acpinternational.org

Click the "Find a Career Services Expert" box and your geographic region to bring up a search tool that can find an expert in areas such as assessment, coaching, personal development, family/spouse relocation, financial planning, and retirement planning. Each listing includes a biography with contact information.

Career Guide to Industries
www.bls.gov/oco

The Bureau of Labor Statistics' *Occupational Outlook Handbook* offers information about various occupations within industries, training and advancement requirements, earnings, and working conditions.

CareerOneStop
www.careeronestop.org

This U.S. Department of Labor site is a comprehensive source of information on an assortment of career issues. You can browse occupations by state and view current wage and salary information. You can also view the skills and abilities required to work in a particular job or profession.

International Coach Federation
http://internationalcoachfederation.
com/ICF/For+Coaching+Clients/
Find+a+Coach

> The "Coach Referral Service" feature offers a searchable directory of the ICF's 12,000 members in 42 countries.

National Board for Certified Counselors (NBCC)
www.nbcc.org/counselorfind

> The counselor-certifying board offers an online search tool that can help you find a professional career counselor. Check the "Career Development" box (or any other category you're interested in) to gather a list of names in your area.

National Career Development Association
www.ncda.org

> Click on "Career Center" and "Need a Career Counselor?" to view a list of qualified professionals, along with their websites and e-mail links.

Occupational Outlook Quarterly Online
www.bls.gov/opub/ooq/ooqhome.htm

> This online newsletter, based on the print periodical *Occupational Outlook Quarterly,* outlines various trends in work and labor, and includes an archive going back to 1999.

6

WHAT ARE MY OPTIONS?

Here are 20 callings to consider on the road to finding the work you love

DISCOVERING WHAT YOU WANT TO DO with the rest of your life—or even the next few years—is a daunting proposition. One way to demystify a career move (and increase its odds for success) is to gather all the information possible before you take the plunge. Though the only true way to experience a job is to actually do it, of course, the ability to pore over labor trends, job requirements, and hiring statistics can help you find your rightful place in the scheme of things.

The Internet is expanding the boundaries for self-discovery. These days, you can slice though vast databases and glean detailed information about thousands of potential careers. Facts and figures that were available only to career counselors and the business elite a few years ago are now accessible at the click of a mouse. This includes profiles of different careers, working conditions, earnings, education and training requirements, advancement options, future outlook, and similar occupations. You can also view the skills, knowledge, abilities, work activities, and tools that you would use in a particular line of work.

This chapter examines 20 careers ideal for boomers and other older workers. These jobs have a high percentage of workers age 50 and up.

They are not physically overtaxing. Many of them are ideal for those seeking self-employment or part-time work. Some are high-value jobs that may provide a greater sense of meaning, and all of them are likely to be in demand over the next several years. The list of jobs that appear in this chapter—compiled using data supplied by the Bureau of Labor Statistics, O*Net Online (operated by the U.S. Department of Labor), and the U.S. Census Bureau—can serve as a starting point for any career-change initiative.

Understanding Your Work Personality
Before we delve into some of the best careers for boomers, let's take a look at a few key issues. One of them is what O*Net describes as "interests." It might help to think of these as personality factors. Individuals typically fall into one or more of the six categories listed below. Although the categories cannot predict who will succeed in a particular career, they serve as a general indicator for the type of person who is attracted to the job—and will likely be the happiest and most productive in it.

Realistic. The work usually involves practical and hands-on approaches. Many of these professions involve craft-type jobs and focus on outdoor work rather than paperwork or team-based work.

Artistic. These individuals prefer to work with forms, designs, and patterns. They often enjoy self-expression and prefer to work without strict rules or regulations.

Social. Working in the company of others brings a sense of satisfaction. Oftentimes, those who choose to work in these careers enjoy helping others.

Investigative. Ideas, thinking skills, and problem-solving are at the center of work for individuals who fall into this group.

Conventional. Those who work in these occupations typically favor set rules, policies, and procedures. They prefer order and routine. Many of these individuals enjoy detail-oriented work.

Enterprising. Ingenuity and resourcefulness are key traits of those who fall into this group. These individuals like to make decisions, start and carry out projects, and enjoy risk and rewards.

Know Thy Skills
There's no denying the need for skills. And in today's information-intensive world, the demand for a more robust skill set seems to grow more urgent every day.

In some cases, you may already possess the expertise required to perform well in a chosen (new) career. If not, you may have to go back to school, or seek out the required training on or off the job. The aptitudes listed under "SKILL LEVEL NEEDED" on pages 115-137 are not exhaustive, but most 21st-century jobs are likely to call for some combination of them.

Do I really understand what's required in a job or career? It's one thing to imagine working in a field. It's another thing entirely to dive into the field. Research careers online, then match the possibilities you find with personality tests and other self-assessments.

What does it take to build a career map? Information is a good thing, but it can also create problems. You must figure out how to use all those facts (which often diverge). At this stage, it's essential to consider how your recareering style, personality, and skills match up. Even if they don't, you may choose to pursue a career that interests you, but you should expect the road to be bumpier.

Have I explored all my options? It's best to spend a good deal of time reviewing career profiles. If there's a possibility you might proceed, contact the relevant professional associations. They can often provide additional information, including brochures, booklets, and packages. They can also provide detailed information about education, training, and licensing requirements.

10 Careers Ideally Suited for Recareering Boomers

Now let's take a look at some of the best careers for older workers. These positions rose to the top based on a number of factors, including the ability of older workers to perform well, projected labor demand over the next several years, value to society, quality of working conditions, and flexibility (the chance to work part-time or on a self-employed basis). Several categories offer ratings from one diamond to four, including an overall recareering rating, outlook, working conditions, part-time availability, and how friendly the career is for those 50+. Keep in mind that these criteria may be quite different from those most prized by a twentysomething college graduate. (Yes, age sometimes matters!)

K-12 School Teacher

OVERVIEW K-12 schoolteachers must serve as solid role models and be comfortable dealing with active (and sometimes rebellious) young people. They engage in interactive and hands-on instruction that encompasses lecture, discussion, activities, and props to teach often abstract and complex subject matter, including writing, reading, mathematics, science, and social studies. They also encourage students to learn social skills and teamwork, and to master new technology. Teachers at the middle- or high-school level might teach art, music, foreign languages, and physical education. As school populations grow more and more diverse, teachers are increasingly called upon to work with students from different backgrounds, languages, and value systems. Today, many older individuals find greater meaning and purpose in teaching.

RECAREERING RATING: ♦♦♦♦ Virtually anyone from any profession can transition into teaching in midlife. Although additional education is required, fast-track credentialing programs make it possible to become a teacher within a year. If that's not an option, substitute teaching may be a possibility. Most districts and schools do not require substitutes to be credentialed.

ANNUAL EARNINGS: $48,700 for elementary; $49,470 for middle and high school (range: $31,000-$73,000)

PERSONALITY FACTORS: SOCIAL, ARTISTIC, INVESTIGATIVE. You must enjoy working with young people and have considerable patience—particularly when unmotivated or disrespectful students are among your charges. Must also deal with a growing array of accountability standards and testing criteria. Creativity and enthusiasm are essential.

RECAREERING STYLE: OPPORTUNIST, CHANGE AGENT, REINVENTOR.

EDUCATION: General education teachers must earn a bachelor's degree and complete an approved teacher training program, with the number and type of subject and education credits varying from state to state. They must also participate in a supervised practice-teaching program. Some states also demand technology training and the attainment of a minimum grade-point average. Twenty states and many school systems dictate that teachers obtain a master's degree in education, either as a prerequisite or within a few years of entering the field.

SKILL LEVEL NEEDED: High. INSTRUCTING, READING & COMPREHENSION, COMMUNICATION (WRITTEN AND/OR VERBAL), LISTENING, MONITORING, TIME MANAGEMENT, CRITICAL THINKING.

JOB REQUIREMENTS: States have different criteria for issuing regular licenses to teach kindergarten through grade 12. However, all 50 states and the District of Columbia mandate that public school teachers be licensed and credentialed (though private schools often bypass this criteria).

OUTLOOK: ♦♦♦♦ The demand for teachers will grow at an 18 to 26 percent rate (587,000 additional positions) through 2014*.

WORKING CONDITIONS: ♦♦♦♦ Most schools offer pleasant working conditions. However, some teachers may find that crowded classrooms and ongoing accountability standards create stress and burnout. Most teachers work a traditional 10-month schedule (with summers off), though some districts use a year-round schedule that dictates eight weeks of work followed by a week off (and a five-week break during the winter).

* Demand figures are based on the period from 2004 to 2014.

WORKERS AGE 50+: ♦♦♦♦ 30%

PART-TIME: ♦♦♦♦ 9.3%

SIMILAR OCCUPATIONS: Teacher assistant; teacher helper; postsecondary teaching.

FOR MORE INFORMATION

Bureau of Labor Statistics, *Occupational Outlook Handbook*
www.bls.gov/oco/ocos069.htm

American Federation of Teachers. 555 New Jersey Avenue NW, Washington,
D.C. 20001. 202-879-4400. www.aft.org.

National Council for Accreditation of Teacher Education. 2010 Massachusetts
Avenue NW, Suite 500, Washington, D.C. 20036. 202-466-7496.
www.ncate.org.

National Center for Alternative Certification. 1901 Pennsylvania Avenue NW,
Suite 201, Washington, D.C. 20006. 202-822-8280. www.teach-now.org.

National Education Association. 1201 16th Street NW, Washington, D.C.
20036. 202-833-4000. www.nea.org.

Registered Nurse

OVERVIEW For a growing legion of older workers, nursing is a healthy career
choice. A registered nurse (RN) diagnoses and treats patients; educates
patients and their families; provides support to doctors and advice to
patients; administers tests; and operates equipment and machinery. RNs
often specialize in specific areas, including pediatrics, oncology, trauma care,
and cardiac care. Most RNs work as staff nurses in medical centers, though
some work independently in clinics. These include: clinical nurse specialists,
nurse anesthetists, nurse midwives, and nurse practitioners. Others teach,
or work as consultants, public-policy advisors, pharmaceutical and medical-
supply researchers, salespeople, and medical writers or editors.

RECAREERING RATING: ◆◆◆◆ If you'd like to do something meaningful and help others, nursing may be your ticket to fulfillment. A growing number of boomers are recareering into the field. The huge demand for professional nurses ensures that not only will you have work, but you are likely to be able to exert a high degree of control over where you work and what hours you work.

ANNUAL EARNINGS: $57,280 (range: $43,000-$75,000)

PERSONALITY FACTORS: SOCIAL, INVESTIGATIVE. Nurses must be comfortable working in a high-stress environment and adept at dealing with doctors, patients, families, and other medical professionals. They must be aware of potential problems and be comfortable handling a variety of tasks.

RECAREERING STYLE: OPPORTUNIST, CHANGE AGENT, REINVENTOR.

EDUCATION: Must earn a bachelor of science degree in nursing (BSN) or an associate degree in nursing (ADN), or earn a diploma through a hospital program. BSN degrees take approximately four years to complete. Advanced specialties require at least a master's degree. Most of these programs last about two years and require a BSN degree; some programs require at least one to two years of clinical experience as an RN for admission.

SKILL LEVEL REQUIRED: High. LISTENING, READING & COMPREHENSION, CRITICAL THINKING, INSTRUCTING, COMMUNICATION (WRITTEN AND/OR VERBAL), TIME MANAGEMENT, MONITORING, DECISION-MAKING.

JOB REQUIREMENTS: Degrees only.

OUTLOOK: ◆◆◆◆ As the boomer population of the United States approaches Medicare eligibility, employment for registered nurses is projected to grow at a rate of 18 to 26 percent (1,203,000 additional positions) through 2014.

WORKING CONDITIONS: Most nurses work in clean, well-lit environments. Some work in home health (visiting homes, schools, community centers, and clinics). Nurses typically spend a lot of time on their feet, and may work night shifts and overtime. Some may also work on an on-call basis. Nurses are often exposed to sick patients (some carrying transmittable diseases), and may suffer injuries due to lifting and moving patients.

WORKERS AGE 50+: ◆◆◆◆ 25.4%

PART-TIME: ◆◆◆◆ 23% (many employers also offer flexible scheduling and contract work)

SIMILAR OCCUPATIONS: Emergency medical technician; paramedic; licensed vocational nurse; home health aide; radiological technician; occupational or physical therapist.

FOR MORE INFORMATION

U.S. Bureau of Labor Statistics, *Occupational Outlook Handbook*
www.bls.gov/oco/ocos083.htm

American Academy of Nurse Practitioners, P.O. Box 12846, Austin, TX 78711.
512-442-4262. www.aanp.org

American Association of Colleges of Nursing, 1 Dupont Circle NW, Suite 530,
Washington, D.C. 20036. 202-463-6930. www.aacn.nche.edu

American College of Nurse-Midwives, 8403 Colesville Road, Suite 1550,
Silver Spring, MD 20910. 240-485-1800. www.midwife.org

American Nurses Association, 8515 Georgia Avenue, Suite 400,
Silver Spring, MD 20910. 800-274-4262. http://nursingworld.org

National League for Nursing. 61 Broadway, New York, NY 10006.
800-669-1656. www.nln.org

Pharmacist

OVERVIEW: Pharmacists dispense drugs and devices prescribed by physicians and other medical practitioners. They advise patients how to use medications correctly, and they help physicians understand proper dosage, interactions, and side effects. Pharmacists oversee confidential records and are responsible for the accuracy of both records and prescriptions. Some pharmacists now work in nontraditional settings, such as pharmaceutical firms or public health agencies.

RECAREERING RATING: ◆◆◆◆ Demand for pharmacists is increasing rapidly and it's a job that has many desirable qualities for boomers and other older workers. If you can handle the educational requirements, it could be the career for you.

ANNUAL EARNINGS: $94,520 (range: $68,000-$119,000)

PERSONALITY FACTORS: CONVENTIONAL, REALISTIC, INVESTIGATIVE. You must be comfortable working with medical professionals and the public. Analytical thinking and an ability to conduct research are essential.

RECAREERING STYLE: OPPORTUNIST, REINVENTOR.

EDUCATION: A doctor of pharmacy degree from an accredited college of pharmacy. The Pharm.D. requires at least six years of postsecondary study (two years of college and a four-year pharmacy-studies program). It focuses on managing pharmaceutical products and communicating with patients and other healthcare providers about drug information and patient care, professional ethics, and public health issues. Participants boost their knowledge though classroom instruction and on-site learning that takes place under the supervision of licensed pharmacists.

SKILL LEVEL REQUIRED: High. LISTENING, COMMUNICATION (WRITTEN AND/OR VERBAL), INSTRUCTING, READING AND COMPREHENSION, MATH, TIME MANAGEMENT, RESEARCH, CRITICAL THINKING.

JOB REQUIREMENTS: It's mandatory to pass an exam and obtain a state license.

OUTLOOK: ◆◆◆◆ Expect employment for pharmacists to expand at a rate of 18 to 26 percent (101,000 additional positions) through 2014, as population ages and new and more drugs are introduced.

WORKING CONDITIONS: ◆◆◆◆ Most pharmacists spend a lot of time on their feet and some must work weekends and night hours. Pharmacists must also take special precautions, such as wearing masks and gloves when handling and mixing medicines.

WORKERS AGE 50+: ◆◆◆◆ 25.8%

PART TIME: ◆◆◆◆ 21%

SIMILAR OCCUPATIONS: Pharmacy technician; pharmacy aide.

FOR MORE INFORMATION

Bureau of Labor Statistics, *Occupational Outlook Handbook*
    www.bls.gov/oco/ocos079.htm

Academy of Managed Care Pharmacy, 100 North Pitt Street
    Suite 400, Alexandria, VA 22314. 800-827-2627. www.amcp.org

American Association of Colleges of Pharmacy, 1426 Prince Street,
    Alexandria, VA 22314. 703-739-2330. www.aacp.org

American Pharmacists Association, 1100 15th Street NW, Suite 400,
    Washington, D.C. 20005. 202-628-4410. www.pharmacist.com

American Society of Health-System Pharmacists, 7272 Wisconsin Avenue,
    Bethesda, MD 20814. 301-657-3000. www.ashp.org

National Association of Boards of Pharmacy, 700 Busse Highway,
    Park Ridge, IL 60068. 847-698-6227. www.nabp.net

National Association of Chain Drug Stores, 413 North Lee Street, P.O. Box
    1417-D49, Alexandria, VA 22313. 703-549-3001. www.nacds.org

Clergy

OVERVIEW: Leads a congregation in worship or provides counseling services to others, including the sick and dying. Performs last rites. Helps others achieve spiritual and personal enlightenment, confront personal problems, and grapple with ethical issues. Administrative and management skills are also required to keep the parish operating efficiently.

RECAREERING RATING: ♦♦♦♦ For the religiously devout, work in the clergy can be a deeply meaningful pursuit in the second half of life. Although the financial rewards aren't great, the work is ideally suited to older individuals who are willing to put in longer hours. Working conditions are generally good.

ANNUAL EARNINGS: $43,060 (range: $21,000-$70,000)

PERSONALITY FACTORS: SOCIAL, ARTISTIC, ENTERPRISING. You must be honest, ethical, and empathetic toward others. Requires strong emotional control and the ability to cooperate with others. A positive attitude is essential.

RECAREERING STYLE: OPPORTUNIST, CHANGE AGENT, REINVENTOR, FANTASY SEEKER.

EDUCATION AND TRAINING: Some denominations or congregations require a university degree, others do not.

SKILL LEVEL REQUIRED: High. COMMUNICATION (WRITTEN AND/OR VERBAL), LISTENING, READING AND COMPREHENSION, CRITICAL THINKING, PROBLEM SOLVING.

JOB REQUIREMENTS: No certifications or licenses, though some denominations and congregations may require a degree or specialized learning or training at a monastery or university.

OUTLOOK: ◆◆◆◆ Employment in the clergy will grow at a rate of 9 to 17 percent (139,000 additional positions) through 2014.

WORKING CONDITIONS: ◆◆◆◆ Must be willing to work nontraditional hours and be available when and as problems or emergencies occur.

WORKERS AGE 50+: ◆◆◆◆ 38.1%

PART-TIME: ◆◆◆◆ 9.4%

SIMILAR OCCUPATIONS: Psychological counseling; teaching.

FOR MORE INFORMATION

O*Net Online. http://online.onetcenter.org/link/summary/21-2011.00

Aish HaTorah (Jewish). One Western Wall Plaza, P.O. Bpx 14149, Old City, Jerusalem 91141, Israel. 972-2-628-5666. www.aish.com

Buddha Dharma Education Association (Buddhist). 78 Bentley Road, Tullera, via Lismore NSW 2480, Australia. 61-612-6628-2426. www.buddhanet.net

Archdiocese of New York (Catholic). 1011 First Avenue, Floor 20, New York, NY 10022. 212-371-1000. www.archny.org

Islam.com (Islamic). www.islam.com. info@islam.com

National Council of Churches USA (Christian). Suite 880, 475 Riverside Drive, New York, NY 10115. 212-870-2141. www.ncccusa.org

World Council of Churches (Christian). 150 route de Ferney, P.O. Box 2100, 1211 Geneva 2, Switzerland. 41-22-791-6111 www.oikoumene.org

Bookkeeping, Accounting, or Auditing Clerk

OVERVIEW: If you're good with numbers, then working as a bookkeeping, accounting, or auditing clerk may add up to a great career. Typically, you oversee an organization's financial records. You update and maintain these records—including transactions, receipts, accounts payable, accounts receivable, and reports—as needed. At a small business, a bookkeeper will often oversee all processes and records, and manage payroll and bank deposits. At a larger firm, an accounting or auditing clerk is likely to handle a specific task or group of tasks. Clerks with greater knowledge and experience may handle more advanced tasks, including invoice review, account reconciliation, billing vouchers, and managing accounting codes. Today, most bookkeepers and accounting or auditing clerks use software to manage financial records on personal computers.

RECAREERING RATING: ◆◆◆◆ Those with math and computers skills can excel in this field. With a high number of 50+ individuals working in the profession and an ability to work part-time, it's ideal for many boomers looking to maintain an income stream or downshift.

ANNUAL EARNINGS: $31,780 (range: $20,000-$46,000)

PERSONALITY FACTORS: CONVENTIONAL, ENTERPRISING. Honesty and character aren't optional. Individuals working in this field must also be able to follow set procedures and handle repetitive tasks. It's also necessary to sit for long hours and deal with deadlines.

RECAREERING STYLE: ADAPTER, ACTIVE RETIREE.

EDUCATION AND TRAINING: A high-school degree is usually required; a few employees may require a two-year or four-year college degree. Many bookkeepers and accounting or auditing clerks are trained on the job.

SKILL LEVEL REQUIRED: Medium. MATH, COMPUTER, TIME MANAGEMENT, READING AND COMPREHENSION, LISTENING, COMMUNICATION (WRITTEN AND/OR VERBAL).

JOB REQUIREMENTS: No certifications required.

OUTLOOK: ♦♦♦♦ Bookkeeping, accounting, and auditing clerks accounted for more than two million jobs in 2004. However, the profession is forecast to grow only 0 to 8 percent through 2014 (503,000 more positions).

WORKING CONDITIONS: ♦♦♦♦ Virtually all bookkeepers work in an office environment. Forty-hour workweeks are common, though many smaller businesses use bookkeepers on a part-time basis. Evenings and weekends may be required (especially at restaurants and stores), and during end-of-month closings or during tax season, employers often ask clerks to work overtime. Because of the long hours sitting and entering data, physical issues—including neck, back, and eye strain—can be a problem.

WORKERS AGE 50+: ♦♦♦♦ 30.8%

PART-TIME: ♦♦♦♦ 25%

SIMILAR OCCUPATIONS: Bill and account collector; billing and posting clerk and machine operator; brokerage clerk; credit authorizer, checker, and clerk; payroll and timekeeping clerk; procurement clerk; and teller.

FOR MORE INFORMATION

Bureau of Labor Statistics, *Occupational Outlook Handbook*
    www.bls.gov/oco/print/ocos144.htm

O*Net Online. http://online.onetcenter.org/link/summary/43-3031.00

American Institute of Professional Bookkeepers, 6001 Montrose Road, Suite 500, Rockville, MD 20852. 800-622-0121. www.aipb.org

Real Estate Appraiser or Assessor

OVERVIEW: If determining the value of real estate—including homes and commercial structures and properties—sounds appealing, then the job of an appraiser or assessor may be on the money. These estimates are used to set the fair-market value for buying and selling property, tax purposes, and loans. Assessors and appraisers examine a property closely, noting additions, improvements, and changes. Appraisers usually work for independent firms or provide services on a self-employed basis. Assessors work for local governments and develop valuations based on site inspections and computer programs. The job may require driving, an ability to understand data on specialized maps, and the ability to tabulate data and write reports.

RECAREERING RATING: ◆◆◆◆ For those with math skills and a detail-oriented personality, working as an appraiser or assessor might prove ideal. The profession attracts many 50+ individuals and is not physically demanding.

ANNUAL EARNINGS: $51,110 (range: $24,000-$86,000)

PERSONALITY FACTORS: CONVENTIONAL, ENTERPRISING. You must be able to follow procedures and routines. The ability to start and complete projects is essential.

RECAREERING STYLE: ADAPTER, ACTIVE RETIREE, OPPORTUNIST, REINVENTOR.

EDUCATION AND TRAINING: No formal degree required, though states have different requirements in place for training and trainee periods.

SKILL LEVEL REQUIRED: High. LISTENING, READING AND COMPREHENSION, COMMUNICATION (WRITTEN AND/OR VERBAL), MATH, CRITICAL THINKING, RESEARCH.

JOB REQUIREMENTS: Almost all positions require a state-issued license or certification. You can view the requirements at your state's Web site. For example, California operates an Office of Real Estate Appraisers (www.orea.ca.gov). In addition, existing professionals in these fields must partake in continuing education, typically 14 hours or more per year.

OUTLOOK: ◆◆◆◆ Despite the subprime mortgage crisis of 2007, overall demand for appraisers and assessors is expected to grow at a faster than average rate of 18 to 26 percent per year (45,000 more positions by 2014).

WORKING CONDITIONS: ◆◆◆◆ The 40 percent of assessors and appraisers who are self-employed work from small offices or home offices. Many use computers; and most drive a vehicle to locations in order to conduct an analysis. Independent professionals in these fields often work more than 40 hours per week, and all appraisers and assessors may find it necessary to work evenings and weekends.

WORKERS AGE 50+: ◆◆◆◆ 37.8%

PART-TIME: ◆◆◆◆ 8.9%

SIMILAR OCCUPATIONS: construction and building inspectors; real estate brokers and sales agents; claims adjusters, appraisers, examiners and investigators.

FOR MORE INFORMATION

Bureau of Labor Statistics, *Occupational Outlook Handbook*
www.bls.gov/oco/ocos300.htm

O*Net Online. http://online.onetcenter.org/link/summary/13-2021.02

American Society of Appraisers, 555 Herndon Parkway, Suite 125, Herndon, VA 20170. 703-478-2228. www.appraisers.org

Appraisal Foundation, 1029 Vermont Avenue NW, Suite 900, Washington D.C. 20005. 202-347-7722. www.appraisalfoundation.org

Appraisal Institute, 550 West Van Buren Street, Suite 1000, Chicago, IL 60607. 312-335-4100. www.appraisalinstitute.org

National Association of Real Estate Appraisers, 1224 North Nokomis NE, Alexandria, MN 56308. 623-580-4646. http://narea-assoc.org

International Association of Assessing Officers, 314 West 10th Street, Kansas City, MO 64105. 816-701-8100. www.iaao.org

Archivist, Curator, or Museum Technician

OVERVIEW: It's the job of archivists, curators, and museum technicians to acquire and preserve important documents and other valuable items for permanent storage or display. They work for museums, governments, zoos, colleges and universities, corporations, and other institutions that collect items or artifacts. These documents and collections may include works of art, transcripts of meetings, coins and stamps, living and preserved plants and animals, and historic objects, buildings, and sites.

Archivists collect, organize, and manage a collection of documents or records—either on paper on in a computer. They may also establish educational programs and public outreach initiatives.

Curators typically oversee a museum or similar institution. They're responsible for purchases, sales, and evaluating and authenticating pieces. They're also involved with fundraising and public outreach.

Conservators preserve, treat, and restore documents, art, and other items.

Museum technicians help set up exhibits, maintain collections, and provide support in archiving items in a collection.

RECAREERING RATING: ♦♦♦♦ These positions can prove intellectually stimulating. In many cases, it's possible to gain valuable experience by volunteering or working as a docent (an unpaid guide) to gain knowledge about a museum or other institution. In some cases, a second degree may help land a position.

ANNUAL EARNINGS: ♦♦♦♦ Archivist, $44,400 (range: $24,000-$73,000); curator, $49,980 (range: $26,000-$80,000); museum conservator or technician, $38,060 (range: $21,000-$61,000)

PERSONALITY FACTORS: ARTISTIC, INVESTIGATIVE. Curators and archivists must enjoy research and intensive thinking. They must feel comfortable making decisions and accepting responsibility. Creativity and innovative thinking are a plus. Museum technicians and conservators may also require hands-on skills for building exhibits.

RECAREERING STYLE: OPPORTUNIST, REINVENTOR, FANTASY SEEKER.

EDUCATION AND TRAINING: An undergraduate degree and sometimes a master's or doctorate degree is required.

SKILL LEVEL REQUIRED: High. LISTENING, READING AND COMPREHENSION, COMMUNICATION (WRITTEN AND/OR VERBAL) CRITICAL THINKING, TIME MANAGEMENT, INSTRUCTING, DECISION-MAKING, HANDIWORK.

JOB REQUIREMENTS: No certifications or licenses required.

JOB OUTLOOK: ♦♦♦♦ Because many individuals find these jobs desirable, there's a good deal of competition for museum positions. Employment opportunities for archivists, curators, and museum technicians are thought likely to continue expanding at a 9 to 17 percent rate through 2014 (approximately 10,000 additional positions).

WORKING CONDITIONS: ◆◆◆◆ Most individuals in these fields spend a good deal of time on their feet and interacting with the public or other museum employees. A few conduct research and spend most of their working hours in relative seclusion. Those who install exhibits may require the physical strength to lift and carry heavy objects. Curators for larger institutions may travel extensively.

WORKERS AGE 50+: ◆◆◆◆ 31.7%

PART-TIME: ◆◆◆◆ 11.8%

SIMILAR OCCUPATIONS: Artists and related workers; librarians; and anthropologists and archaeologists, historians, and other social scientists.

FOR MORE INFORMATION

Bureau of Labor Statistics, *Occupational Outlook Handbook*
www.bls.gov/oco/ocos065.htm

American Association of Museums, 1575 Eye Street NW, Suite 400, Washington, D.C. 20005. 202-289-1818. www.aam-us.org

American Institute for Conservation of Historic and Artistic Works, 1717 K Street NW, Suite 200, Washington, D.C. 20006. 202-452-9545. http://aic.stanford.edu

Society of American Archivists, 527 South Wells Street, 5th Floor, Chicago, IL 60607. 312-922-0140. www.archivists.org

Academy of Certified Archivists, 90 State Street, Suite 1009, Albany, NY 12207. 518-463-8644. www.certifiedarchivists.org

National Association of Government Archives and Records Administrators, 90 State Street, Suite 1009, Albany, NY 12207. 518-463-8644. www.nagara.org.

USAJOBS (Official job site for the U.S. Federal Government), 703)-724-1850. www.usajobs.opm.gov

Chief Executive Officer (CEO)

OVERVIEW: Chief executive officers make key decisions about how to run an organization. They set policies and implement methods for measuring success. They manage executive staff and, at many companies, interact with a board of directors. They also set budgets and ensure that the organization is complying with laws and regulations. CEOs work at large, medium, and small companies, as well as not-for-profit organizations.

RECAREERING RATING: ♦♦♦♦ Many people who have worked in the business world for 20 years or longer may have the knowledge and ability to run a company, particularly a smaller firm or a nonprofit organization. Although the job can be demanding, it can also prove challenging and rewarding.

ANNUAL EARNINGS: $144,600 (range: $62,000-$190,000)

PERSONALITY FACTORS: ENTERPRISING, CONVENTIONAL, SOCIAL. Essentials include: strong leadership skills; an ability to deal with stress; high levels of integrity, dependability, persistence, and independence; and a willingness to cooperate with others and adapt to constant changes.

RECAREERING STYLE: ADAPTER, OPPORTUNIST, CHANGE AGENT, REINVENTOR.

EDUCATION AND TRAINING: A college degree is usually required; some chief executives have graduate degrees (such as executive MBAs) and/or a law degree. Must have considerable managerial or entrepreneurial experience.

SKILL LEVEL REQUIRED: High. COMMUNICATION (WRITTEN AND/OR VERBAL), LEADERSHIP, CRITICAL THINKING, MONITORING, READING AND COMPREHENSION, LISTENING, NEGOTIATING, PROBLEM SOLVING.

JOB REQUIREMENTS: No certification or license required.

JOB OUTLOOK: ♦♦♦♦ Because of the high profile and prestige associated with serving as a CEO, competition for these positions is keen. Demand for CEOs will expand at a 9 to 17 percent rate through 2014 (approximately 150,000 additional positions).

WORKING CONDITIONS: ◆◆◆◆ Chief executives usually enjoy a spacious office, numerous support staff, and plenty of perks. However, they may work long hours and weekends, and the position may require travel. There's also enormous pressure to perform well. Those who underperform financially or operationally will find their jobs in jeopardy.

WORKERS AGE 50+: ◆◆◆◆ 41.3%

PART-TIME: ◆◆◆◆ 5.3%

SIMILAR OCCUPATIONS: Marketing director; CFO; treasurer and controller; human resources director; industrial production manager; operations manager; school superintendent or administrator; postmaster or mail superintendent.

FOR MORE INFORMATION

Bureau of Labor Statistics, *Occupational Outlook Handbook*
www.bls.gov/oco/ocos012.htm

O*Net Online. http://online.onetcenter.org/link/summary/11-1011.00

American Management Association, 1601 Broadway, 6th Floor, New York, NY
10019. 877-566-9441. www.amanet.org

National Management Association, 2210 Arbor Boulevard, Dayton, OH
45439. 937-294-0421. www.nma1.org

Landscape Architect

OVERVIEW: Prepares site plans, handles cost estimates, manages specifications, and oversees procurement for proposed land features and structures at public and private buildings, homes, parks, zoos, airports, and other locations. Works with clients, engineers, and others to integrate desired features into a project. May work at a company or on a self-employed basis (just under 25 percent of landscape architects work for themselves).

RECAREERING RATING: ◆◆◆◆ A great career if you're creative, relish being outdoors, and want to remain active. You may need to go back to college for two years to obtain a degree (if you already have a four-year degree), and you will likely be required by your state to pass an exam in order to be certified.

ANNUAL EARNINGS: ◆◆◆◆ $60,480 (range: $34,000-$95,000)

PERSONALITY FACTORS: ARTISTIC, REALISTIC, INVESTIGATIVE. Must have an artistic flair and be good with spatial relationships. At the same time, it's essential to have practical, hands-on ability to solve problems. The ability to conduct research, pay close attention to detail, and work with others, including government officials and engineers, is also crucial.

RECAREERING STYLE: OPPORTUNIST, CHANGE AGENT, REINVENTOR, FANTASY SEEKER.

EDUCATION: A four-year college degree in environmental design or landscape architecture is necessary. Computer skills such as a working knowledge of computer-aided design (CAD) may also be necessary.

SKILL LEVEL REQUIRED: Medium. COMPUTER, MATH, TIME MANAGEMENT, COMMUNICATION (WRITTEN AND/OR VERBAL), CRITICAL THINKING, PROBLEM SOLVING.

JOB REQUIREMENTS: Most states require landscape architects to be licensed or registered. Licensing is based on the Landscape Architect Registration Examination (L.A.R.E.), sponsored by the Council of Landscape Architectural Registration Boards.

JOB OUTLOOK: ◆◆◆◆ The profession is expected to grow at an 18 to 26 percent rate (8,000 additional positions) through 2014.

WORKING CONDITIONS: ◆◆◆◆ Because landscape architects work outside and in the field, they may experience heat, cold, and inclement weather. Requires lots of standing and sitting.

WORKERS AGE 50+: ◆◆◆◆ 25.9%

PART-TIME: ◆◆◆◆ 5.5%

SIMILAR OCCUPATIONS: Surveyor; material engineer; electrical drafter; civil-engineering technician; commercial and industrial designer; interior designer; set and exhibit designer.

FOR MORE INFORMATION

O*Net Online. http://online.onetcenter.org/link/summary/17-1012.00

American Society of Landscape Architects, Career Information, 636 I Street NW, Washington, D.C. 20001. 202-898-1185. www.asla.org

Council of Landscape Architectural Registration Boards, 144 Church Street NW, Suite 201, Vienna, VA 22180. 571-432-0332. www.clarb.org

Personal and Home Healthcare Aide

OVERVIEW: Personal and home healthcare aides assist the elderly, ill, and disabled (both physically and mentally). They typically work in homes or at a residential care facility. Aides clean clients' houses, do laundry, and change bed linens. Aides may plan meals (including special diets), shop for food, and cook. They also may help clients get out of bed, bathe, dress, and groom. Some accompany clients to doctors' appointments or on other errands. Physicians, physical therapists, registered nurses, and others oversee aides.

RECAREERING RATING: ◆◆◆◆ Individuals looking to help others and engage in meaningful work should consider working as a personal or home healthcare aide. Though demanding, the work is rewarding. It also lends itself to part-time work. And it requires minimal skills and education. However, the pay for these positions is typically low.

ANNUAL EARNINGS: ◆◆◆◆ $20,100 (range: $15,000-$27,000). Those providing home healthcare services average $6.99 per hour, while individuals working with the mentally retarded or in substance-abuse facilities earn an average of $9.09 per hour.

PERSONALITY FACTORS: SOCIAL, REALISTIC. Must be comfortable working around people, including the ill and their families, and have the ability to display empathy. The job may require hard work and tasks related to hygiene. It requires a realistic and practical approach.

RECAREERING STYLE: ADAPTER, ACTIVE RETIREE, CHANGE AGENT.

EDUCATION AND TRAINING: No formal education is required. Most companies provide training to employees.

SKILLS: LISTENING, READING AND COMPREHENSION, COMMUNICATION (WRITTEN AND/OR VERBAL), MONITORING.

JOB REQUIREMENTS: No licensing or certification required.

JOB OUTLOOK: ◆◆◆◆ Personal and home healthcare positions will expand at a 27 percent or higher rate through 2014, as boomers age and healthcare needs increase.

WORKING CONDITIONS: ◆◆◆◆ Aides may work in the same home for several weeks or months or change locations on a regular basis. Some of these homes may be clean, well lit, and pleasant; others may be dirty and cluttered. Likewise, some patients and families show appreciation and affection; others become combative, angry, or even abusive. Work can be physical and lead to exhaustion. Aides must travel to patient sites, typically by car.

WORKERS AGE 50+: ◆◆◆◆ 38.1%

PART-TIME: ◆◆◆◆ 34%

SIMILAR OCCUPATIONS: Childcare worker; nursing and psychiatric home healthcare aide; physical therapy aide or assistant; occupational therapy aide; social and human services assistant.

FOR MORE INFORMATION

Bureau of Labor Statistics, *Occupational Outlook Handbook*
www.bls.gov/oco/ocos173.htm
O*Net Online: http://online.onetcenter.org/link/summary/31-1011.00

10 Other Careers to Consider

Medical Assistant

ANNUAL WAGE: $27,190

DEMAND: ♦♦♦♦ 27% or higher*

PREPARATION: Medium

RECAREERING STYLE: ADAPTER, ACTIVE RETIREE.

WHAT YOU SHOULD KNOW: The demand for medical assistants is huge. Because the job requires neither a formal education nor substantial training, it offers a quick career transition.

Pharmacy Technician

ANNUAL WAGE: $26,510.

DEMAND: ♦♦♦♦ 27% or higher

PREPARATION: Low

RECAREERING STYLE: ADAPTER, ACTIVE RETIREE.

WHAT YOU SHOULD KNOW: If two to four years of additional schooling are out of the question, consider becoming a pharmacy technician. They assist pharmacists by preparing prescribed medication for patients, such as counting tablets and labeling bottles.

Library Technician

ANNUAL WAGE: $27,910

DEMAND: ♦♦♦♦ 9-17%

RECAREERING STYLE: ADAPTER, ACTIVE RETIREE.

PREPARATION: Medium

WHAT YOU SHOULD KNOW: It's a great way to keep your mind active, and interact with librarians and visitors.

Demand figures are based on the period from 2004 to 2014.

Surveying or Mapping Technician

ANNUAL WAGE: $34,590

DEMAND: ♦♦♦♦♦ 9-17%

RECAREERING STYLE: ADAPTER, ACTIVE RETIREE, OPPORTUNIST.

PREPARATION: Medium

WHAT YOU SHOULD KNOW: Surveying and mapping remain in demand. These positions are suitable for older workers who enjoy work in the field and are not intimidated by computers.

Bill or Account Collector

ANNUAL WAGE: $30,640

DEMAND: ♦♦♦♦ 18-26%

RECAREERING STYLE: ADAPTER, ACTIVE RETIREE.

PREPARATION: Medium

WHAT YOU SHOULD KNOW: It's not a career for everyone, but if you have the right personality and temperament (including a willingness to work in a call center), collections can be interesting and rewarding—whether you're tracking down a deadbeat parent for the government or negotiating the payment schedule for a hospital bill on behalf of an HMO.

Loan Counselor

ANNUAL WAGE: $41,840

DEMAND: ♦♦♦♦ 18-26%

RECAREERING STYLE: ADAPTER, ACTIVE RETIREE, OPPORTUNIST.

PREPARATION: Considerable

WHAT YOU SHOULD KNOW: If you have a financial background and you're computer-literate, you might find this line of work interesting.

Public Relations Specialist

ANNUAL WAGE: $53,760

DEMAND: ♦♦♦♦ 18-26%

RECAREERING STYLE: ADAPTER, ACTIVE RETIREE, OPPORTUNIST, CHANGE AGENT, REINVENTOR.

PREPARATION: High

WHAT YOU SHOULD KNOW: These days, everything is about PR—and the demand for individuals with solid communication skills is substantial.

Interior Designer

ANNUAL WAGE: $48,000

DEMAND: ♦♦♦♦ 9-17%

RECAREERING STYLE: OPPORTUNIST, CHANGE AGENT, REINVENTOR, FANTASY SEEKER.

PREPARATION: Medium to high (apprenticeship and license may be required)

WHAT YOU SHOULD KNOW: If you have design flair and you're able to work with specific requirements, interior design may be your ideal job. It's possible to design home spaces, businesses, airplanes, trains, and public areas.

Animal Caretaker

ANNUAL WAGE: $20,230

DEMAND: ♦♦♦♦ 18-26%

RECAREERING STYLE: ADAPTER, ACTIVE RETIREE, FANTASY SEEKER.

PREPARATION: Low

WHAT YOU SHOULD KNOW: If you love animals, consider pet sitting, dog walking, and tending to other animals. The work is often flexible and lends itself readily to the self-employed and those seeking part-time work.

Floral Designer

ANNUAL WAGE: $23,040

DEMAND: ◆◆◆◆ (9-17%)

RECAREERING STYLE: ADAPTER, ACTIVE RETIREE, FANTASY SEEKER.

PREPARATION: Low

WHAT YOU SHOULD KNOW: Floral design is an easy transition for anyone with a bit of creativity and a little design flair. Most florists work at shops, full-time or part-time, and prepare arrangements for weddings, funerals, parties, and corporate events.

Career Options by the Numbers

A great supersite for exploring jobs is CareerOnestop (www.careeronestop.org), which lets you define a search and explore fastest-growing occupations, occupations with the largest overall employment, occupations with declining employment, highest-paid occupations, and job projections.

Moreover, you can select your state, designate the level of education and training you have, and view specific occupations in terms of employment numbers, job openings, and the state's rank. You can also click on a particular occupation—"Postsecondary teachers," say—and select an occupational profile, such as "Biological Science Teachers," then view an occupation description, career video, and state and national trends.

Don't miss these links on CareerOnestop's main page:

Top 50 Fastest-Growing Occupations

You can view each occupation, employment numbers over a 10-year span, the percent change, an earnings chart, and the training required to work in the field. Click on a specific occupation to view data state by state.

Top 50 Highest-Paying Occupations

Lets you view jobs based on hourly wages and annual income. Click to see the state rank, then drill down for career details.

Most Openings

Displays occupations with the most openings, along with earnings level, and education and training levels needed.

Salary & Benefits Tool

Sort through hundreds of career options and view national or state data about wages and income.

Compare Wages by Metropolitan Area

You pick the occupation and metro area you wish to examine, then view that area's wages compared with U.S. averages.

Make a Federal Case of It

Here's another recareering possibility that is often (but un-accountably) overlooked: working in government.

With 1.8 million employees, the U.S. federal government is the nation's largest employer. Beltway bandits, every one? Hardly: 9 out of 10 federal employees work outside Washington, D.C. Add state- and local-government jobs to that list, and the total number of government workers extends into the millions.

Not surprisingly, government agencies face the same set of issues as do organizations in the private sector. Federal agencies will need to hire 550,000 people—one-third of their full-time workforce—to fill "mission-critical" positions through 2013.

Although 7 in 10 workers age 50 to 64 consider government "inefficient," toiling in a bureaucracy does confer certain bonuses. Stability is one; government jobs have historically been less subject to layoffs. Benefits are another; the federal government (and some state and local branches) allows employees to carry health insurance into retirement. Currency is a third—not the kind made at the U.S. Mint, but rather the "best practices" that governments are starting to adopt from the business world.

In January 2008, the Partnership for Public Service (www.ourpublicservice.org) announced "FedExperience Transitions to Government," a pilot program designed to persuade workers retiring from private-sector jobs to consider "encore careers" in government service. The Internal Revenue Service and the Small Business Administration have also begun working with AARP to raise their profile with older adults as members of its National Employer Team (www.aarp.org/money/careers/findingajob/featuredemployers/info.html).

The bottom line? As the red-white-and-blue turns gray, your knowledge and skills may be in demand in a place you never considered.

For more information, visit www.usajobs.gov.

Books

100 Fastest-Growing Careers: Your Complete Guidebook to Major Jobs with the Most Growth and Openings, by Michael Farr, JIST Publishing Inc., 2006. Serves up profiles of hot careers.

175 Best Jobs Not Behind a Desk, by Michael Farr and Laurance Shatkin, JIST Publishing Inc., 2007. Provides information and resources about "active" jobs, organized by activity level, amount of time outdoors, earnings, education, growth through 2014, openings, interests, self-employment, part-time work, gender, age, and personality type.

225 Best Jobs for Baby Boomers, by Michael Farr and Laurence Shatkin, JIST Publishing Inc., 2007. This book offers detailed descriptions of careers and jobs suited to boomers.

Over-40 Job-Search Guide, by Gail Geary, JIST Publishing Inc., 2004. Offers profiles of high-activity jobs and professions.

More Resources

O*Net Occupational Information Network
http://online.onetcenter.org/find

Analyze different jobs and professions by knowledge, skills, abilities, work activities, interests, and work values.

U.S. Census Bureau Census 2000 Equal Employment Opportunity Data Tool
www.census.gov/eeo2000/index.html

Lets you examine demographic data (the percentage of older workers in a given field, for example) and earnings data through customized database searches.

U.S. Department of Labor, Bureau of Labor Statistics, Occupational Employment Statistics
www.bls.gov/oes/current/oes_stru.htm#00-0000

Offers detailed wage and earnings data for hundreds of jobs. The data are also broken out by region.

U.S. Department of Labor, Bureau of Labor Statistics, Occupational Outlook Handbook
www.bls.gov/oco

Discusses what workers do on the job, training and education requirements, earnings, expected job prospects, and working conditions.

◆◆◆

SECTION III

BUILDING A FOUNDATION
FOR YOUR FUTURE

7

BACK TO SCHOOL, FORWARD TO WORK

Advanced planning + additional education = blueprint for success

CHANGING CAREERS MAY INVOLVE MONTHS or years of planning. It may require a return to school to take specialized courses or earn a degree. In the end, it may test your will and make you wonder why you ever wanted to embark on such an odyssey in the first place. But like most good things in life, the hard work sweetens the eventual accomplishment—in this case, a new career.

If you've ever taken a long road trip, you know how crucial it is to do some serious planning before you grab the steering wheel and head out on the highway. Your pretrip preparation can determine whether you drive on smooth roads, stay at nice inns, and eat good meals—or wind up on a bumpy road to headache and heartburn.

By the same token, traveling from Point A to Point B in the professional landscape requires a career map that can deliver you to your destination with a minimum of detours and breakdowns. Those who spend the time and energy necessary to plot out their route through the territory ahead are likely to experience a smoother, more enjoyable journey.

Let's take a closer look at some tactics you can use to move your career-planning initiative into the fast lane.

Laying the Groundwork
for a Career Move
Allow me to revisit that road-trip meta-phor for a moment. Imagine that several time-saving shortcuts to your objective exist. They don't appear on any map, however, so only a very few people know about them. Those not fortunate enough to discover these shortcuts by chance simply motor along the road they have always known and trusted. They whiz past potential gains.

That's a fanciful description of today's job market, to be sure—but it's not too far-fetched. If you're actively considering a career change—or simply feeling unsettled about what lies in store in your current job—it's best to chart your course now, before you're forced "out on the road again" by a downsizing, a dismissal, or some other traumatic event over which you have no control.

The following preemptive strategies can help you raise your profile within an industry and build connections to potential employers in the new field you have targeted.

Tap into the power of (old-fashioned) networking. Many otherwise successful individuals overlook the benefits of building a professional net-work. For them, the very term "networking" may conjure up outdated images of a used-car salesman or real estate agent handing out cards at a party and pressing the flesh with annoying zeal. In reality, networking is as simple as staying in touch with people you know—friends, family, and former colleagues—and making a concerted effort to meet new people who share your interests and goals. Here again, preemption is the career-changer's best friend: It's wise to develop and maintain a solid network long before you need it.

One way to do that might be termed "anticipatory reciprocity": You can help others find jobs in your organization or industry, or take the extra step needed to connect them with business opportunities. Stay in touch by phone and e-mail, and don't hesitate to meet friends, acquain-tances, and professional associates for coffee, lunch, or an evening drink.

It's not uncommon for excellent leads to stream in from an individual's social circle—sometimes at the most unexpected (but opportune!) times. Keep in mind that the more you give over the years, the more you will receive when you finally need it yourself.

Use social-networking sites. We'll examine online networking and various sites in greater depth in Chapter 11, but it's never too early to mention that constructing a virtual network can yield enormous dividends. For example, LinkedIn (www.linkedin.com) allows you to build a professional network by—you guessed it—linking to others online and being granted access to view their circle of trusted acquaintances. The idea is that by establishing groups of professional colleagues, it's possible to create connections that will lead to different jobs, new clients, better business opportunities, and more. (Just as it takes time to build a network in the physical world, however, you must lay a foundation in the virtual world well before you need it.) Other services, including ZoomInfo.com and Congoo.com, let you create or edit a profile and search for job leads. Recruiters often use these sites to spot promising job candidates.

Connect with a corporate alumni group. More than 500 major companies and organizations now operate alumni groups in one form or another. The list includes such corporate titans as Hewlett-Packard, Microsoft, TimeWarner, and Ernst & Young. Those belonging to an alumni group find that staying in touch with former colleagues often generates new business, deepens networking opportunities, and occasionally leads to a new job.

Corporate alumni networks operate in much the same way as university alumni groups: Participants hold regular events and meetings, host job-referral programs, publish alumni directories, offer professional training sessions, and provide career-placement services. Some groups encourage former employees to attend meetings, parties, and other functions that keep them tuned into business developments and industry trends. And many now use newsletters, websites, and social-networking tools to ratchet up the interaction. You can find out more about corporate alumni groups at www.corporatealumni.com.

Get involved with an industry association or local business group. Joining a professional organization—and participating in it (especially volunteering to serve on or chair a committee)—will likely raise your profile among colleagues and prospective employers. Moreover, attending meetings, mixers, and other events makes you more visible to others. Although this approach often works best for individuals seeking a new job in the same field, it can also open up new career vistas among those hoping to reinvent themselves in a new field.

Another possibility: Join your local chamber of commerce and get to know the most active businesspeople in your community. This approach is particularly effective if you're considering starting a business of your

---

Key Questions

Have I laid the groundwork for a career change? Changing careers can take time and require patience. But it's possible to expedite the process by building a network and conducting the requisite research.

How committed am I to addressing skill and knowledge gaps? Trade schools, community colleges, and four-year universities are no longer the exclusive domain of the under-30 crowd. If you have identified a career track and you've compared your present knowledge and skills with what you need to succeed, you can upgrade your education and achieve your goals.

Do my expectations jibe with reality? It's easy to let enthusiasm run wild or launch a career-change effort with a burst, only to watch it fade away. Staying motivated is tough over months or years, so make sure you're in it for the long haul. If you've done your research up front, you will be prepared for the expected and unexpected eventualities bound to pop up along the way.

own. You're apt to find a ready-made customer base and learn about other businesses that cater to your needs.

Look for fast-track opportunities. You may be able to use your existing education, experience, and knowledge to transition to a new career—without spending the usual amount of time in the classroom. In the education arena, for example, alternative certification of teachers has become commonplace. The U.S. Department of Education (DOE) reports that 20 percent of today's teaching force is made up of novice teachers from alternative-route programs. These initiatives, which also encompass fields such as information technology and professional consulting, are designed to fill shortages in key areas (such as math, science, special education, and English as a Second Language) or boost an organization's competitive standing. You may already have the skills needed to make a quick transition or you may, as with teaching, need only a bachelor's degree and some additional coursework, which you can tackle part-time and online. This makes it possible to prepare for a career change while continuing to work in an existing job or profession.

Such was the strategy adopted by 58-year-old Douglas Peterson of Alexandria, Virginia. Back in 1972, Peterson had graduated from the University of Oregon with a bachelor's degree in community service and public affairs. He then went to work for a string of city governments—including those of Salem, Oregon, and Carmel-by-the-Sea, California—before attending graduate school at the University of Southern California. Armed with a master's degree in public administration, Peterson eventually landed in Washington, D.C., where he signed on as a policy analyst with the National League of Cities.

Twenty years later, Peterson was still on the job. Increasingly restless and burned out, he quit in 2005. A few months later, he decided to teach at a local church—and immediately took to the profession. Then, at a career fair in Richmond, Peterson discovered that the state of Virginia offers a fast-track program designed to funnel individuals with work and life experience into teaching. He enrolled in a program at nearby Regent University that ran from May through August 2006, then took a job as a substitute teacher. After that, Peterson underwent a year of supervised teaching and took a battery of required exams, which he passed.

Today Peterson teaches English at Mark Twain Middle School in Fairfax County. "It's an adjustment," he concedes. "To keep up with middle schoolers takes a lot of stamina. But I feel like I'm doing something stimulating and meaningful."

If you're interested in sharing your own accumulated knowledge, an organization such as the National Center for Alternative Certification (www.teach-now.org) can put you on the right track. In addition, private schools often hire teachers based on experience rather than certifications or other credentials. (Many public and private schools likewise hire substitutes without requiring teaching credentials.)

Explore
Your Options
When it comes to learning about job possibilities, career-changers today can pursue multiple avenues of inquiry. Spending the time required to learn what's out there can expand your view like a wide-angle lens. It can help you spot opportunities that many job seekers overlook. Here are a few alternatives to consider:

Job fairs. College grads aren't the only ones being wooed by the corporate world. Today, senior job fairs have become wildly popular. A growing array of organizations, including Boeing, Dillard's, Marriott International, and Nationwide Mutual Insurance Company, are using these events to find experienced workers. The job fairs take place all over the country and often include workshops on topics such as writing a résumé, selling yourself to your next employer, managing your finances during uncertain times, and weathering job and life transitions. Many organizations hire directly through these fairs. You can find them by searching online and checking job sites such as Monster.com (http://resources.monster.com/

job-fairs) and CareerBuilder.com (www.careerbuilder.com/JobSeeker/ CareerFairs/default.aspx). You can also search "senior job fairs" at Google to find organizations sponsoring job and career fairs specifically for seniors.

Sampling a job or career. What better way to learn about a job or career than take it for a test-drive? VocationVacations, a Portland, Oregon organization founded in 2004, offers an array of opportunities to sample real jobs at real companies. For a few hundred to a few thousand dollars, you can sample just about any calling, from art-gallery director to animal therapist, from trucker to riverboat tour guide. Participants spend two or three days immersed in doing the actual work.

"There's a big difference between changing jobs and changing careers," says Brian Kurth, founder and president of VocationVacations. "This is a hands-on environment that gives you a realistic sense of what the work

Cultivate Lifelong Learning

Here are four basic steps to keep your mind active—and boost your marketable skills—at every stage of your life:

Subscribe to magazines and read books. In addition, read blogs and visit websites pertinent to your area(s) of professional and personal interests. A good place to find blogs on almost any subject is Blogcatalog.com (www.blogcatalog. com). It boasts links to more than 100,000 blogs on topics ranging from career & jobs to finance, and from business to volunteering.

Create to-do "learning lists" and follow through on things that are important to you.

Take a course at your local adult school, community college, or university extension program.

Attend workshops, seminars, and conferences. Sit in on sessions or purchase recordings of those you can't attend.

is like." About three-quarters of the firm's "vocationers" are seeking a career change, Kurth estimates, and approximately 20 percent make a professional transition after participating in the program. More and more of these individuals are in their 40s, 50s, and 60s.

Internships and volunteer positions. Companies have long offered internships to help students and others gain experience and learn about a career. Some of these positions are paid; others are volunteer only, or they grant credits. Increasingly, companies are enthusiastic about connecting to older workers.

An internship offers a good way to get a realistic but low-risk "dose" of a business or industry. Likewise, volunteering as an aide in the medical arena or as a docent at a museum may help you better understand what's required to land paying work in the field; in some cases, it can even help you decide whether or not you should return to school for a degree.

Internships and volunteer stints also confer experience that can help you snag a desired position later on. More than a few individuals have worked their way up to dream jobs after first getting noticed as interns or volunteers. Not to mention that being "inside" an organization is often the best way to gain the figurative inside track to a position.

Trade magazines and trade associations. Another way to gain valued insider status—or at least knowledge—is through the pages of the trade magazines that cover various professions and careers. Hundreds of major publications exist, and many of these are available online. In addition, trade associations often provide a wealth of more direct information about various careers (some of this takes the form of pamphlets, brochures, or backgrounders). Search for these organizations through Google or Yahoo! Or visit your local public library, which should keep a copy of the *Encyclopedia of Associations* in its reference collection. In addition, Yahoo! offers a trade-magazine directory with hundreds of listings (http://dir.yahoo.com/Business_and_Economy/Business_to_Business/ News_and_Media/Magazines/Trade_Magazines/).

Someone who works in the career you're considering. Remarkably, one of the best methods for gleaning knowledge about another career is also the most frequently overlooked: It's good old-fashioned human intelligence, gathered by talking with someone who currently works in the field. If you know someone who serves as a veterinarian or a stockbroker, for example, and you think one of those fields might be beckoning you, consider yourself fortunate. Have a casual conversation with the vet or broker, or schedule some time when the two of you can talk. Invite the person out for coffee or lunch.

In the absence of such a personal contact, you may have to identify a person who works in a field you're interested in, then try approaching that professional via a polite request to chat for 10 or 15 minutes by phone or in person. The worst the person can say is "No." More likely, you will find that many professionals are flattered by the attention (or heartened that others want to join the industry) and will therefore take at least a few minutes to respond.

Afterward, be sure to thank the person and ask what you can do to help them. Who knows? It could be the start of a fruitful long-term relationship.

Out of the Cube and into the Class
If you identified a skill or knowledge gap in Worksheet #3 on page 107, you should also have listed an accompanying solution. More often than not, the need for a skill upgrade will shunt you directly into an educational environment. If you want to become a certified public accountant, for instance, you will need to take requisite coursework and pass the CPA exam for your state of residence. If you long to become an aerospace engineer, you will have to earn a bachelor of science degree from a specialized school, such as Embry-Riddle Aeronautical University.

If you aspire to become a computer consultant, on the other hand, you can set up shop without taking any classes—though the flaws in this

Extend Your Education

Matching your interests and desires with suitable educational programs can be challenging, if not overwhelming. Here are two sites that can help you narrow down your schooling options.

CareerOneStop Education and Training Finder

http://www.careerinfonet.org/edutraining/default.aspx?searchMode=occupation

Locate regional, state, and local training and education opportunities by occupation, or search by keyword. The database provides information about schools and training programs, including how to gather more information.

Senior Resources Center

http://www.retiredbrains.com/Education/Index

Offers an extensive list of professions, with links to schools and other institutions that provide degrees, certifications, and general learning.

approach are fairly obvious: Just because formal learning is not required for a profession does not mean it's inadvisable. Today, the knowledge base of just about every occupation is growing at such a prolific pace that it's almost impossible to market oneself as a generalist. If you're a "geek on call," for example, you might specialize in PCs or Macs, Linux or Unix. You might dedicate yourself to networking, Internet telephony, or any of a dozen other fortes. Not surprisingly, savvy customers will want to see proof of your accreditations—and reassure themselves that you know your stuff—before they let you probe the soul of their machine.

For many older workers—particularly boomers—going back to school is no problem. That's because these forty- to sixty-somethings eagerly anticipate resuming their studies. In 2005, the Department of Education reported, 141,648 individuals over age 50 were full-time students in undergraduate, graduate, and first-professional (that is, law and medicine) programs; another 523,021 were part-time students. These numbers have swelled by more than 20 percent since the beginning of the decade.

As boomers and other older Americans pursue new careers, the look and feel of the classroom is changing. No longer is it an oddity to see 50- or 60-year-olds sitting in classrooms at a trade school, community college, or four-year university. The number of students age 30 and older swelled from approximately 15 percent of all students in 1973 to nearly 25 percent in 2003. That's about four million older students now attending colleges and universities nationwide—and the numbers continue to grow.

Boomers Go to College, a 2007 study conducted by AARP Oregon and Portland Community College, reports that 4 out of 5 older students attend college for more than personal enrichment. Most are "intent on completing their studies in a relatively short time frame to enable them to translate their education into meaningful employment," the report says. Yet whereas boomers are "motivated learners"—they believe they will meet their goals—80 percent conceded that the complexities of life in middle and older age intensify the task. Juggling work, school, and family is a typical challenge for them.

Some schools get the message that older students have different attitudes —and different needs. As a consequence, these institutions have begun creating customized programs for older students, including orientations, mentoring, and shared coursework. At Central Florida Community College in Ocala, Florida, for example, the Living, Learning, and Serving curriculum targets students 50+. It features a Retired Services Volunteer program for those seeking work in not-for-profit organizations; a Lifelong Learning program for those who want intellectual stimulation but have no desire to return to work; and a Life Services program that helps older students improve their job skills in order to secure new employment or enter a new career.

Central Florida Community College is not alone. In August 2007, think tank and program incubator Civic Ventures teamed with the MetLife Foundation to provide $25,000 grants to 10 community colleges across the country (listed below and on the opposite page). These schools will develop programs that help older workers gain the skills demanded by careers in education, healthcare, and social services. These "Encore Colleges," as Civic Ventures has dubbed them, will offer specialized curricula and teaching methods designed for boomers and others. They will also introduce mentoring programs and career counseling.

Learning to Change

Attitudes and values are evolving. Christina Butler, a librarian at Ohio Dominican University from 1986 to 2003 (and the wife of Ken George, profile on pages 156–157), was drawn to the subject

Get Schooled

These 10 Civic Venture schools (see above) offer programs customized for older students:

Baltimore City Community College (Baltimore, Maryland) Offers an executive outplacement model to help African-American women over age 50 develop individual plans to transition into new careers.

Broward Community College (Fort Lauderdale, Florida) Provides free seminars and career counseling to inform boomers about local encore careers and service opportunities.

Central Piedmont Community College (Charlotte, North Carolina) Has established a leadership training program to support boomers interested in transitioning from careers in the for-profit to the nonprofit sector.

Coastline Community College (Fountain Valley, California) Features online and classroom courses for those over 50 preparing for careers in gerontology and eldercare.

Collin County Community College (Allen, Texas) Helps train boomers laid off from engineering, technology, and other careers to become certified high-school math teachers in one year.

GateWay Community College (Phoenix, Arizona) Collaborates with local employers to help boomers segue into careers as caregivers. The employers provide instructors, tuition support, and flexible jobs.

Owensboro Community and Technical College (Owensboro, Kentucky) Trains retiring nurses to become adjunct nursing faculty at the community-college level.

Portland Community College (Portland, Oregon) Offers a peer-mentoring program for students age 50 and up who are enrolled in the school's gerontology certificate or degree program.

Virginia Community College System (Richmond, Virginia) Has developed a statewide recruitment effort to attract more boomers with college degrees to its existing statewide, fast-track teacher-licensing programs. Partners include the state's 23 community colleges, the Virginia Department of Education, and K-12 schools.

Washtenaw Community College, (Ann Arbor, Michigan) Offers outreach and support programs for mid-career professionals who want to use their training and business experience to address social problems.

Traditional colleges and universities aren't the only game in town, however. Increasingly attractive to older workers are trade schools, which teach topics as diverse as culinary skills, court reporting, and computers. In many instances, they provide the desired knowledge and skills in weeks or months rather than years. What's more, trade schools are relatively inexpensive, offering certificate programs in the hundreds of dollars. A Google search using the name of your city and "technical or trade school" usually suffices to serve up results.

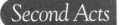

HELPING OTHERS ATTAIN "AHA!"

KEN GEORGE, *from computer programming project manager to math tutor*

I WORKED AS A COMPUTER PROGRAMMER and manager for the state of Ohio for almost 27 years. I liked the work, but the job became incredibly stressful over the last few years (managerial changes had led to political games and nonsense). I was having migraine headaches and stomach problems that made me unable to come into work at least a couple of days every week. Fortunately I had sick days available, but the situation wasn't good. One day my wife, Mary Ellen, sat me down and confronted me with the situation. It wasn't worth sacrificing my health, she said—and perhaps shortening my life.

When I thought about it I realized she was right, so I decided to retire. But by retiring a few years early, I would take a financial hit. If I had stayed at my job the full 30 years, I would have received a full pension. Ohio structures the program so that each year beyond 25 contributes disproportionately to your retirement. For me, the difference was $800 to $1,000 per month in retirement income.

For a long time I was in denial. I feared the unknown, and what I would do with the rest of my life. But when I finally made the decision to leave, I felt this immense load lift from my shoulders. Suddenly, the stress was gone. I felt great; all my symptoms cleared up. Even though I worked for another six months—I wanted to finish a project I was involved in—I could see the end in sight. It made me realize that a lot of stress is self-imposed.

When I retired, on December 31, 2004, I wanted only to de-stress and decompress. I wanted to get my head on straight and enjoy the basic things in life. Well, that lasted all of two weeks. I realized I can't handle sitting around doing nothing. I decided to attend a recareering seminar with my wife. It really helped me focus my attention on what brings me happiness, on what I want to do with my life. We participated in a number of exercises and addressed the issue, What's next? The exercises helped us think about things like: What makes me feel fulfilled? What are my passions and talents? What makes me really happy? It made me realize that we often get so busy in our jobs that we don't think about these things. I realized that I wanted to help other people learn. (I had always enjoyed mentoring and working with others that way.) But I also knew I didn't want to teach in a classroom. What appealed to me instead was the idea of teaching in a one-on-one situation.

My degree was in computer science, but in college I minored in math. I resolved to go back and get a second degree in mathematics so I could tutor high-school and college students. I was fortunate because my wife is a librarian at Ohio Dominican University, which offers immediate family members free tuition. (In my case, that was close to $20,000 a year.) I enrolled in fall 2005 and will graduate in the winter of 2008-2009.

I'm taking six hours of classes per week, and I spend an equal amount of time on homework and take-home tests. I also work in the university's math lab, where I put in about 12 hours per week. I see the college students in the morning and the high-school students later in the day. I really enjoy the work. A lot of people struggle with math, so helping others attain that "Aha!" moment energizes me—and reassures me I'm on the correct path.

When I graduate, I would like to tutor about 20 hours a week. I want to earn some extra money, but I also want to have more free time. I earn $8.50 per hour in the lab and $20 an hour for private students. Many people charge much more than that for private tutoring, but I'm not doing it to get rich.

It was somewhat intimidating as someone in his late 50s, sitting in class with students as young as 17. Fortunately, over time, I discovered that it was possible to make friends with some of the students. We've gone through several classes together, and we respect each other.

Making the transition has not been easy. I kept the whole thing quiet for a while because I was afraid to admit to anyone that I wanted to make such a big change in my life. When I finally told my friends, they were surprised but then supportive; only a few acted disappointed. I explained to them that I needed to do this for myself and that I wanted to contribute to the greater good.

We are getting by, but the career change has forced us to sacrifice on the financial side. We don't have any cushion now, so we're very cautious about what we spend money on. But I now understand that you have to pay a price either way: A person's emotional well-being and psychological health have value, too. Quality of life is important, and I'm now a lot closer to how I want to live my life.

of late-life education and began attending workshops and seminars on the topic. In 2002, after earning a Ph.D. in higher education administration from Ohio State University College of Education, Butler founded Over 60 Learning, a think tank and support organization that promotes learning later in life. Today, at age 61, she has marched into a bold new career—and, through a website and career coaching, she is helping others to follow her enterprising path. "As people live longer and they're healthier later in life," says Butler, "they're looking to earn more money, stay engaged in work, and participate in lifelong learning. Many people would like to do something positive or give back to society, but they can't do it on their retirement income alone."

Butler sees a growing number of people in their 60s, 70s, 80s, and even 90s heading back to school. Yet it's not always easy to make the round-trip from work to school and back to work again. Some run into resistance from family members who question why the person is heading back to the classroom later in life. ("Family attitudes still trail the realities of today's workplace and lifestyle requirements," Butler explains.) Others find it difficult to find meaningful work once they complete their curriculum or earn a new degree.

Nevertheless, many are forging ahead—and succeeding. One of them is Mercedes Pellet, who in 1979 started a translation business with her husband, Michael, so the two of them could spend more time with their five young children. Pellet, a native of Colombia who now lives in Maryland, parlayed her knowledge of Spanish into a $5 million, 55-person firm named M2. Its clients included major multinationals such as Texaco and American Airlines, and the company eventually offered translation services in 16 languages.

Pellet's true passion all along, however, was caring for abandoned or abused animals. When her Yorkshire terrier died in 2004, she began exploring opportunities to act on that interest. "When I investigated what it would take to become a veterinarian," says the 63-year-old grandmother, "I realized that eight years of intensive study was going to be too much." Pellet still went back to school, but she set her sights on a more realistic career goal: becoming a registered veterinary technician. She enrolled at Fairmont State Community & Technical College (now Pierpont Community & Technical College) in Fairmont, West Virginia, taking classes in chemistry and microbiology—and quickly discovering she was in over her head. "In my first chemistry class," she recalls, "all I understood from the instructor was 'Hello' and 'Good-bye.' I thought I had made a terrible mistake. In addition, none of the 18- and 19-year-old students bothered talking to me. Even the professors were younger."

But after finding a tutor and acclimating to college ("I eventually became their friendly grandmother"), Pellet found her balance. She completed her coursework, passed the national board exam, and—after she and Michael sold their translation business in 2006—began searching for a compatible animal-adoption agency. She now works at Homeless Animal Rescue Team, a shelter in Oakland, Maryland.

Reflecting on her journey of reinvention, Pellet stresses the importance of viewing the road traveled through a lens of one's own: "When I told my mother about the career change, she thought I was crazy. Friends and family thought I had flipped. But my husband always supported me. He gave me the confidence to make my dream happen.

"And wonderful things have happened since I made the change. By making a difference in the lives of animals, I feel as though I have accomplished something significant."

Going back to school at 50 is not the same, of course, as matriculating at 19. For one thing, learning styles are different—older students are likelier to prefer books and to learn through repetition, while younger students generally embrace technology, interactivity, and multitasking. For another thing, age differences and social interaction can prove somewhat daunting. For instance, a 55-year-old may find himself assigned to a study group with 20-year-olds who have very different ideas about how best to prepare for exams and make presentations. They may be thinking all-night cram sessions and PowerPoint slides while you're more comfortable with weekend studying and flip charts. There's also the fact that an older student will probably have to balance family obligations with studying and other school-related activities. Younger students may place a premium on dating, partying, and having fun.

Not surprisingly, the *Boomers Go to College* study found that a strong support system is vital for older individuals heading back to the classroom. If you're interested in resuming your learning, check with the community college or university you're considering attending to see if it offers mentoring, tutoring, career counseling, or academic advisory services. These can help you stay on track and achieve your goals.

Spending some time analyzing your situation—and taking steps to expand your career options and opportunities—can deliver you to the threshold of a new career. The next agenda item will be to scrutinize your finances in order to understand how—or whether— your pocketbook and lifestyle can support a career-change campaign.

Books

The Complete Idiot's Guide to Discovering Your Perfect Career, by Rene Carew, Alpha, 2005. Guides readers through the process of trading in their unfulfilling career for a more rewarding one.

Do What You Are: Discover the Perfect Career for You through the Secrets of Personality Type, by Paul D. Tieger and Barbara Barron, Little, Brown and Company, 2007. Helps readers understand their personality type and how and where they fit into the workplace.

Happy About Online Networking: The Virtually Simple Way to Build Professional Relationships, by Liz Ryan. Happy About, 2006. Strategies for successful networking online to raise your career visibility.

I'm on LinkedIn—Now What???: A Guide to Getting the Most OUT of LinkedIn, by Jason Alba, Happy About. The lowdown on using the wildly popular social-networking site to your career advantage.

I'm on Facebook—Now What???: How to Get Personal, Business, and Professional Value from Facebook, by Jason Alba and Jesse Stay, Happy About, 2008. Provides insights into networking on this ever-more-influential site.

It's Only Too Late If You Don't Start Now: How to Create Your Second Life at Any Age, by Barbara Sher, Dell, 1999. A primer on how to make the transition to a new career—and how to realize your unfulfilled expectations at any age or stage of life.

Never Eat Alone: And Other Secrets to Success, One Relationship at a Time, by Keith Ferrazzi and Tahl Raz, Doubleday Business, 2005. Examines the art of networking by moving beyond handshakes and business cards to developing rapport with colleagues, acquaintances, and others.

More Resources

AARP
Boomers Go to College
http://community.aarp.org/n/pfx/forum.aspx?msg=132.1&nav=messages&webtag=rp-or

Examines the growing trend of older workers returning to campus.

Aging Horizons Bulletin Newsletter & Educational Webzine
www.aginghorizons.com

Offers articles, news, and insights focusing on the latest trends and research in aging.

Civic Ventures

www.civicventures.org

A not-for-profit organization examining how older Americans c an contribute to society through work, volunteerism, and other activities.

Goliath Jobs

www.GoliathJobs.com

This free online employment service for students and alumni invites employees to list their job openings on college websites.

National Center for Alternative Certification

www.teach-now.org

Serves as a clearinghouse for information about alternative routes to teaching. The site includes a searchable database showing the requirements for the 48 states in which programs currently exist.

Over60Learning
Education in the 3rd Age

www.over60learning.com

Serves as a resource for older individuals looking to enhance their education and knowledge.

Quintessential Careers
Quintessential Careers Assessment Test Review

http://www.quintcareers.com/online_assessment_review.html

Provides an overview of the various personality, career-assessment, and skills-testing methods available online.

The World Bank Group
Lifelong Learning

http://www1.worldbank.org/education/lifelong_learning/

Offers information and sources for skills and knowledge development in the 21st century.

CHAPTER

8

MONEY MATTERS

*Anchor your future with some selective
financial planning in the present*

IT'S NEVER WISE TO MAKE A MAJOR LIFE TRANSITION without forecasting its
financial implications, but changing careers can be especially tricky. You
may find yourself out of work for months. You could wind up spending
tens of thousands of dollars or more on career counseling, education,
and accreditations. And if you decide to start your own business or open
a franchise, you may need to shell out a six-figure sum just to get things
off the ground.

With the definition of retirement getting blurrier by the day, planning
your financial future grows commensurately more complex. No longer is
it possible to conduct a straight-line projection for exiting the workplace
at age 65 with a predictable pension securely in hand. Given their longer
lifespans and more active mindsets, today's boomers and other older
workers must dovetail their planning for retirement with their planning
for a new career.

Ron Manheimer knows all about that. The noted author and lecturer
serves as director of the North Carolina Center for Creative Retirement,
a research institute at the University of North Carolina, Asheville. "We
are now in a time when that static picture of retirement is gone for many

people," observes the author of the book *A Map to the End of Time: Way-farings with Friends and Philosophers*. "People are exploring different combinations and different degrees of continued work, leisure, and volunteering."

Sometimes the process seems like a three-dimensional chess game in which moving one piece has a ripple effect on all the other levels of a person's life—including the options available for future career moves. The ability to manage your money effectively often determines whether a recareering effort succeeds or falls flat. (You can't pursue your dream if you can't make the numbers work.)

The starting point for any recareering project is to determine what assets you have now, how much money you will need to engineer the transition, and how a new career will influence your future financial status. "We no longer talk about retirement planning these days," says Wayne Starr, a Certified Financial Planner in Kansas City, Missouri. "We talk about whole-life planning." Whether you choose to examine the financial aspects of a career change on your own or turn to a professional for guidance, the key is to engage in as much up-front planning as possible.

Yet it's not *only* about money. It's also about attaining a state of mind

Making Social Security Count

Death and taxes may be the only things certain in life, but Social Security ranks a close third. Those who have worked and earned income for 40 quarters are eligible to claim benefits early, at age 62. Indeed, that's just what about half of all individuals do. But waiting to start your retirement benefit at a later age may make more sense.

Here's why: If you continue to work after age 62 and earn more than a certain annual limit (it was $13,560 in 2008), the Social Security Administration will deduct $1 in benefits for every $2 you earn above that cutoff. When you reach full retirement age, however, the penalty drops substantially: In 2008, for instance, the penalty for 65-year-olds who continue to work is $1 for each $3 you earn above the much higher limit of $36,120. In other words, don't stop working—but do understand the consequences before you opt to collect.

If you'd like to analyze your situation, here are some valuable resources:

AARP Bulletin - Social Security
www.aarp.org/bulletin/socialsec

This site provides news, information, alerts, profiles, and message boards related to Social Security. It is filled with useful tips on how to navigate the complex and often confusing world of retirement benefits.

Center for Retirement Research at Boston College
http://crr.bc.edu

Offers assorted articles and *The Social Security Fix-It Book,* a guide to addressing the problems facing Social Security.

National Committee to Preserve Social Security and Medicare www.ncpssm.org

Offers news, information, and an array of resources focused on Social Security. There's also a form for submitting questions to "Mary Jane," an expert on Social Security, and archived columns in which the answers appear.

Social Security Administration www.ssa.gov

It's the official word on everything related to Social Security. The site offers an array of resources, including a description of benefits, an online benefit application, a mechanism for requesting records and statements, retirement planners, Medicare information, and other facts and tools.

Social Security Benefits Handbook
www.socialsecuritybenefitshandbook.com

Author Stanley Tomkiel offers a comprehensive guide to the jumble of Social Security rules and regulations, including eligibility requirements, benefit amounts, and how to troubleshoot problems and submit appeals.

in which you can feel economically secure. One person or couple may find an income of $40,000 a year comfortable enough to lead a middle-class lifestyle. In another household, $400,000 may not cover the monthly expenses—particularly when country-club memberships, luxury travel, and courtside NBA season tickets are factored into the equation. A June 2007 survey by Discover Financial Services found that 1 in 4 consumers would be unable to maintain their current standard of living for more than a month if they lost their income.

Getting started with financial planning can intimidate the bravest soul. Because—unpardonably—the discipline is not yet taught in schools, most of us aren't completely comfortable plugging in numbers or playing with retirement calculators. The bewildering array of modern investment vehicles—bonds, equities, annuities, and so on—can also conspire to disorient us.

Additionally, planning for the future necessarily entails a great deal of uncertainty—and therefore may favor those adept at "fuzzy thinking." We're not sure how much we will need for the simple reason that we cannot know in advance how long we will need it for. Adding a career change to the mix further muddies the waters. Finally, there's the challenge of actually living by a plan—something that can dispirit even the most disciplined person. Today's consumerist epidemic—its symptoms ranging from $5 daily lattes to $10,000 home-theater systems—can make it extraordinarily difficult to reach goals. A plan may even be perceived as a roadblock to happiness.

This chapter examines how a career change is likely to affect your financial picture: Can you use certain untapped assets to finance a career change? How might your current situation and needs shape your career planning and financial planning? The chapter also spotlights specific situations not uncommon to older individuals—divorce, health problems, the illness or death of a spouse—and discusses how these events can trigger (willingly or otherwise) a career change.

The net message: A little bit of financial planning now can go a long way toward helping you find the work you will love in the future.

Assessing
Your Situation

It's easy to overlook the fact that changing careers can derail (or at least sidetrack) your retirement planning. If you wind up in a job that pays less, for example, you'll have to increase your retirement savings or plan to work later in life. Most financial advisors believe you should be able to live on 70 to 80 percent of your preretirement income once you retire—provided that you've paid off your mortgage, don't have children at home, aren't saddled with lingering education bills, and live within your means.

For most people, Social Security, pension plans, and self-directed retirement savings (a 401(k), a 403(b), a SEP-IRA, or a Roth IRA) will compose the bulk of retirement income—or at least supplemental income if you plan to shift careers and keep on working for several more years. If you opt to take Social Security at age 62, you will receive reduced benefits. A retirement planner (and chart) is available at www.ssa.gov/retire2/agereduction.htm. It displays how benefits vary for different ages, and how age reductions affect a spouse survivor's benefit. You can use it to gauge how much money you're likely to receive in Social Security benefits now and in the future.

No less important is understanding how your retirement savings affect your financial picture—and your ability to change careers. Prematurely withdrawing money from a retirement account will cost you: It triggers taxes and penalties. Any funds you take from a self-directed retirement plan before age 59 ½, for example, are subject to ordinary income tax plus a 10 percent penalty. (For medical emergencies and certain other situations, hardship exemptions now exist.) If you are 59 ½ or older, by contrast, you can begin withdrawing money from a self-directed retirement account without paying a penalty (though you will have to pay taxes on the deferred income). You can also opt to take a lump-sum distribution, which could help finance the launch of a new business. You must begin withdrawing money from the account by the time you reach age 70 ½.

Plenty of excellent information exists for retirement planning (see Resources, pages 189-190). Yet the process often involves other factors that may erode your finances. These include caregiving services provided to family members (which could interfere with work), childcare (whether you're a parent or a grandparent), and volunteer commitments to religious

Expected & Actual Sources of Income in Retirement

Unfortunately, expectations and reality often collide on the path to retirement. Many individuals significantly underestimate the money they will need to make a go of retirement.

EXPECTED	REPORTED
Personal savings (net)	
Workers: 50%	Retirees: 24%
A workplace retirement savings plan, such as a 401(k)	
Workers: 28%	Retirees: 6%
Other personal savings or investments	
Workers: 22%	Retirees: 18%
Social Security	
Workers: 14%	Retirees: 40%
A traditional employer-provided pension	
Workers: 13%	Retirees: 21%
Employment	
Workers: 11%	Retirees: 2%
The sale or refinancing of a home	
Workers: 2%	Retirees: 2%
Something else	
Workers: 3%	Retirees: 4%
Don't know/Refused	
Workers: 6%	Retirees: 5%

Source: Employee Benefit Research Institute and Mathew Greenwald & Associates, Inc., 2007 Retirement Confidence Survey.

or social-service organizations. Consider these factors—and their direct and indirect costs—before you make any career-change decision. They could dictate the type of job you take, the place where you choose to work, and the nature of the benefits you will require, including work schedule and personal days off.

A 2002 Cornell University study, for example, found that working wives in late midlife are *five times* likelier to retire early in order to care for a disabled husband than wives who are not caregivers. Men who are caregivers, on the other hand, tend to defer their own retirement much longer. Unanticipated disruptions in work patterns and earnings can take a correspondingly severe toll on your income levels and lifestyle. They can also alter—or entirely short-circuit—your plans to change careers. Every family or household must therefore find its own path—but planning ahead can avert stress and frustration.

Worksheet #1: Calculate Career-Change Costs

Let's get down to the nitty-gritty—and get a fix on just how much it may cost you to recareer. Fill in the chart below with your best estimates. If you're contemplating more than one career-change possibility, you'll want to examine the numbers for each of those situations.

Recareering Expense	AMOUNT
Career counseling	
Education	
Equipment, tools, and technology	
Monthly expenses while out of work	
Stationery and supplies	
Other expenses	
TOTAL EXPENSES	

Understanding Your Assets
& Borrowing Options
Getting a fix on your assets can be a relatively straightforward process, especially if you rely on a software application such as Intuit's *Quicken* or *Microsoft Money*. These programs help you track various assets and total their dollar value. They also provide sophisticated reporting capabilities, budgeting tools, and the ability to forecast various scenarios based on projections. For those who are less than proficient on a computer, however, it's equally possible—if a bit more methodical—to accomplish the task using good old pencil and paper.

To conduct a more detailed analysis, consider relying on the expertise of a Certified Financial Planner. The Financial Planning Association (www.fpanet.org/plannersearch/search.cfm) is among the organizations that provide referrals. Keep in mind, however, that it's wise to check (and double-check) references in order to ascertain whether or not the financial specialist you're considering has the knowledge, expertise, and objectivity to put you on the right track.

No matter which approach you use, spend some time understanding your situation. Some assets, such as a house, may allow you to take advantage of equity without selling. Others, such as jewelry or art, may have to be sold in order for you to monetize them—that is, convert their value to cash. Still others, such as stocks, may fluctuate in value in lockstep with market gyrations. Get a handle on the liquidity of your various assets—particularly if you anticipate converting them to cash at some point in the recareering process.

Likewise, carefully weigh the cost of taking out a personal loan, using credit cards, or tapping into a line of credit. Each offers pros and cons. What works for one person may prove disastrous for another. One advantage of personal-finance software is the ability to get a quick read on your assets and liabilities. If you need to do so manually, use Worksheet #2, on the opposite page (you may need an additional sheet of paper to list your personal property).

Worksheet #2: **Estimate Your Net Worth**

Assets

	PRESENT ESTIMATED VALUE
Cash in the bank (checking and savings accounts)	
Money that's owed to me	
Stocks/bonds/mutual funds	
Other investments, including annuities and real estate	
Retirement savings	
Pensions	
Home	
Second home or vacation property	
Property (vehicles, jewelry, collections, collectibles, etc.)	
TOTAL ASSETS	

Liabilities

Mortgage	
Bank loans	
Vehicle loans	
Credit-card debt	
Lines of credit	
Alimony and/or child support	
Amounts owed to others	
Taxes (income, property, other)	
Other liabilities	
TOTAL LIABILITIES	

Net Worth

Total Assets	
(minus) Total Liability	
NET WORTH	

Factor in Your
Financing Choices
Now let's take a closer look at various assets and how they might be used to finance a career change.

Your house. If you own a house, you could be sitting on at least some potential capital. Despite ongoing fluctuations in real estate values—including a lagging real estate market and the subprime mortgage mess that blindsided the market in 2007—the average home in the United States rose in value 136 percent, to $185,200, from 1990 to 2006. Depending on your recareering choice and your financial requirements, a home may generate the wherewithal to see you through.

Using your equity. A home equity line of credit (HELOC) might allow you to meet education costs or ongoing living expenses—and deduct from your taxes whatever interest you pay the lender. It's crucial to comprehend, however, that any money thus borrowed adds to your monthly debt. If you continually tap an equity line, you could find your minimum monthly payment inching up to hundreds of dollars. Remember, too, that an equity line often comes with an adjustable interest rate: In that case your interest payments will rise even if your debt principal stays the same.

What about using a HELOC to fund a start-up business or buy a franchise? It's often done, but never without risk: An inability to repay the principal decreases your future net worth, and if you're unable to make payments at some point, you could lose your house. What's more, in the event of a sharp downturn you could wind up with negative equity. This will leave you owing money to the bank even if you sell the house for more than its purchase price.

A reverse mortgage. In simplest terms, a reverse mortgage is a loan you take out against the equity in your home. You can receive a lump sum or a monthly payment, or you can withdraw money as you need it. The bank simply reduces the equity value of the home and subtracts the borrowed principal (plus interest and fees). When you die or sell the property, the bank collects on the loan.

A primary advantage to this type of loan is that there's no need to qualify based on your income or ability to repay. If you own your home, have equity, and you're at least 62 years old, you are eligible to apply for a reverse mortgage. The disadvantage is that banks usually charge considerable interest and fees, and the continuing withdrawal of principal lowers the proceeds from the eventual sale. Still, a reverse mortgage may help finance ongoing living expenses, especially for those looking to work part-time or volunteer into older age.

Selling and downsizing. For many empty-nesters and other older individuals, the idea of downsizing exerts a powerful pull. For those considering a career transition, there may be an additional benefit: Selling your abode

How to Make a Severance or Buyout Work for You

It's not unusual for large companies to tender buyouts or severance packages to union workers and executives. In February 2008, for example, General Motors announced it would offer buyouts as high as $140,000—along with full retirement benefits—to offset its $38.7 billion loss for the year. GM's goal: to replace higher-paid workers with younger, lower-paid ones. Other companies have dangled packages valued at several hundred thousand dollars—or more—in front of executives.

Can you up the ante if you're facing a buyout or severance offer? First, determine whether you truly wish to leave. If the answer is no, stay put. If the "itch to switch" to another career is compelling, however, look hard at the numbers: A six-month severance probably won't cover the expenses of a career move, including education or training, general job-search costs, and living expenses. The equivalent of 12 to 18 months' salary is more likely to pave the way to a successful career change.

Here are some more actions to consider taking:

Retain a labor attorney, if possible. You're likely to fare better if you bring expertise and objectivity to the situation.

Don't accept the employer's first offer. You may be able to push the numbers up with some negotiation. Try to secure four weeks of severance for every year of employment.

Ask for the money in a lump sum, payable immediately rather than in installments.

If you're close to the end of the year, consider pushing the payout into the following year to diffuse your tax liability.

Negotiate to receive medical, dental, and other insurance coverage while you're receiving the severance.

Make sure you're paid for unused vacation, sick days, and personal days.

Receive any year-end bonuses now or negotiate to receive them within the package.

For more information about severance and buyouts, visit:

FindLaw. *Negotiating Strategies to Maximize Post-Termination Severance*
http://employment.findlaw.com/articles/2560.html

Vault. *The Whats and Whens of Negotiating Severance*
www.vault.com/nr/newsmain.jsp?nr_page=3&ch_id=421&article_id=9695043&cat_id=81

The Ladders. *Negotiating Severance Packages*
www.theladders.com/career-advice/Articles/NONE/Negotiating+Severance+Packages

and buying a smaller one can unlock equity without incurring the interest and fees associated with a HELOC or reverse mortgage.

Selling can create concerns and issues beyond that, of course. For one thing, you could face a tax bill. The Taxpayer Relief Act of 1997 offers a maximum tax exemption of $250,000 for singles and $500,000 for couples on profit from the sale of a primary residence. If you're over this limit, you will have to pay capital-gains tax. And you're allowed to take the tax break only if you've owned the home and lived in it for at least two years. For another thing, you will probably wind up forking over a commission to a real estate broker (unless you opt to sell the home yourself—a complex and time-consuming process). Seven percent is the standard fee—though it's often possible to negotiate the commission downward by a percentage point or two. Selling a $500,000 house, for example, will throw off a $35,000 fee—which is deducted from your proceeds from the sale.

Stocks and other investment assets. If you're fortunate enough to hold stocks, bonds, and other securities, they may afford another potential way to finance a career change. These assets are highly liquid and, depending on your investment skills (or your broker's acumen), they represent a viable savings pool to draw from. Consult a professional financial planner to review the potential tax liabilities before placing any sell orders with your brokerage firm.

Your 401(k) or SEP-IRA is another potential funding source. You may have saved hundreds of thousands of dollars—money that could fund a new business. Depleting your retirement savings, however, could undermine your retirement if the business venture doesn't pan out. In other words, weigh the possibilities—and risks—before you take the leap.

Savings. In early 2008, the personal savings rate in the United States had dipped into negative territory. This means that collectively, the U.S. population had no savings and was in fact in debt. If you've managed to set aside money of your own, however money markets and CDs could play at least a supplemental role in bankrolling a start-up business. In the event you have funds available but aren't certain just when you will need them for a career move, it's probably best to stash the savings in a money-market account, or use a "laddering" strategy that allocates equal sums to separate accounts that mature on a quarterly or semiannual basis. (You may want to avoid CDs with a specific maturity date, such as six months or a year, which make your money inaccessible for that span of time.)

Insurance and annuities. If you have taken out an annuity in the past, particularly a deferred annuity, you may have an opportunity to receive payments in a lump sum or on a monthly basis. Some annuities also include a survivor's benefit, which guarantees your partner or other beneficiary a payout if you die. Similarly, a life-insurance policy may provide income or death benefits. The latter could be important if you have incurred substantial debt from the start-up of a business but do not want to saddle your survivors with financial obligations.

Other property. Have you accumulated art, antiques, or collectibles over the years? These possessions could be worth anywhere from a few hundred to thousands of dollars—or more. The question, of course, is whether you're willing to part with these items—especially if they hold sentimental value or have been passed from one generation to the next within a family.

Credit cards. It's tempting to view credit cards as a source of quick cash. To be sure, there's no easier way to borrow. But depending on the cash-advance fee and interest rate charged by the issuing bank, you could quickly find yourself drowning in debt. Annualized interest on cash advances may top a mind-boggling 50 percent, while many cards exceed an annual interest rate of 25 percent, and a few top 30 percent. What's more, certain card issuers have been known to charge exorbitant late fees—sometimes upward of $39 on a balance as low as $250. And unlike an equity line on a house, the interest on a personal credit card is not tax-deductible. It's best to view credit-card advances as a last resort: Use them sparingly—if at all. Otherwise you will almost certainly wind up paying dearly in the long run.

Explore an Alternative Lifestyle It's easy to fall into predictable patterns—owning a home, holding down a conventional job. But for those open to changing careers and lifestyles, cost-saving alternatives abound. For some, it may be possible to sell a home in a larger city or more expensive region and move to a rural community where housing is a fraction of its urban price. Others may decide to rent a smaller apartment

Making Things Compute

Financial planning may not be your favorite pastime, but you'll have to transcend the shoebox-and-check-ledger system to achieve your career and retirement goals.

All sorts of programs—including stalwarts *Quicken* and *Microsoft Money*—promise to help you do just that. Almost every financial-planning program will download transactions from financial institutions, let you pay bills electronically, track investments, and generate reports (such as budgets and forecasts). As your income or spending patterns change, the programs tweak your financial portrait to keep pace. Calculators built into the programs also invite you to model what-if scenarios.

Are they worth it? "An accounting application can help an individual or business gather and manage information," says former IRS agent Steven Duben, CPA, now in private practice. "It eliminates the number-crunching and moves straight to the answers." These leading programs all offer free trials:

iBank. *IGG Software. $59.99. Mac.* Provides a comprehensive e-finance and e-banking solution in an intuitive, easy-to-use package. Offers budgeting, retirement, and other financial-planning tools, including graphs and charts.

Intuit Quicken Premiere. http://quicken.intuit.com. *$89.99. Windows (Mac version also available).* Puts all your financial matters under one roof, painting a complete picture of your net worth. Includes retirement-planning tools and a "wizard," which walks you through the steps needed to cut spending and boost savings.

Microsoft Money Plus Premium. www.microsoft.com/money. *$49.99. Windows.* Handles everything from balancing a checkbook to budgeting, reporting, and retirement planning. Helps you manage spending and understand investments and net worth.

Moneydance. www.moneydance.com. *$29.99. Windows, Mac, Linux.* Powerful features include online banking and bill payment, budget management, portfolio tracking, and reporting that can assist in retirement planning.

in the same area to free up capital for a business venture. Still others may cut back on dining out, keep an old car running, or borrow books and videos from the local library rather than buying or renting them.

A few career changers go so far as to live a vagabond lifestyle. They may sell or stash their belongings and roam the globe, tending bar in Thailand or guiding tourists in Costa Rica. With the kids grown, some money in the bank, and few responsibilities to tether them in place, they can explore the world and live the life they've always imagined. They rent an apartment or a house when they arrive at a destination, carry an ATM card, and make friends across the globe. They may volunteer for the Peace Corps or embrace numerous other volunteer opportunities.

That's what Stan and Marcia Klein decided to do. After retiring from careers in real estate and social work in 1997 at age 60, the couple sold their house in suburban Connecticut, shed almost all their worldly possessions, and moved to "everywhere." Their first adventure was a two-year hegira through Japan, Southeast Asia, India, Nepal, China, Africa, and finally Mexico, where they house-sat for four months. They stayed in youth hostels, budget hotels, and with local families all along the way, "traveling second-class at a pace that suited us," in Stan's words, "without advance reservations or hard plans."

The trip profoundly reshaped their perspectives. "We learned so much about ourselves and the world we live in," says Stan. "Possessions we had accumulated through the years suddenly seemed less valuable." When the Kleins returned stateside, they translated that new outlook into a more austere lifestyle. They also took on odd jobs that let them save money for a more permanent, travel-filled retirement. "We had assumed that a more budget-conscious life would be a sacrifice," says Stan. "Instead, it turned out to be a benefit: Once we stopped spending, we were really much happier."

Globe-trotting may not be your gig, of course, but adjusting your lifestyle to work fewer hours or start a new business holds universal appeal.

Paul Green, a 61-year-old chef who lives in Center Tuftonboro, New Hampshire, did both. In his main career as an executive sous-chef, Green had worked at premier restaurants such as the Signature Room in Chicago and the Aspen Lodge in Colorado. As he grew older, troublingly, Green had difficulty finding regular work. "I love cooking and I'm not ready to hang it up," he says. "But a lot of kitchens want a working chef—and to be a line chef is a young person's job."

In 2002, Green hit bottom. Suffering from severe depression, he spent two nights in jail after being arrested for drunk driving. He got sober, moved to New Hampshire, and downsized his life. He now rents a cabin in the woods for $550 a month and meets his expenses with a military pension and Social Security.

With simplicity came new vistas. In 2008 Green launched Temporary Chef.com, which matches experienced chefs with restaurants, hotels, catering firms, and private individuals seeking short-term chefs. Green takes a 20 percent commission on every placement. "I've had the Porsche and the sailboat," Green reflects, "so I'm now quite comfortable living at a more basic level and enjoying my time. I live and breathe the culinary arts—this is the continuation of a lifelong passion."

A New Career Changes the Equation
More than teaching you the net cost of changing careers in the here and now, financial planning can reveal how a different career will reshape your long-term financial outlook. A good starting point is the *Occupational Outlook Handbook*, published by the Bureau of Labor Statistics. It is available at www.bls.gov/oco. This site lets you search hundreds of job categories and view a detailed description (plus the current earnings range) for each one. The site also offers job outlooks with employment projections through 2014.

Of course, any change in career is also likely to alter your commuting expenses, tax payments, retirement savings, and possibly health insurance

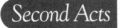

LEARNING TO FEEL

Ellen Robling, *from graphic designer to massage therapist*

After graduating from Carnegie Mellon University in Pittsburgh, I went to work as an assistant art director at *Ranger Rick* nature magazine. That was in 1972. A few years later I went to work at Time-Life Books in Alexandria, Virginia. I worked there for 18 years, gradually rising through the ranks to a management position. I enjoyed graphic art and design, but as time went on I was no longer using these skills, so I enjoyed the work less and less. At age 45, I was downsized out of my position. That was in 1996. Thankfully, Time Inc. gave me 52 weeks of severance pay.

There had been a lot of layoffs before then, so it wasn't entirely unexpected. In fact the grim joke at the time was that only the pathological optimists on staff didn't have a layoff plan. Well, I had one, but it had grown out of some wrenching life circumstances a couple of years before. My father, who had prostate cancer nine years back, had developed bone-marrow cancer in 1993. He did not want to undergo chemotherapy or radiation therapy, so he went to a hospice where he could manage the pain. The oncologist predicted, "It will be a short run."

I went to Pittsburgh every weekend from Washington. At the time, I was getting a massage every three weeks, and it was really helping me deal with the strain of my father's cancer and the burden of managing a department of creative but difficult people.

The hospice was managing my dad's pain well, but he still felt a sense of powerlessness. I suggested that I massage him on the dining-room table and mimic the massage that my therapist had been giving me for two years. I had more or less memorized her massage. It turned out to be a remarkable experience because he would really relax; he would become comfortable in a body that was debilitated. He was someone who didn't talk a lot, but he would start talking to me in a sort of stream-of-consciousness.

I gave him two massages a weekend. It shifted our relationship dramatically. I really got to know him. So that was a gift.

The other gift was that he lived 18 months—after the oncologist said that he would live only three or four months. The doctor said, "We don't know what you are doing, but keep doing it." I realized that there was still another gift here: My ability to make people feel better. So, about a year after my father died in 1994, I decided to go to massage school. I picked Santa Fe, a mecca for natural and alternative healing. I'm a recovering alcoholic, and at the time I felt I needed to take more risks. In February 1996 I found a renter for my condo in Dupont Circle, and everything just fell into place. I graduated from massage school six months later and have been doing this ever since. Two years later I sold my condo, and I've never looked back.

Now, 10 years later, I'm earning a third of what I used to make but I'm happier than I've ever been in my life. It was a fabulous transition. What I really like is that people always leave happy after they receive a massage. There's no critique, no analysis, no long discussion about the quality of the work, as there was in the days when I was working as a graphic designer. It just appeals to people on a very basic and primal level. I put in about five hours a day, and I feel great. I hope to keep my massage business going for many years.

costs. If you use financial-planning software, you can simplify the analysis process by creating dynamic budgeting reports that instantly adjust to changes in actual and projected income and expenses. If you've decided to stick with paper and pencil, don't fret. You're likely to spend more time conducting your analysis but still gain valuable insights into your financial health and ways to free up cash for a career-change endeavor.

Spending plan. If you have money saved and can use it to cover living costs and other expenses while recareering, great. If not, you'll have to find a way to tighten your budget. Worksheet #3 on page 183 helps you track year-to-date income and spending. (You may need to add line items to reflect your own situation.) This worksheet can help you identify places to save and provide insights into how you might adjust your lifestyle in order to recareer. Once you know your household income, you can use current spending and budgeted spending to find ways to trim costs and free up funds for training, coaching, job searching, and other expenses likely during the transition period.

Once you have a handle on your income and expenses, you can begin to understand how a career move will affect your overall financial picture. In some cases, cash savings or a home-equity line may provide the cushion needed to recareer. In other instances, you may need to make immediate or ongoing sacrifices in order to take the job you want in the field you covet. The key is to avoid big surprises—and sidestep mounting debt.

Ultimately, career planning and retirement planning must go hand-in-glove. If you're willing to accept a lower standard of living and make some mid-course corrections, you should be happy and comfortable—assuming you've invested time in the decision. But if you intend to trade in a $150,000 job (and its attendant perks) in the corporate world to earn $40,000 a year as an elementary-school teacher, you can't expect to maintain the same lifestyle or squirrel away as much savings. If the psychic gain is adequate compensation, that's great. If not, you're likely to solve one problem in your life only to watch another one emerge.

Balancing the time-money equation is one of the profound challenges of our era. Whether you turn to a Certified Financial Planner, a software application, or a paper worksheet, it's up to you to examine the numbers and use them to guide your thinking and actions. Ultimately, those who strike the right balance and downshift smoothly are far more likely to glide into a new career than have their lives erupt in chaos. And those who manage their finances and steer clear of excessive debt are likely to enjoy far broader options and opportunities over time.

Addressing Healthcare-Coverage Risks

For many Americans, particularly older workers, healthcare coverage ranks as a key consideration in choosing work. It's bad enough for those who lack coverage because an employer or a particular job simply doesn't offer it. But those who make a conscious

Worksheet #3: Track Income & Expenses

Income	PRESENT ESTIMATED VALUE
Salary or self-employed income	
Partner's income	
Social Security or retirement income	
Other income (including investments)	
TOTAL INCOME	

Expenses	BUDGETED COSTS	ACTUAL COSTS	DIFFERENCE
Clothing			
Groceries			
Household/home			
Phone/Internet/cable TV			
Dining			
Entertainment			
Utilities			
Car/gas/repairs			
Travel			
Charity			
Mortgage/rent			
Property tax			
Income tax			
Insurance (auto and home)			
Health insurance			
Retirement savings			
Other savings			
Miscellaneous			
Other liabilities			
TOTALS			

decision to limp along without insurance coverage until they qualify for Medicare are playing with fire. A 2005 study conducted by Harvard Law School found that nearly half of all bankruptcy filings were triggered by unanticipated major medical problems.

Obtaining coverage in the workplace or after retirement grows more nettlesome by the month—thanks to rising costs and round after round of corporate cost-cutting initiatives. In 1993, 46 percent of employers with 500 or more employees offered healthcare benefits to early retirees. By 2006 that figure had plummeted to 29 percent. In 1997, approximately 31 percent of all workers in the private sector were employed by firms that offered retiree health benefits. By 2003 only 22 percent enjoyed that protection. Worse still, expectations and reality remain oceans apart. Nearly half of all workers (47.4 percent) ages 45 to 64 expected retiree health benefits upon retirement in 2002; only 28.7 percent received them.

So if you hope to change careers, consider your care options cautiously. If a spouse has employer-sponsored family coverage, you may be in luck—as long as he or she continues in that job. If you qualify for COBRA, it's generally wise to obtain the policy—even though it is expensive. (Formally known as the Consolidated Omnibus Budget Reconciliation Act of 1985, COBRA gives certain employees the option to pay for health-insurance coverage for a specified period after they leave a job.) Otherwise, if you're not yet eligible for Medicare, factor in the cost of private health insurance or use the potential price tag as part of the decision-making process. And if you're not able to obtain coverage at all (because of a preexisting condition, for example), consider whether you have sufficient money set aside to cover any health expenses. Many experts estimate hat figure at somewhere between $200,000 and $300,000 at any given moment, after age 55. If you fall into this category, you may need to save more—or make a quick transition to a new job or career that offers insurance benefits.

The Challenge
for Women
For many women—singles in particular—a career change and its attendant financial planning create additional challenges. In general, women earn 25 to 30 percent less than men over the course of their work lives. Because of child-rearing responsibilities and eldercare, many women also spend fewer years working. This regrettable dynamic translates into scantier retirement savings—a triple whammy that leaves about one-third of all single older women poor or on the verge thereof. Worse, about four times as many non-married women 65 and older are poor compared with their married counterparts. For blacks, Hispanics, and other minorities, the numbers are higher still.

Nor can we overlook that women live longer than men, on average (80.1 years compared with 74.8, according to a 2005 report from the Centers for Disease Control). As a result, they will likely have to support themselves longer. Factor in divorce, health problems, and the care of grandchildren or eldercare for aging family members, and the equation becomes even more complex.

If you lack the knowledge or wherewithal to conduct your own analysis, consider turning to a qualified financial advisor or planner. (Doing nothing is a choice, but it can only defer the problem, not dispose of it.)

Retirement:
The End Game
At some point, it's likely that your work will become less desirable—or even less feasible. That's when the "R" word enters the vocabulary. Regrettably, most Americans do an inadequate job of preparing themselves for retirement. According to a 2007 survey conducted by the Employee Benefit Research Institute and Matthew Greenwald & Associates, almost half of workers saving for retirement report that their savings and investments (excluding the value of their primary residence and any defined-benefit pension plans) total less than $25,000. Seven in 10 admit they have accumulated less than $10,000.

How a new career will affect your retirement—even your phased retirement—is a key question. Though conventional wisdom holds that you can finance a comfortable retirement on just 70 to 80 percent of your pre-retirement income, that formula does not address the unique needs of an individual or household. You may be the miracle worker who can subsist on 50 percent, enabling you to work fewer hours in midlife or leave the

Key Questions

Do I understand how a career move will transform my lifestyle and retirement? Without detailed number-crunching and financial analysis, you're flying blind. As a result, you could find your recareering effort derailed—or wind up in financial quicksand yourself.

How will I finance a career change? Consider which assets you can leverage—or part with. Also consider lifestyle changes, such as buying a used rather than new car and investing the difference. Many small sacrifices can add up to significant cash.

Have I balanced the financial considerations of a career change with a sense of purpose? For most individuals, the essential goal of a midcourse career change is to invest their lives with greater balance and meaning. It's vital to run the numbers, yes—but you have to keep an eye on quality of life, too.

Could a financial advisor shed light on my career planning? An objective expert can provide insights you might overlook. This person can also help you overcome an aversion to risk or a reluctance to diversify investments. However, make sure you find a professional adviser who is honest, impartial, and represents your best interests. Seek references from family and friends, or start your search at the National Association of Personal Financial Advisors (www.napfa.org) or CPAdirectory.com.

workforce a few years earlier than the norm. On the other hand, you may not be willing to part with a luxury car or exotic vacations every year. If that's the case, you may have to meet the resulting financial demands through longer hours, or by holding down a job into your 70s or 80s.

Retirement planning is a complex task—and, in truth, far beyond the scope of this book. However (and I realize you've heard this before), it's best to save early and save often—particularly if you want to maximize your recareering options in the future. If you are 45 years old with an annual salary of $100,000 and want to retire on 70 percent of that income by age 65, your nest egg could conceivably reach $622,404. But that's if you start saving today with an initial deposit of $5,000, tuck away 20 percent of your income each year, earn an annual return of 7 percent (5 percent post-retirement), and are lucky enough to see the inflation rate stay at a meager 3 percent during those 20 years. Yet even with your projected annual Social Security benefit of $18,192, you would still fry your nest egg by age 78. (Again, this assumes you can live on 70 percent of what you were earning at age 65.) To make your money last to age 82, you will need to save $25,000 a year. And if you expect to live to age 90, you will have to ramp up your annual savings to a whopping $33,000.

If you've already started saving, however—and let's say you're currently age 50—the process needn't be so painful. Assuming you have $250,000 saved and you contribute 10 percent of your income annually ($10,000), you could have $1,106,883 by age 75. If you're willing to postpone retirement until that age (not unreasonable these days), you will have enough money to live until age 96—even if each year you withdraw 90 percent of your pre-retirement annual income. Moreover, you will leave behind more than $367,000. If you want to examine your own situation and play with the numbers, visit an online retirement calculator, such as http://moneycentral.msn.com/retire/planner.aspx, www.bloomberg.com/invest/calculators/retire.html, or www.aarp.org/money/financial_planning/sessionseven/retirement_planning_calculator.html.

Of course, a house and other assets—including annuities and various investments—can provide additional income during the latter stages of one's life. The twofold key to success, says Certified Financial Planner Wayne Starr, is to take the time to crunch the numbers but also to think clearly about your strategies, methods, and tactics. It's essential to manage risk appropriately: Avoid not just highly speculative investments but the temptation to play it too safe, which can yield subpar returns. Shun individual stock-picking, which threatens to ensnare you in the stock market trend du jour, in favor of index funds that benefit from the market's overall gains and flatten out the market's vagaries. And look realistically at how large or little a role Social Security benefits can play as a source of your retirement income.

Some financial planners point out that the emphasis on saving and building a sizable nest egg—fanned by the multitrillion-dollar financial-services industry—overlooks one of the most fundamental and obvious retirement-planning strategies: Trim spending. By reducing overhead and cutting expenses—curtailing big-ticket purchases, eating out or traveling less frequently—it's often possible to eliminate several hundred dollars in costs each month. This simple change might slide recareering from the questionable category to the highly feasible.

Goal-centric planning is Starr's mantra. The better you understand your desires, he says, the easier it will be to build a sound financial plan. For one person, that may equate to never setting foot in an office again and playing golf four days a week. For another, it may involve working part-time, volunteering part-time, and spending several hours a week with grandchildren. Navigating and planning for a career change might begin years before the actual switch takes place—or you may decide to reinvent your life on the spur of the moment. Either way, financial planning is imperative.

Books

The AARP Crash Course in Creating Retirement Income, by Julie Jason, AARP Books/Sterling, forthcoming. A comprehensive guide to saving money and achieving a desired lifestyle in retirement.

Ernst & Young's Financial Planning for Women: A Woman's Guide to Money for All of Life's Major Events, by Elda Di Re, Andrea S. Markezin, Sylvia Pozarnsky, et al., Wiley, 1998. Addresses women's financial-planning issues for a wide range of scenarios and income levels.

Executricks, or How to Retire While You're Still Working, by Stanley Bing, Collins, 2008. For late-blooming slackers—or work shirkers of any age, really—comes this satirical prescription for how to "retire" while you're still on the job.

The Motley Fool's Money After 40: Building Wealth for a Better Life, by Tom Gardner and David Gardner, Fireside, 2006. Provides advice and action plans for handling an array of financial issues in middle age and beyond.

The Number: What Do You Need for the Rest of Your Life, and What Will It Cost?, by Lee Eisenberg, Free Press, 2006. A look at life issues and achieving goals through effective financial planning.

Personal Financial Planning, by G. Victor Hallman and Jerry S. Rosenbloom, McGraw Hill, 2003. Provides an array of tools and techniques to help you better understand, define, and achieve your financial goals.

The Wall Street Journal Guide to Planning Your Financial Future, 3rd Edition, by Kenneth Morris and Virginia B. Morris, Fireside, 2002. Offers text, charts, and diagrams—with clear and straightforward explanations of financial issues, terms, tools, and strategies.

What Color Is Your Parachute? for Retirement: Planning Now for the Life You Want, by Richard Nelson Bolles and John E. Nelson, Ten Speed Press, 2007. A comprehensive guide to planning your financial future.

Work Less, Live More: The New Way to Semi-Retirement, by Bob Clyatt, Nolo Press, 2007. Supplies tips on how to balance work and financial planning to create a less demanding work schedule.

More Resources

AARP Financial Planning and Retirement
www.aarp.org/money/
financial_planning/

This site provides in-depth news, information, planning, and analysis materials on a range of retirement-oriented topics. It also provides numerous other resources.

About.com: Financial Planning
http://financialplan.about.com

Offers a breadth of articles, tips, and tools on various aspects of financial planning, including retirement.

National Association of Personal Financial Planners
http://www.napfa.org/

Furnishes information about financial planning. Don't miss the "Find an Advisor" feature.

Retirement Living Information Center
www.retirementliving.com/

Lists great places to retire, taxes by state, retirement communities and senior housing, as well as news, information, and tips.

Retirement Resources
http://taxtopics.net/retirement.htm

This site provides extensive information about Social Security benefits and offers retirement-planning information and calculators.

Social Security Online
www.ssa.gov

This site delivers detailed information about Social Security benefits, retirement planning, Medicare, survivor's benefits, and much more.

Wachovia Ernst & Young's Financial Planning for Women
www.wachovia.com/personal/page/
0,,505_513_1094_1291,00.html

Written by female Ernst & Young partners, this site provides news, information, case studies, and worksheets that can guide the financial-planning process.

Yahoo! Finance—Retirement
http://finance.yahoo.com/retirement

Provides information on retirement trends and strategies. The site also offers calculators, how-to-guides, and a glossary.

9

A QUESTION
OF BALANCE

*Alternative work options are
redefining today's workplace*

CHANGING ATTITUDES AND DEMOGRAPHICS have revolutionized the
workplace. Although companies no longer guarantee employment, they
must remain inviting enough to attract top talent. In an economy fueled
largely by information and knowledge, nothing less will do. Even among
employers in service industries such as hospitality and retail, there's a
crying need to find and retain dependable, motivated people.

As a result, many companies have begun to offer alternative benefits
and other work incentives. Among these are flextime, job sharing,
telecommuting, contract work, sabbaticals, leaves of absence, phased
retirement, home offices, on-site gyms and childcare, and free lunches.
Some let employees bring their kids—even their pets—to work.

Not surprisingly, a number of these arrangements benefit older workers
—as well as those eager to take on a new career. They provide a foundation
for meaningful work, minus the time demands and commuting pressures
of a traditional full-time job. A flexible work schedule may also furnish
the time and latitude a person needs to explore one job while holding
down another. It can also restore that essential work-life balance, allowing
a person to juggle volunteerism, social activities, and hobbies.

Flextime A quarter-century ago, the idea of workers deviating from a traditional 9-to-5 schedule seemed outrageous, if not downright seditious. The corporate "command and control" mentality in force at the time dictated that managers oversee employees and make sure they engaged in meaningful (at least as defined by the organization) tasks.

However, the advent of computers and networking has created new ways to think about work and schedules—particularly in white-collar fields. Flextime, as its name implies, allows employers and employees to carve out nontraditional work arrangements. For individuals providing childcare, eldercare, or otherwise coping with a challenging daily schedule, flextime can pay enormous dividends.

An employer might stipulate that an employee be present in the office from 10 a.m. to 2 p.m., for example, leaving the remainder of the day flexible. A person might arrive in the office at 6 a.m. and leave at 2 p.m., or arrive at 10 a.m. and leave at 6 p.m. Essentially, the employee decides when to work—as long as the hours add up to the weekly or monthly

How to Sell an Employer on a Flex-Work Format

Not all employers rush to embrace the idea of flexible work environments. In fact, some are not even aware of the possibilities and how they can benefit both the company and its workers. It may therefore fall to you to get the issue on the radar of key managers or executives. Here are some concrete steps that may help you transform the flextime ideal into a workplace reality.

Point out that a flexible work schedule improves morale and reduces turnover. The cost of recruiting, hiring, and training a new employee can cost $10,000 to $20,000 at small- to medium-size organizations, and up to $50,000 or more at larger firms. Flextime bends so people don't break.

Map out job duties and workload responsibilities. Show how various tasks will be covered during business hours and off hours. Show that a flexible work schedule will not undermine accountability.

Work to formalize policies with the HR department. Or, if you're at a smaller firm, volunteer to help develop an employee handbook covering flextime-scheduling policies and procedures. Guidelines give an organization an objective and impartial way of applying flextime; this in turn averts power plays and squabbles.

Make all requests in writing. People forget, misunderstand, or manipulate. A verbal request for flextime leaves too much latitude for problems. A thoroughly documented request (and agreement, should you reach that stage) obviates the possibility of any misinterpretation of what you're asking for—and receiving.

requirements and the work gets done. In some cases, employers combine flextime with a flexplace policy. This approach lets employees choose where they will work—at home, in the office, or at a coffee shop.

Older workers are prime candidates for both flextime and flexplace work. Although jobs in the service sector or manufacturing don't lend themselves to flexible arrangements, the dynamics increasingly favor alternative scheduling. Fortunately, a growing number of employers recognize the value of a less rigid schedule. According to the Boston College Center on Aging and Work, approximately one-third of employers offer flexible work options to a "limited extent." Only 7.6 percent provide no option at all.

Demographics and attitudes will soon collide. Marcie Pitt-Catsouphes, co-director of the Center on Aging and Work, believes that older workers who want to remain gainfully employed find the standard 5x8 workweek too confining. They want to have time for themselves, their families and friends, and the business of running their life. Employers who lack flexible work options may find themselves breathing the exhaust fumes of other companies passing them by. "They may be missing important opportunities to enhance both their business performance and their employees' engagement," notes Pitt-Catsouphes.

Job Sharing Although society has traditionally operated on

the principle that a single person holds down a job, that's changing too. Starting around 1990, job sharing emerged as a viable alternative opportunity. Typically, two people hold down the same position at the same company—each present during different days, or during hours within the same day. In some cases, an employer may match a candidate *with* someone else. In other cases, it's up to an individual to find his or her own job-sharing partner in order to win the employer's approval of a job-sharing proposal. Participants might range from an older executive working with a younger executive attending graduate school to two nurses who don't want to log full workweeks.

Job sharing can involve different scenarios, including each participant's putting in two and a half days per week, or partners' splitting the week by working two full days each and overlapping on a third full day. The latter is considered a 1.2-employee arrangement, with each person receiving 60 percent of the total salary.

In common with, say, a solid marriage, job sharing requires substantial effort, constant coordination, and excellent communication. The two individuals involved must be able to handle a single position as efficiently as one. Although working mothers pioneered job sharing, the trend is now fanning out to include older workers and others as well.

Employees aren't the only ones who benefit from job sharing. Some companies find that it provides an alternative to layoffs and a steady stream of temporary help, smoothes over gaps caused by vacations and sick days, improves morale, increases productivity, lowers training and overtime costs, and provides better job coverage. In some cases it's possible to match a person who is good at customer interaction with another who excels at administrative functions, thus creating a more well-rounded job profile. Although some positions aren't sharable and not everyone is suited for splitting duties with another person, the two-for-one approach is redefining the concept of a job.

Telecommuting & the Virtual Office
Workers have always lugged projects home in their briefcases and backpacks ("graveyards of good intention," in proletarian argot). A few have spent one or two days each week handling tasks from their den or a home office. Telecommuting as a formal concept, however, was not born until 1973. That's the year former University of Southern California professor Jack Niles—now an independent consultant and author of *Making Telecommunications Happen*—coined the phrase to describe an emerging group of workers who rely on telecommunications and computers to accomplish their jobs remotely.

Over the years, the telephone has morphed into e-mail, instant messaging, texting, videoconferencing, and collaboration software. As technology "flattens the world," to reprise Thomas Friedman's phrase, more and more people are trading in their corner office for a corner of the den. Today, according to the Maryland-based International Telework Association & Council, more than 20 percent of the American workforce engages in telecommuting. And don't subscribe to the canard that to be visionary you must be large: Mom-and-pop shops are likewise sending their workers home—to work.

In some cases, this remote alternative is becoming the rule rather than the exception. Look at Alpine Access, a Denver, Colorado firm that manages call-center operations for companies such as J. Crew, Vermont Teddy Bear, and ExpressJet. It relies on equal doses of technology and innovation to redefine the workplace. Call-center agents—many of them

Key Variables in the Motivation Equation

Many companies have woken only slowly to this stark reality: Today's marketplace demands creative new ideas. But others have adapted nicely, thank you very much, and though not every organization can land on a list of best employers, many have found that the right mix of programs, perks, and other benefits can ratchet up productivity and pay dividends.

Through boom times and bust, the philosophy at SAS Institute—the world's largest privately owned software firm—has remained "Keep the employees happy." The formula works: SAS has stayed profitable since its inception in 1976, consistently limiting employee turnover to less than five percent—far below the industry norm.

It's not difficult to understand why. SAS offers flexible work hours, ample exercise time, and employee-recognition programs for top performers in R&D and other departments. All of these perks boost morale immeasurably. The firm also provides on-site day care, an in-house medical facility, subsidized meals, and transportation reimbursements for workers at its satellite locations. These programs require an investment from the company, but the return on that investment is substantial.

"Creating a work-life balance is one of the ways we differentiate ourselves," says Mike Gallagher, director of human resources at SAS. "We want to make flextime, exercise breaks, and personal time available to the 98 percent of the employee population that will utilize it but not abuse it. We can deal with the remaining 2 percent on an individual basis." Yet even the more expensive programs pay for themselves, Gallagher notes, through greater productivity, improved loyalty, and fewer distractions.

At Boston Beer Company, incentives and rewards are more than corporate froth. Almost everything revolves around brewing beer. The winner of the company's yearly home-brewing contest, for example, receives a free trip for two to the world's premier beer event: Munich's Oktoberfest.

It's a winning proposition for everyone involved. "We could provide tickets to the Super Bowl or Disney World," notes Jim Koch, founder and chairman. "But a person isn't going to learn about beer and brewing at those events. The contest winner returns from Oktoberfest more enthusiastic than ever about beer and the culture surrounding it." More than 90 percent of the firm's employees take part in the contest. "The more knowledgeable, enthusiastic, and happy our workers are," says Koch, "the better off we are."

Koch has rolled out a welter of other measures to motivate workers: flexible scheduling; quarterly parties at the brewery; company-subsidized meals; paid adoption aid; and a week of parental leave for spouses, namely men, with newborns. What's more, Boston Beer grants employees 17 to 22 personal days a year, which they can use for any purpose—vacations, sick days, a day at the ballpark, or time off to watch their child's piano recital. "Boston Beer Company doesn't make the beer," in Koch's view, "people do. So it's essential to have great employees. And if they're happy and motivated, we will see better bottom-line results."

stay-at-home mothers or career-changers—work from their residences for 15 to 40 hours a week, thus escaping traffic-clogged roads, sky-high gasoline prices, dry-cleaning bills, and winter blizzards. Although it maintains no central facility, Alpine Access has found that these virtual workers are one-third more productive than those who slog their way to an actual, physical work site.

Alpine also experiences 50 percent less turnover than its competitors, states CEO Chris Carrington. "This approach provides access to quality workers," he says. "We can tap into groups, such as those who are 50 or older and want to re-enter the workforce, who would never in a million years come into a 'bullpen'—that is, a call center with 500 other people with an average age of 22. But when you make it clear they can do that work from the comfort of their own homes, suddenly they are interested."

Indeed, more than one-fifth of Alpine's 7,500 agents are 50 or older. Carrington expects that proportion to spike in the years ahead. "We seek out this group of workers," the CEO explains, "because we have found that we benefit from their maturity, their empathy, and their ability to leverage 20 to 30 years of job experience. Most of them are dependable and self-motivated. They show up for work on time."

Adrianne Vaiser is among those in the age 50+ category who have figured out that home is where the work is. The 56-year-old mother of two girls—ages 18 and 12—decided to head back to work in 2007 after an 18-year child-rearing hiatus. Vaiser had previously worked as a travel agent, a reservations agent for Club Med, an airport agent for Braniff Airlines, and an independent travel consultant. Surfing the Web one day, she spotted an article that mentioned Alpine's virtual call center. *"I could do this,"* she recalls thinking at the time. *"It would fit perfectly with my schedule and provide some money for college tuition."*

Vaiser applied online, dispatched an e-résumé, submitted to a phone interview, and began working as a reservation agent for ExpressJet in June 2007—all without a single face-to-face meeting with anyone from Alpine Access. "It has turned out to be an ideal job," says the small-town Colorado resident. "I go downstairs to my office, log onto my computer, switch the phone to route personal calls to voicemail, and begin answering calls and assisting people with reservations."

Vaiser's typical workweek comprises 15 to 20 hours. At any time, however, she can check online to see if the company needs more agents—and, if so, log in. "I don't have to deal with office politics and gossip," she says. "I can get the kids to sports and after-school activities. I can get to the doctor and dentist. I don't have to buy lunches out, and I go to work in my sweats. At this point in my life, I don't want to work in an office."

As it has been for Adrianne Vaiser, the intersection of telecommuting and recareering is an ideal fit for many older workers. The business and social benefits are clear: They range from a need for less office space to reduced energy demands and air pollution. Yet many organizations now see telework as a way to find top talent and land key prospects. As telecommuting becomes more common in the business world and individuals grow more comfortable using collaboration tools and technology, fewer workers will consent to disruptive, job-related moves. And as boomers and others start second or third careers that hinge on virtual work from a home office, certain spots are emerging as telework meccas. They include Bend, Oregon; Charlottesville, Virginia; and Asheville, North Carolina.

Contract Work
In years gone by, the employment contract was a corporate lure designed to lock up key executives for a specified time. Today, by contrast, workers in many fields sign contracts to serve a company for three months, six months, a year—whatever they desire. This cyclical work allows an individual to alternate bursts of work with stretches of leisure.

Nowhere is the future more visible than in the nursing profession. A remarkable 55 percent of nurses surveyed say they intend to retire between 2011 and 2020. Yet with boomers aging, the demand for health services will only rise. What's more, nurses are getting older too. In 2004, the average age of the RN population was estimated to be 46.8—more than a year older than the average age of 45.2 estimated in 2000, and more than four years older than in 1996, when the average was just 42.3. As if all this isn't adequate cause for concern, some states, such as California, have imposed nurse-to-patient staffing-ratio requirements.

It doesn't take a highly paid analyst to figure out that anyone with a nursing degree is going to be among the most popular girls (or boys) at the recruiting dance. Healthcare providers are responding with offers for higher pay, better pensions, and more clout. A few have even offered free

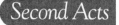

CULTURAL IMMERSION

KAY BURCH, *from foundation manager to social-service worker*

I DEVELOP PARTNERSHIPS AND ALLIANCES for the AARP Foundation. I've been at AARP for about five years and was hired as the foundation's chief development officer. I like my work, but I will be 65 in November 2008, and I am planning to go to Mexico and work for a volunteer organization there.

Right now, I am downshifting. Rather than serving as Chief Development Officer, I am working in a support role that entails fewer responsibilities. In years past I worked 55 to 60 hours a week, on average. Now I would say I'm working only about 47 to 52 hours per week. I'm also coaching other members of the staff.

Going to Mexico didn't just pop into my mind on the spur of the moment. It has evolved over time. It grows out of my desire to learn about another culture and actually experience that culture. I have a master's degree in Latin American politics and a doctorate in comparative politics. Every time I have experienced another place while traveling—such as India, Indonesia, and Latin America—it has added value to my own life and work. The idea of cultural immersion really excites me.

I want to work in the southern Mexico region of Oaxaca and focus on microenterprise issues. There is a lot of poverty and a lot of social issues, including literacy, that need to be addressed. I'm attracted to Mexico and neighboring areas such as Guatemala, but it's also appealing to work there because it's closer to the United States and it's fairly easy to go back to see family and friends. I'm hoping to have my 85-year-old mother, my 40-year-old daughter, and my 7-year-old granddaughter join me for the first year. It will be an educational experience for all of them too.

My daughter is learning to be a jeweler, so there's intergenerational recareering going on. She is moving away from managing retail stores. I am just starting to do research on organizations, living arrangements, and schools for my granddaughter.

As my retirement gets closer, I will begin applying for positions or simply volunteering to help organizations with their fund-raising. I don't expect to make any money doing this. In fact, it will probably be the other way around: I'll spend my own money in order to volunteer.

One complicating factor is that my mother has dementia. At first I wasn't sure how to handle the situation. But she's in remission to some degree, so she is capable of interacting and enjoying certain things.

Overall, I am very excited about this move. I'm looking forward to making a difference in the lives of others—and embarking on a new and exciting stage in my own.

tuition or new cars. Meanwhile, many hospitals are willing to hire RNs on a contract basis, typically for three- to six-month stints. At some facilities, 60 percent of the nursing staff enjoys the flexibility of such contracts.

Yet contract work offers opportunities far beyond the world of medicine. Today, skilled professionals from a range of fields—engineering, software development, IT systems integration, finance—find themselves able to call the shots. In the years ahead, as the knowledge economy expands and older workers become the focus of recruiting and retention efforts, cyclical work is likely to go mainstream.

Sabbaticals The concept of a sabbatical—a one-year respite from work every seven years—cropped up at Harvard University in the late 1800s. Since then, universities, research institutions, and medical establishments have relied on the practice to retain talented staffers. Not all is altruism, however; by enabling essential workers to periodically recharge their batteries, such a breather can ratchet up their productivity. Sabbaticals are gaining acceptance in the corporate arena as well. Companies that have offered them include Autodesk, Charles Schwab, DuPont, L.L.Bean, McDonald's, Nike, Ralston Purina, TimeWarner, and Apple.

According to the Society for Human Resource Management, 18 percent of companies presently offer some sort of unpaid sabbatical leave. Four percent provide paid sabbaticals. The practice is more common at larger companies and within certain industries, such as technology and the biosciences, where long hours and intense projects are the norm. But the self-employed are getting into the act, too.

For those ensconced in a career, a sabbatical may offer an opportunity to pursue a lifelong ambition—writing a novel or traveling to India, for example—or the time needed to explore other options. Meanwhile, whether or not a company offers a sabbatical may be the deciding factor for those contemplating a change of jobs or employers. A sabbatical can be the deciding coin that brings balance to the work-life scales.

AARP, for one, offers a "Renewal" program for those with seven years of consecutive employment. Individuals who receive positive evaluations are eligible for four weeks' paid leave. (They can also add accrued vacation.) According to an official explanation of the program's goal, "Taking dedicated time to rebuild our physical, emotional, and spiritual vitality is good stewardship of resources—both for the employee and for AARP— resulting in a more refreshed, engaged, and productive employee."

Gilbert Chavez can certainly attest to the power of a sabbatical. The 65-year-old from Gold Beach, Oregon had worked as a professional musician in his 20s, playing nightclubs and other venues in Las Vegas and California. Approaching 30, he went back to school to earn a high-school diploma, then a bachelor's and a master's degree. Finally, after 30 years as a librarian in southern California and Oregon, Chavez sold his house, quit his job, and joined the Peace Corps—a lifelong ambition.

In 2000 Chavez headed off to Mongolia, where he taught English at Orkhon University for two years and helped develop library systems in the capital city, Ulaanbaatar. "It was an opportunity and a privilege to make a tiny contribution," he reflects. "It was a way to complete my purpose in life. I came back feeling recharged and refreshed."

Chavez now works as a library director in Curry County, Oregon. Although he has no plans to retire, "serving in the Peace Corps is something I may want to do again at some point in the future."

By Your Leave—
of Absence, That Is
Older workers are more likely to require a leave of absence than their younger counterparts. Their own health—or that of a spouse or parent—may come into play. Prolonged caregiving responsibilities or the death of a family member may boost the need for time away from work. Although the Family and Medical Leave Act, signed into law by President Clinton in 1993, provides up to 12 unpaid weeks during a 12-month period, some employers recognize that a leave makes good business sense. Because the cost of hiring and training a new employee often runs into the tens of thousands of dollars, adding staff is typically 150 percent to 200 percent more expensive than keeping a current employee. Not only that, but the departure of a valued employee often creates a knowledge vacuum, putting an even higher premium on minimizing turnover.

Phased Retirement
The notion of walking away from work at age 65—and pocketing an ample pension on your way out the door—is, deplorably, fading into the dustbin of history. Many workers are therefore experimenting with phased retirement instead, which lets them ease into retirement by assuming a less taxing role in the waning months of their working lives.

The Society for Human Resource Management defines "phased retirement" as "a work-schedule arrangement that allows employees to gradually reduce their full-time hours over a period of time." In practical terms, this approach might translate into working fewer weeks per year, or fewer hours per day. It might mean taking on new duties that are less stressful, such as mentoring younger employees or working in a support role.

There's no single approach to phased retirement. For many longtime workers, it's all about downshifting—moving forward at a reduced speed more compatible with their age and interests. A 2005 Merrill Lynch survey

Taking the Bite out of the Generational Sandwich

Raising children or caring for aging parents takes time, money, and resources. The situation is especially daunting for those who work full-time. For boomers who put off starting a family until their 30s or 40s, a new challenge has emerged as well: They must provide care for an elderly parent, hold down a job, and rear their children at the same time.

Experts have labeled this group the "sandwich generation." According to Margaret Neal and Leslie Hammer, professors at Portland State University in Oregon and authors of *Working Couples Caring for Children and Aging Parents,* 9 to 13 percent of U.S. households with two or more people age 30 to 60 tend to elders at least three hours a week while raising children. According to another study, 77 percent of Americans expect to care for an older loved one within the next five years, and 70 percent of those who provide care must take time off from work to do so.

It's no small matter. "Working couples report greater stress, increased levels of work-family conflict, slightly higher levels of depression, and in some cases financial challenges," Hammer explains. "Maintaining a job while managing family responsibilities has become a major issue for much of today's workforce."

Caregiving has always been a collective obligation of our species, yet it now affects more people—and it affects them more profoundly, says Donna L. Wagner, director of Towson University's gerontology program. Not only have basic demographics changed, but more women have entered the workplace. Families are more dispersed. And many workers have no financial safety net to catch them when they fall: Even with the provisions of the Family and Medical Leave Act, which provides 12 weeks' annual unpaid leave for a birth or family health condition, they simply can't afford to take time off.

Too often, individuals caught in the middle find themselves unprepared to deal with the mélange of practical and emotional issues that caregiving brings. Already stressed by work and children, their time and energy are at a premium. Meanwhile, says newspaper columnist and expert on aging Carol Abaya, "Many individuals aren't equipped to handle the role reversal of becoming a parent to their parent. Coping with financial and legal issues as well as juggling phone calls, visits, and in-home care can affect [their] work and relationships."

For those on the verge of a career change, it's vital to examine a caregiving situation before taking any major steps. A couple—or a family—may need to divvy up caregiving roles and responsibilities more equitably. (Often this will require that children lend a hand.) Additionally, you may benefit from taking "caregiving classes" at a school or online. Finally, consider an employer that allows a flexible or alternative work schedule, or one that offers personal days or dependent-care assistance. Children's Memorial Hospital in Chicago, for example, reimburses family members for up to 80 hours per year of the in-home care they provide.

So what's the bottom line for those on the front line? Caregiving should not stop you from recareering, but your plans will have to accommodate it carefully if you want to successfully negotiate a change.

found that 42 percent of boomers would like to cycle between work and leisure. AARP, for its part, discovered that 1 in 8 older workers (those aged 63 to 73) are currently "phasers."

However, be aware of the impact that a phased-retirement program could have on your plans for recareering or retirement. Current federal statutes—and some state laws as well—limit the circumstances under which an individual can work part-time and receive pension or retirement benefits. A phased retirement might also dictate whether or not an employee receives healthcare coverage. The Internal Revenue Service is proposing to loosen the rules, but it's always best to check with your employer in advance.

A New Generation
of Perks
In the quest to retain workers—and knowledge—more and more companies are turning to new and sometimes unusual benefits. In recent years, information-technology firms have garnered a good deal of attention for gourmet cafeterias, on-site childcare, exercise facilities, grocery stores, gas stations, libraries, even doctors and dentists on location. These and other perks, including the right to bring pets to work, are becoming more common across the corporate landscape. Some firms are also offering special dinners and parties, home makeovers, and free trips for contest winners. In many instances, these policies aim to offset the rigors of today's workaday world and create a more flexible, less stressful environment. And they're often ideal for older workers eager to reduce driving time or improve their overall quality of life.

Thinking Big,
Working Small
The modern corporation isn't the only place undergoing radical change. Americans are increasingly bidding adieu to a 9-to-5 job with a steady paycheck and venturing out on their own. In some instances, they're providing the same services they would inside a corporation—though handling the work independently. In other cases, they're competing against the same companies that employed them earlier in their career. In almost every scenario, these individuals are embracing their hobbies and passions while chasing their dreams. A few of their methods are detailed below.

Free agency. The traditional relationship between employers and employees isn't the only thing undergoing fundamental change. Since the mid-1990s, as information technology has seeped into every corner of society, the free-agent economy has burned white-hot. It shows no signs of cooling. Consultants, graphic artists, writers, Web designers, software developers, financial analysts, project managers, meeting planners, and even chief executive officers now work on an independent basis—without landing on any particular company's payroll. This new world order has dramatically changed the working world—and the way people view employment. More than 10 million independent contractors exist in the United States, up from 6.7 million in 1995.

Businesses pursue independent contractors because they lower overall costs, increase flexibility, and can reduce a company's exposure to lawsuits. Meanwhile, many individuals find the arrangement ideal because they're able to choose whom they work with, how much they work, and when they switch off the computer and mobile phone. Those looking for a part-time work arrangement, particularly older workers, may find that independent relationships—and the flexible hours they bring—are ideal. Not surprisingly, it's a direction enthusiastically embraced by many individuals seeking to change careers.

More than a name or a mindset, free agency represents a new way of conducting business. As Daniel H. Pink points out in his 2001 book, *Free Agent Nation*, Starbucks becomes the office, FedEx the shipping department, Staples the procurement service, and Barnes & Noble the R&D unit. The barriers to entry, including up-front capital costs, are often low (at least by historical standards), though the key to survival is to keep jobs coming in—a task that requires excellent marketing skills, a dedication to networking, and the ability to provide desirable and affordable services.

It's certainly a different world that the one William H. Whyte skewered in his 1956 critique of blind corporate fealty, *The Organization Man*. Free agents, on the other hand, trade job security (or whatever remains of it) for a foot-pounding, life-on-the-edge reality show in which they are the star players. There are substantial risks—and commensurate rewards. Although free agents may have to weather bouts of unemployment and constantly learn new skills, they're able to change, morph, and evolve in a way that simply was not possible in the past. A linear career path has been replaced by rich opportunities to recareer.

In order to flourish, consultants, freelancers, and others in the free-agent economy must possess technology skills as well as specialized expertise in a particular field, whether it's publishing, marketing, or education. The most successful among this category have spent time in a particular field and have inside knowledge of how projects unfold.

A restaurant manager, for example, might emerge as a dining consultant—providing expertise on menus, seating arrangements, and food preparation. Or a technical writer may be able to make the leap to generating articles for trade magazines and journals. For many who change careers in midlife or after an initial retirement, free agency provides a breath of fresh air.

Mind your business! A variation on the free-agency theme—and one with tremendous appeal for veterans of the workforce—is the idea of starting a business. More than 28.5 million small businesses exist in the U.S.—and that figure is rising at an annual clip of nearly four percent. Remarkably, nearly 20 million of these businesses are owned and operated by individuals who have no paid employees. One study found that 63 percent of Americans desire self-employment.

No longer is it a euphemism for "unemployed" to report that you're a consultant or an independent graphic artist, Web designer, writer, pet trainer, or seamstress. In fact, some employers actively seek out "retirees" and consultants in order to create a pool of on-demand labor. A good starting point for finding these firms is the AARP Best Employers site at www.aarpmagazine.org/money/2007_best_employers.html.

With an attractive website, business cards, a phone line, broadband Internet access, and some talent, it's possible to eclipse the pay scale that comes with a corporate job. Even better, many view their own business as a ticket to greater happiness. They're able to pursue a passion and get paid. They're able to work on their own terms.

For some, Suite 101 is the home office, which serves as headquarters for a scrapbooking business, an online sports-collectible store, or a transcription service. For others, a fancy storefront on a fashionable boule-vard is a place to sell candy, pet products, burgers—you name it.

Whereas some individuals go the independent route, others embrace a small business or franchise operation. These days a dizzying array of franchise options exist, including fast-food restaurants, sign stores, mail-box-and-shipping services, craft boutiques, computer shops, do-it-your-self art-framing centers, and exercise studios.

According to the Center on Aging and Work at Boston College, 50+ workers have significantly higher rates of self-employment (17 per-cent compared with 12 percent) and small-business ownership (9 pecent compared with 5 percent) than their younger counterparts. No less im-portant: Older workers prize their independence. Among all age groups, 32 percent of those self-employed and 14 percent of small-business owners would prefer to have regular jobs. Among the 50+ set, the numbers drop to 21 percent and 7 percent respectively.

Operating a small business can prove incredibly satisfying. For starters, you're the boss. You get to reap the spoils of your hard work. You can shutter the shop when you want to go on vacation—and, blessed with a good employee or two, take time off for an afternoon walk or to watch a grandchild's ballet performance.

On the other hand, owning a business requires dedication and persist-ence. Half of all new small businesses fail within five years, according to the Small Business Administration. You are the CEO, but you may also wind up playing the roles of accountant, marketing specialist, reception-ist, IT administrator, inventory clerk, and customer-service agent. You may spend long hours running the business and dealing with a tangle of frustrations and problems.

Sara Rix, a senior policy advisor at AARP, believes that older adults eyeing entrepreneurship should think carefully before committing money and resources. Not only is there a risk of burning through your savings, she says, but starting a business and running it effectively can prove mentally and physically taxing. Long hours and infrequent days off are the norm.

Nonetheless, entrepreneurship continues to galvanize older individuals. A 2005 study found that older entrepreneurs now make up 54 percent of self-employed workers—a jump from 48.5 percent in 2000.

Take the case of Toni Cory. The 52-year-old woman from Mt. Pleasant, Iowa worked at Motorola for a quarter-century as an engineering technician. There it was her job to program machines that attach microchips to printed circuit boards. In 2002, Motorola sold the company to Celestica. Then, just three years after that, Celestica decided to shutter the plant and ship its operations to Mexico. Cory received a first-hand lesson in global economics: It took the form of a pink slip.

Fortunately, Cory and her husband, Paul, who runs his own construction business, had seen the proverbial writing on the wall. "We had a feeling the company would announce a downsizing," Cory remembers, "so we launched our own downsizing initiative." The Corys unloaded their

7 Steps to Breaking Away

If you're considering starting your own business, here are a half-dozen issues and challenges you cannot ignore:

Follow your interests and passions. If you eagerly anticipate the end of each workday, you're primed for change. Find something that excites and satisfies you—whether it's opening a sports-card shop or a computer-repair service.

Do your research. Explore whether the business is viable and you will find yourself on the right track well before you hang out your shingle. Check out Entrepreneur.com and its print publication, *Entrepreneur* magazine. It offers lots of tips, advice, and information on how to start a new business or fine-tune an existing one. Other useful sites include the United States Small Business Administration (www.sba.gov) and Franchising.com.

Draft a business plan. Whether you're starting a business in your office or on Main Street, outline how you will raise the necessary capital, what you will spend it on, who your customers or clients will be, who your competition is, and how you plan to market yourself.

Make sure you have adequate capital and reserves. The most common reason for deferring self-employment is a lack of capital and cash. Save your money, and understand that it's not unusual for a business to take a year or two to turn a profit. You must carefully weigh every expense but also understand how to invest in the business.

Be prepared mentally and physically. It's easy to get carried away with visions of glamour and success. But launching a new business is a stressful enterprise that demands long hours—particularly at the outset.

Ensure that you have support. Your spouse and family must be supportive—and it's great if they're willing to help out in emergencies. Also, try to find employees you can trust to keep the operation running when you're not there.

Stay informed. Read trade publications. Subscribe to online newsletters. Attend conferences. In short, do whatever it takes to keep up with the latest industry trends—and to understand your customer base.

house, a boat, and other assets to chisel down debt. They also began mapping out their future. "Any other manufacturing job would clearly have just as little job security," she explains. "Their pay and benefits might be good, but they just couldn't offer much of a future."

The couple had long fantasized about opening a daycare facility for dogs. A couple of years earlier, in fact, Cory had taken a fast-track business course at her local community college, which taught her how to construct a business plan, manage capital, and oversee employees. But her biggest lesson came from a local banker, who had asked the class: "Why should we invest in you if you aren't willing to invest in yourself?"

That message struck a chord in Cory. In October 2005, thanks to VocationVacations—an organization that enables people to test-drive other careers for a fee (see also pages 149–150 and 217–218)—she traveled to Cedar Rapids and worked at a "doggie daycare" for a day. Though the pay-to-play holiday set her back $350, it honed her yen for the work. Then, in January 2006, Cory spent five months at a professional dog-training school in St. Louis to become an accredited trainer.

Finally it came time came to get serious about the canine daycare business. Toni and Paul cashed in their 401(k)s to the tune of $200,000, then scraped together the additional funds they would need to launch the business and pay their living expenses. "Other people thought we were foolish to risk our retirement," Toni admits. "But when I remember the advice of the banker who spoke to our business class, I don't feel funny saying we're investing in ourselves rather than in stocks and bonds from major corporations."

The Corys also required a loan—and landed $200,000 in additional financing from that selfsame banker. They bought a piece of undeveloped land four miles outside Mt. Pleasant, built a 24-by-24-foot log cabin for a living space, and began constructing the facility. The doors to Almost Home Dog Daycare and Boarding swung open on October 9, 2006.

"I wanted to be in control of my destiny," says Cory, "and now I am." She's happier than ever, but at the same time she concedes that the road to entrepreneurial success is paved with reckoning and readjustment. On the lifestyle front, for example, the couple has had to drastically curtail their spending. The business is growing rapidly (Almost Home now has four employees), but Cory has also missed the occasional loan payment—with the blessing of the bank. "Last summer we were fully booked," she reported in July 2008. "I'm putting in 90-hour weeks, but the business is taking off, so it's an exciting and wonderful time."

Key Questions

Do I understand my recareering style? Am I prepared for an era of swift and unrelenting change? Potentially acute labor shortages—and the increased interest in older workers that is likely to result—do not necessarily translate into a dream job. It's essential to keep up on education, training, and professional networking in order to stand out as a top-tier candidate.

What do I want out of my job and career as I grow older? The traditional 9-to-5 work routine is fading into history. In its place, home offices, mobile work, and flexible schedules are emerging as pillars of the digital-employment era. Today's employees—boomers among them—are therefore in a good position to bargain for desirable working conditions and working hours that fit their lifestyles.

Do I understand my basic needs? Before you opt for a particular type of business or career decision, understand how you function best. Do you thrive in a home office? Or would you be more productive in the field and around people? Are you a self-starter, or do you need a boss monitoring your progress in order to stay on track?

Is flexible work part of my future? Those on the verge of a career shift should consider whether a particular industry or a specific employer offers flexible work programs—or is willing to make other scheduling concessions to older workers.

Do I understand how to present a convincing case for a flexible work arrangement? Many an employer has yet to jump on the flextime bandwagon. You may have to craft a proposal of your own, then sell the concept to an existing boss or a new employer. If you find yourself in this situation, do the research required to demonstrate the advantages of this approach.

Making Sense
of the Change
It's not your grandfather's workplace. Heck, it's not even your father's or your mother's: Job security is gone, mandatory retirement is fading into history, and the ability to learn new skills and knowledge is the baseline for staying employed. There are greater options, opportunities, and risks. There are new business models and unfamiliar workplace relationships.

In the emerging workplace of the 21st century, the ideas and concepts that drove individual and organizational success in times past will become quaint landmarks on the road to success and self-actualization. The corporate pyramid—tied into vertical promotions and titles based on rank—could well collapse under the weight of a flatter, more decentralized work model. "The problem with a vertical structure is that it doesn't work efficiently in a knowledge-based economy," business consultant and author Tamara Erickson observes. Already, "It's not mathematically possible to tie many of the most highly valued activities and accomplishments into a vertical promotion."

For those seeking to embark on a new career in midlife, the landscape of work now emerging offers remarkable opportunities. Not only will individuals with skills and talent attract previously unimaginable attention and job offers, they will find the dynamics of work turned topsy-turvy. Organizations will have to find ways to tie compensation to breadth of experience rather than to seniority or rank. They will have to discover methods of engaging employees and independent contractors—from project to project and from position to position. For those looking to change directions and find a new career, the prospects are rich.

Books

The Baby Boomer's Guide to the New Workplace, by Richard Fein, Taylor Trade Publishing, 2006. Offers insights into navigating today's changing workplace.

Finding a Job After 50: Reinvent Yourself for the 21st Century, by Jeannette Woodward, Career Press, 2007. Focuses on finding the right job in midlife and making yourself the best candidate for it.

Harvard Business Review on Work and Life Balance, by Stewart D. Friedman, et al., Harvard Business School Press, 2000. Examines leading work and lifestyle trends, including telecommuting, alternative work environments, and how to avoid burnout.

Life Matters: Creating a Dynamic Balance of Work, Family, Time & Money, by A. Roger Merrill and Rebecca Merrill, McGraw-Hill, 2004. Two time-management experts offer creative solutions for balancing what they see as the four pillars of life: family, money, work, and time.

Power Sabbatical: The Break That Makes a Difference, by Robert Levine, Findhorn Press, 2007. Provides a comprehensive framework for making a sabbatical succeed and rejuvenating your outlook. Offers tips and resources, and helps you develop a viable sabbatical plan.

Stop Living Your Job, Start Living Your Life: 85 Simple Strategies to Achieve Work/Life Balance, by Andrea Molloy, Ulysses Press, 2005. Features tasks and tools designed to help you achieve greater balance between work and life.

Striking a Balance: Work, Family, Life, by Robert W. Drago, Dollars & Sense, 2007. Offers a framework for navigating today's working world while maintaining a sense of harmony.

The Work-at-Home Workbook: Your Step-by-Step Guide on Selecting and Starting the Perfect Home Business for You, by Lesley Spencer, Wyatt-MacKenzie Publishing, 2004. Offers an assortment of tips, resources, and stories to help readers achieve entrepreneurial success.

More Resources

AARP

www.aarp.org/money/careers/
employerresourcecenter/best
employers/winners/2007.html

This site lists the winners of AARP's "Best Employers for Workers Over 50" program for the last several years, and includes details on how these organizations manage to excel at attracting older workers.

http://assets.aarp.org/rgcenter/
econ/workers_fifty_plus.pdf

Examines the business case for workers 50+ and dispels stubborn myths about older members of society.

American Telecommuting Association

www.yourata.com/index.html

Provides information and resources on telecommuting and other alternative work options.

Business.com

www.business.com/directory/human_
resources/workforce_management/
flexible_work_schedules/

Supplies an overview of flexible work schedules and employment options.

The Conference Board

www.conference-board.org

Offers research and reports on corporate and workplace trends.

Families and Work Institute

http://familiesandwork.org

A nonprofit organization that conducts studies and analysis on the changing workplace—and how it is affecting families and the communities they live in.

Forbes Work-Life Balance Website

www.forbes.com/2007/03/19/
work-life-balance-lead-careers-
worklife07-cx_db_mn_0319worklife_
land.html

Addresses a cornucopia of work-life issues, including alternative work schedules and sabbaticals, through a series of articles and other resources.

United States Small Business Administration

www.sba.gov

Provides a wealth of information on starting and running a small business.

CHAPTER

10

HIGHER CALLINGS

Finding greater meaning (and often a new career) through volunteerism and social activism

AGE CONFERS PERSPECTIVE—an adage that holds special truth when it comes to careers and the changing thereof. Instead of cranking up our efforts and moving faster, we're more likely to focus our energy as a way to achieve greater results. Not surprisingly, our definition of success also changes with age. In our 50s and 60s, no longer do the corner office and a high-status job hold the same allure as they did in our 30s and 40s. In truth, we're far more likely to measure success in terms of how we touch people's lives and whether we're able to leave a legacy.

These days, career swappers are increasingly shunning the traditional job. Many are opting to volunteer—or at least split their time between a job and a volunteer position. In 2006, more than 61 million Americans contributed time to a worthy cause, such as teaching literacy, helping the poor, or working with disadvantaged children. A 2003 AARP study found that 51 percent of individuals 45 and older volunteer for schools, hospitals, charities, religious organizations, or civic groups. Without the support of these individuals, many of these organizations would collapse.

In some cases, volunteering may precipitate a career change—or serve as the perfect way to explore a career move. For example, Vocation

Vacations in Portland, Oregon (see also pages 149–150 and 212) lets individuals "test-drive" a job or potential career—anything from baker to bootmaker, from horse trainer to hot-rod manufacturer—for one to three days. Another organization, i-to-i, offers volunteer vacations in nearly two dozen countries: You can work with orphans in the Philippines, take part in a conservation project in New Zealand, build homes in Costa Rica, tend to children in Tanzania, or teach English in Vietnam. The agency has worked with "voluntourists" as old as 90. The one- to three-week trips occasionally lead to part-time or full-time jobs.

Embracing the
New Activism   The idea of volunteering—to segue to a new career or simply for the intrinsic good that stems from it—appeals to more and more older workers. Consider Christine Comer, an Alexandria, Virginia woman who worked in human resources for the Federal Aviation Administration (FAA) for 36 years. Comer's father died in a California hospice in 1997. "The hospice chaplain made a tremendous impact on me," she recalls. "She was an incredibly kind person. Our family was in serious distress, with varying points of view about how things should take place, and she had the patience and compassion to guide us through the process.

"At the time, I remember thinking that I would like to provide similar comfort to others some day. So the idea of becoming a chaplain stayed in my mind for several years.

"The year before I was ready to retire, I attended a crossing-over ceremony for a friend who had decided to enter the Episcopal Church after serving as a Catholic priest. By pure serendipity, a woman next to me told me about the Clinical Pastoral Education (CPE) program. It sounded like something I would be interested in. So I researched it, spoke to a supervisor at Sibley Hospital in Washington, D.C. about opportunities for chaplains, contacted the Association for Clinical Pastoral Education, received a packet of information, and began planning for the transition."

After her retirement from the FAA in 2004, Comer was accepted into the CPE program. It covered an array of tough issues, including understanding the dying and grieving process, how to conduct a spiritual inventory, and how to counsel individuals of various religious affiliations. Comer also began volunteering at an in-patient facility for a local clinic in Arlington, Virginia—where, she recalls, she knew she was in the right place the moment she walked in: "I really liked working as part of an interdisciplinary team," she says. "So I decided to work at an in-patient facility rather than in a hospice."

Today Comer volunteers in the pediatric ICU at two local facilities, Sibley Memorial Hospital and Fairfax Hospital in Virginia. The 66-year-old feels more content and centered than she has at any time in her life. "I always liked my work and never clamored for any kind of change," she explains. "But helping people sets my heart on fire. It brings a completeness to my life that I have never felt before."

Clarity via Charity
Transforming a passion into a productive endeavor is at the center of almost all volunteering efforts. For some, it's a deep concern for the environment or a desire for equal educational opportunities that transforms passions into purpose. For others, volunteerism is a chance to aid disadvantaged children or provide medical care to the poor in a developing nation. In short, volunteerism knows few boundaries.

It also cuts across an increasingly diverse segment of society. Although the affluent may have more options—and a lot more time to pursue them—virtually anyone with a desire to effect change can make an impact. "Individuals have a profound collective effect on the success of nonprofits and society," says Arthur Brooks, director of the Nonprofit Studies Program at Syracuse University. "Big-name philanthropists may receive a great deal of attention, but individuals are the backbone of philanthropy and volunteerism."

Yet making the leap from getting paid to working pro bono can be a challenge. You may find yourself subjected to a constant stream of marching orders. The working environment might be spartan, if not downright unpleasant (particularly if you're working in a developing nation or with a group such as the homeless or incarcerated). Or you may confront daily heartache, particularly if you are tending to sick children or serving in a conflict-ridden area. It's important to understand the pros and cons before making any sort of commitment.

Volunteering Checklist

If you're interested in making volunteering part of an overall recareering effort, consider the following factors before you make the leap.

Know your motivation. Are you in it to give something back to society? Do you want to help build a stronger community or have a direct impact on a person's life? Do you want to create a legacy? All of these issues can guide you through the decision-making process. "Through giving and helping others," says Tom Endres, vice president of work & volunteering at the National Council on Aging (NCOA), "people are able to find their heart and passion." Ultimately, this could lead to new opportunities—and, possibly, to a new career as well.

Understand your skills. If you have a particular skill—whether it's writing, computer programming, or carpentry—it's likely that a particular organization stands to benefit from it. If you have a favorite hobby or years of experience leading people or solving problems, you may be able to fill a niche in a charitable organization. This approach maximizes the odds of a solid match and minimizes the amount of training you will need to undergo before you can make an impact.

Find the right match. Be clear on what you want to give and what you hope to get out of a volunteer position. For some, it's enough to help society at large, or a specific community, in any way they can. Others wish only to stay active, be it physically, mentally, or socially. And for yet a third group, nothing short of a passionate cause will do. So research the organization and the position it is offering before you sign on. Also be aware that some organizations will want to interview you, and that many—especially those serving young people—will require background checks.

Know your schedule. Don't overcommit to an organization—it will only lead to burnout. If you have ongoing financial needs, balance your volunteer schedule with your money-making endeavors. Ideally, find an organization that lets you scale hours up or down, as needed. Oftentimes, volunteers see their hours and commitment grow as they get more involved with a cause.

Be realistic. According to the NCOA, 40 percent of volunteers quit within a year. It's important to recognize that change doesn't take place overnight, and that you may not see direct results from your efforts right away. By measuring your success in small but tangible ways, you can more easily maintain the fundamental belief that what you're doing makes a difference.

Equally vital, volunteerism is not a sure-fire ticket to fulfillment. Absent careful preparation, you could find yourself in a position that is not a comfortable fit. You could face the same sort of age bias that afflicts older individuals looking for new jobs or new careers. And hook up with the wrong organization and you may feel that your talents are going to waste.

When the National Council on Aging examined volunteerism among boomers, it found that many charities have fallen short in recruiting and retaining older people. In fact, some groups confessed to such low confidence in the leadership abilities of older volunteers that they had not made it a priority to seek them out.

Volunteer Careers

If you would like to sample volunteer work, either full- or part-time, the following organizations and resources can help you find the right role at the outfit for you:

Corporation for National & Community Service Senior Corps www.seniorcorps.gov

This clearinghouse for information on volunteer organizations is also a catalyst for volunteer efforts. Its search engine lets you pursue particular areas of interest, including advocacy and human rights, children and youth, community, hunger, justice and legal, or seniors. Enter your zip code to view groups that match your criteria. Clicking on the link for a charity displays its location and an overview of its mission. It also includes a phone number and contact person.

DeepSweep www.deepsweep.com

This website bills itself as the largest provider of "nonprofit jobs in one place for free." It features an extensive job bank and allows individuals to post résumés for free. Not-for-profit organizations have been known to comb the site, looking for individuals who match their needs.

Global Volunteer Network www.volunteer.org

This New Zealand-based organization is a clearinghouse for volunteer stints in more than 20 countries, including Cambodia, Ecuador, Ghana, India, Nepal, Tanzania, and the U.S. Its website provides information about volunteer opportunities and connects volunteers to positions that intrigue them.

Global Volunteers www.globalvolunteers.org

If you're looking for a volunteer vacation or a long-term volunteer stint, this organization can help you find the group and position you seek. It offers opportunities to teach conversational English, care for at-risk children, paint, repair blighted buildings, or provide healthcare. It operates links to programs in Costa Rica, Jamaica, Mexico, and the United States.

Idealist.org www.idealist.org

"Action without Borders" is the official tagline for this organization, which lists more than 7,400 nonprofit jobs and nearly 12,000 volunteer opportunities in a powerful search engine. You can look for positions by keyword, country, postal code, or language of posting. You can also include skills you have to offer—from cooking to carpentry to writing—as well as any languages you speak. Clicking a link brings up a detailed profile of the organization. The organization's e-book, *The Idealist Guide to Nonprofit Careers for Sector Switchers,* details how to make the switch to the not-for-profit sector. You can download a copy at www.idealist.org/en/career/guide/ sectorswitcher/index.html.

InterAction www.interaction.org

This entity represents "the largest coalition of U.S.-based international nongovernmental organizations (NGOs) focused on the world's poor and most vulnerable people." You can learn about agencies and opportunities, including international relief and development agencies.

Network for Good www.networkforgood.org

This organization serves as a central hub for volunteer opportunities as well as donations to various charities. If volunteerism beckons, it lets you search by areas of interest, zip code (and other geographic factors), group affiliation, and age (including kids, teens, and seniors). The site also features tips on volunteering wisely and personal stories from those who volunteer.

VolunteerMatch www.volunteermatch.org

Matching "good people with good causes" is the mission of this organization. It boasts more than 3.2 million referrals. Enter your zip code, how far you're willing to travel, and area of interest to view a list of matching opportunities and organizations. Clicking on a link displays a description of the opportunity, including a contact person and a map. You can also create an account to receive e-mail alerts and more in-depth information.

Don't believe it for a second. If you want to embrace volunteerism, take solace in the fact that boomers are leaving the workplace in droves and joining the volunteer world. This social microtrend is almost certain to transform perceptions, thinking, and actions. Think tank and social-advocacy group Civic Ventures found that a majority of Americans aged 50 to 70 want to make their communities better places through volunteerism. And many "leading-edge" boomers—those born from 1946 to 1955—are leading the charge. They want to make social activism central to their lives.

If the times they are a-(still) changin', then add volunteerism to the times. Traditional volunteer modes still exist, yes, but newer notions of this customary calling have moved into the mainstream. For example, some individuals serve as "virtual volunteers"—a calling ideally suited to older individuals who possess typing and computer skills but lack time, mobility, or transportation.

More and more boomers also aspire to become agents of social change. They approach volunteerism in the same way that "venture philanthropists" such as Bill Gates tackle world problems. They want to confront disease, illiteracy, poverty, neglected children, animal abuse, and other social maladies head-on, producing tangible—that is, measurable—results. This new breed of volunteers wants to use its accumulated skills, knowledge, and abilities to lead the charge to a better world.

When it comes to volunteerism, it may well be that society is reaching a tipping point of sorts. Tom Endres, vice president of work & volunteering at the National Council on Aging (NCOA), says that America is transitioning from a traditional pattern of volunteering to a 21st-century model. In the past, Endres points out, many older individuals were happy to donate time to just about any worthwhile cause. Today, by contrast, older volunteers "are much more conscious about how they use their time. It is all about giving time for a higher cause, a clear purpose. They want to see a recognizable result."

Beyond Volunteering:
Taking Activism to the Next Level
These days, an entire world beckons beyond traditional volunteerism. It's possible to start a nonprofit organization or foundation, create a business or for-profit social enterprise that aims to effect change, accept a paid job at a nonprofit, write a book or create a film (or provide the funding for such a creative endeavor), or work as an unpaid political or social lobbyist to help a corporation or government agency bring about change.

One person who embraced this approach is Rick Koca, a 65-year-old ex-Navy lieutenant commander who was shocked by the number of teens he saw living on the streets of San Diego. In 1990, a year before he retired from the military with 30 years under his belt (including 14 years as an officer), Commander Koca decided to do something about it. He began walking the streets and handing out food, clothing, soap, toothpaste, and other essential items to homeless kids. "Very few programs addressed this issue at the time," Koca recalls.

As he interacted with the homeless teens, Koca grew angry at their plight. "It's difficult to believe that we live in a society that lets children live and die on the streets," he says. "There's a belief that they are there because they want to be there. That's like saying, 'Do you want to get hit 10 times or five times?' Well, you want to get hit zero times. Most of these kids—there are more than one million of them across the country—come from troubled households, where they were abused or neglected. They just want to get away. Within 48 hours of hitting the street, 42 percent are forced into prostitution just to survive. Mainstream society doesn't see these kids, but they are out there. They are living under bridges and eating out of Dumpsters. They are being raped."

Koca decided to take direct aim at the problem by starting an organization, Stand Up for Kids. He enlisted the help of a volunteer lawyer, who drafted all the documents required for a registered charity, including a charter and by-laws. Upon leaving the Navy in 1991, Koca began devoting virtually every waking hour to the organization—without paying himself a salary. "I live off my military retirement," he reflects today, "and I'm okay with that. I don't have a lot of wants or needs, and what I am doing here is more important than having money. I wanted to build an organization where people volunteer for one reason only: They care about children."

Today, Stand Up for Kids operates in 41 cities and boasts nearly 2,500 volunteers nationwide (including 1,500 who work directly with teens on the streets). It has grown into the largest organization in the United States addressing teen homelessness. Only three staff members receive a salary. The White House has acknowledged the organization, while Virgin Mobile and others have contributed corporate funding. Volunteers canvass the streets and provide teens with much-needed personal-care items and advice. "We don't care if these kids are white, black, brown, ugly, gay, or deformed," Koca explains. "We try to give them what they need— including the feeling that someone cares about them. If they want to go home, we send them home."

Koca's burning passion ripples through the entire organization. He expects the same dedication and commitment from others. And he isn't one to mince words. "I tell people, 'If you're getting involved in this program to get your ass into heaven, this isn't the program for you. But if you got involved with Stand Up for Kids because kids are living on the streets and dying on the streets, then we need your help. Don't come here because it is the churchy thing to do, or the heavenly thing to do. I have a bigger responsibility to the kids.' "

Koca is equally plainspoken with the recipients of his program's services. "I tell them, 'Nobody pays me to put up with your shit. I'm here because you are out there on the streets and I want to make your life better.' "

A father of three and a grandfather of seven, Koca has no plans to fade into the sunset. "This is who I am. As long as there are homeless children, I will be out there helping them. I've never thought about creating a legacy. This is about caring, and that's all. When people recite the Pledge of Allegiance and get to the words, 'With liberty and justice for all,' they have to understand that there is no liberty and justice for street kids. It's shameful that our society ignores these kids."

Social Responsibility
Means Business
Others are addressing social ills through commercial business ventures of their own devising. Dale Grant, a 65-year-old grandmother from East Hampton, New York, formed Grant Associates, Inc. in 1997, after a successful consulting career. "I had always wanted to do something about inequities in the world," she says. "I call it 'the serendipity of birth': Some of us happen to be born in the right place and grow up with a lot of advantages. Others don't."

From Day 1, Grant Associates' primary mission has been to help welfare mothers find work. After President Bill Clinton and the U.S. Congress radically curtailed welfare eligibility in 1996, Grant realized that major corporations hadn't a clue how to recruit, hire, or train this new labor pool. She sent a letter advertising her services to every company in the Fortune 500 and netted 20 clients. Later she focused on landing government grants. By 2008 Grant had built the business into a 55-person firm, with a presence in New York, Atlanta, and Providence. The firm's revenues have grown an average of 25 percent annually.

Grant started the business with $40,000. "Volunteering is great," she allows, "but it's not for me. I even started my own nonprofit organization back in the mid-1990s [to help women break the glass ceiling at corporations] and ran it for a couple of years. But now I have found my calling. I enjoy managing a business, making it successful, and having a significant social impact. It's the best of all worlds."

Grant forswore a salary for the first year. For the next three years after that, she collected only a reduced salary. She plans to lead the venture for the foreseeable future—working from her home in East Hampton and commuting to the company's office in New York City three days a week.

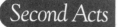

PUTTING STREET SMARTS TO WORK
LUANNE ZURLO, *from Wall Street to philanthropy*

FOR MORE THAN 10 YEARS, I worked as a securities analyst on Wall Street. I spent time at Smith Barney, CSFB, and Goldman Sachs, managing Latin American equity research. For much of that time, I loved the job. It was a perfect fit for my skill set and personality, it paid very well, and the benefits and perks were extraordinary. The work was intense—especially in the 1990s, as emerging markets were opening up and taking off.

Then came the dot-com meltdown and 9/11. It was obvious to me that the party was over. I also realized that I had drifted away from my original passion, which was to make a difference in the lives of people living in developing nations. My father worked for a pharmaceutical company, so I had grown up in different places around the world. I received an international orientation at a young age. Later I earned a bachelor's degree in history from Dartmouth, then a master's degree in international affairs from Johns Hopkins. I spent a year teaching in Spain on a volunteer basis and began to feel a desire to do something that revolved around development. My earlier travels in Latin America, for example, had shown me the abysmally low quality of education there: Huge numbers of people were functionally illiterate, leaving them unable to participate in today's global economy.

But then I decided to attend Columbia Business School instead. There I earned an M.B.A. in finance and accounting. Afterward, somewhat serendipitously, I wound up on Wall Street. One day at Goldman Sachs, I looked at my bonus check and realized that my total income for the year was somewhere around $1 million.

According to the rest of the world's perception, I should have felt on top of the world. But I didn't feel that way—I felt kind of depressed. *Is money all there is to life?*, I recall wondering. Somewhat belatedly, I realized that I desperately needed to reprioritize my objectives.

I left Goldman Sachs on July 2, 2002. By December I had incorporated a new not-for-profit organization, Worldfund, which supports education and literacy in Latin America. I started with a couple of board members; we worked out of my apartment in New York City, and it just grew from there.

Today our annual operating budget is approximately $5 million, and we have a staff of seven people. And this may sound formulaic, but had I known back then how tough it would be to make this organization work, I might never have tried to do so. I lived off my savings and did without a salary for the first couple of years. I pulled together every scrap of knowledge and experience I had gathered in the business world. There were a couple of points where our cash flow was so low we almost didn't make it. But we managed to grow, and now I feel as though we're making a significant impact. It's possible to see the tangible results of our efforts: We are directly affecting the lives of children.

As the executive director of Worldfund, I've had to grow a Teflon carapace and not take everything personally. I hear the word "no" all day long, but it doesn't undermine the positive things we are doing. When I first started out, I found myself riding an emotional roller coaster; the highs were great, but the lows were awful. Now I just try to stay on mission and keep an even approach. Still, it is incredibly uplifting to travel to Latin America and watch our efforts take shape and improve lives. I love interacting with the people—that's what really recharges me.

I'm hoping to build Worldfund into a $10 million-a-year organization. I feel it has the potential to become a major NGO. One of my biggest challenges—and not an uncommon one in the nonprofit world—is encouraging the organization to grow beyond its founder. I don't want Worldfund to be "The Luanne Zurlo Show." At some point, we may need to bring in a more experienced leader. When that day comes, I'll be willing to accept it. The cause is more important than my ego. (I'm a practicing Catholic; without some kind of calling, or a feeling that there's more to life than the material world, I can't imagine exchanging a career on Wall Street for the problems of the developing world.)

I've never been one to develop a five- or 10-year plan. So even though I can't imagine doing this for the rest of my life, right now I am doing what I love. I feel as though I've been endowed with the skills and personality to help Worldfund develop, grow, perhaps even flourish.

This is the place where I can add the greatest value. I consider myself fortunate to have discovered my identity.

"I believe that a person should have a full life at any age and do things that are truly meaningful. It's a recipe for success—and a better world."

From Plan to Action
Volunteering and social activism aren't everyone's cup of tea. You may have to work longer hours. If you join a nonprofit, you'll earn less than your counterparts in the corporate world. According to PayScale.com, mid-level executives in the nonprofit world earn 20 to 25 percent less than their private-sector peers, while executive directors typically earn only half the pay of a CEO.

Compounding the challenge is the difficulty of a sector switch. If you lack training, education, or experience in your target area, you may need to revisit the groves of academe. It's easier to make the leap from teaching English at a public school to leading literacy classes than it is to vault from IT administrator for a Fortune 1000 company to medical-clinic director in a developing nation. So gain a clear idea of your mission and goals— but also know what it will take you to achieve them.

Finally, it's critical to get a sense of the organization you're considering. Hooking up with a well-managed, financially sound organization is vital. If you want to land a job with a certain outfit, spend some time talking to its leadership about how the organization functions. Make sure the two of you are philosophically aligned. According to Idealist.org, "It is important to know the kinds of organizational cultures that help you to flourish. Seemingly small cultural details ... can have a big impact, not to mention more subtle elements such as how decisions get made."

Nonetheless, if you're among the growing wave of boomers yearning to make an impact, you might consider looking beyond the traditional job by volunteering or starting a charitable organization, foundation, or activist business. As charitable organizations become more adept at integrating volunteers, and as older workers become more aggressive in their pursuit of socially significant causes, the number of Americans focusing on the greater good will rise. And that's a good thing for all.

Books

Encore: Finding Work That Matters in the Second Half of Life, by Marc Freedman, PublicAffairs, 2007. Examines how boomers are redefining their identity and lives through more interesting, meaningful, socially significant work.

Career Opportunities in the Non-profit Sector, by Jennifer Bobrow Burns, Checkmark Books, 2006. Offers information and advice on finding work in the not-for-profit sector.

More Resources

Civic Ventures
www.civicventures.org

A not-for-profit organization examining how older Americans can contribute to society through work, volunteerism, and other activities.

Corporation for National and Community Service
www.getinvolved.gov

The CNCS works with community organizations to promote volunteerism in a number of national service programs, including AmeriCorps, VISTA (Volunteers in Service to America), Learn and Serve America, and Senior Corps.

National Council on Aging Work & Volunteerism
www.ncoa.org/content.cfm?sectionID=304

Offers news, information, and opportunities for civic and social engagement.

Urban Institute Volunteer Transitions among Older Americans
www.urban.org/publications/411582.html

This report from the nonpartisan Urban Institute offers insights into the changing patterns of volunteerism, particularly among individuals 55 and older.

World Volunteer Web
www.worldvolunteerweb.org

Serves as a clearinghouse for global news and information about volunteering.

◆◆◆◆

SECTION IV
PUTTING YOUR PLAN INTO ACTION

A Tool Kit for Trading Places

*Using the right resources can boost
your odds of career-change success*

ZEROING IN ON THE RIGHT JOB is more than a numbers game: Rather than mailing off as many résumés and applications as possible, you want to capitalize on opportunities and navigate the process seamlessly—like a Michael Jordan layup or a line of dialogue delivered by Meryl Streep.

Learning to use online job boards and social-networking websites can be perplexing at first. This is a far cry from the world in which many of us grew up, so the temptation is strong to revert to retro mode—mailing off résumés and waiting for responses. It would be a big mistake, however, to forgo the convenience of these 21st-century tools. In many cases they are relatively easy to use, and in almost all instances they can revolutionize the process of finding a job or a new business opportunity. Thanks to on-line communications, what once took months now occurs in minutes.

This chapter examines what it takes to find your ideal job or start your own business. It weighs the pros and cons of competing search strategies —and, if you hope to become an entrepreneur, what it takes to get things off the ground. By adopting the right approach—and by applying some healthy doses of discipline and persistence—you can transform your career dreams into reality. Indeed, doing so may be easier than you think.

How to Locate
Possible Employers
The Internet has profoundly changed the way we identify potential employers. To find one—preferably *the* one—that's right for you in today's job market, you'll need to wield a combination of paper and electronic tools.

Opportunities for employment now extend well beyond the résumé banks that reside—and often lie dormant—at major companies. Savvy job seekers can choose from several methods, detailed below, to increase their exposure and improve their odds of landing the job they aspire to.

Print classified ads. Although the traditional "help wanted" print ad has not disappeared altogether—yet—it is most commonly used within fields such as engineering or nursing, in which job openings are regular and ongoing. Employers anxious to fill positions more quickly usually turn to online classifieds. The Conference Board estimates that U.S. companies now post approximately 4.2 million jobs per month at a variety of online sites, including newspapers, corporate websites, and online job boards. A few job seekers also take a guerrilla job-hunting approach and buy their own ad in a newspaper or trade magazine. It takes guts to go this route, but according to David Perry, co-author of *Guerrilla Marketing for Job Hunters*, it can produce results. "Faced with stiffer competition and tougher hiring requirements," he writes, "companies of every sort are becoming single-minded about productivity and bottom-line performance…. The people who market their talent the best will win!"

Trade magazines. Many employers continue to place ads in highly specialized trade magazines as a way to "narrowcast" their open positions. Whether you want to work as a corporate travel specialist or a university librarian, many trade magazines provide bona fide leads. Finding these magazines may require a bit of creativity; few of them are available at newsstands. In many cases, a Google search, such as "trucking magazine," will yield results. You may also locate trade magazines by searching for a professional field (such as "engineering" or "accounting") along with the

Where the Bosses Are

AARP Best Employers

www.aarpmagazine.org/money/2007_best_employers.html

You can view a list of the best employers in the United States for workers age 50 and older. In addition to profiling each company, the website provides ratings, a description of employee benefits offered, and other key considerations.

Fortune 100 Best Companies to Work For

http://money.cnn.com/magazines/fortune/bestcompanies/2008/full_list/

Glean information about top employers, their demographics and financials, and the benefits they offer.

Hoover's Online www.hoovers.com/free

This site includes data about 43,000 public and private companies from 600 industries. A free service offers basic information, including mailing address and phone number, company profile, and key financial numbers.

Yahoo! Finance Industry Center

http://biz.yahoo.com/ic/ind_index.html

A good starting point for a job search, this free site profiles thousands of publicly owned companies. Click on a category such as "Aerospace" or "Telecom Services," then on a "Company Index" tab to view the firm's address, financials, and competitors.

word "association." (To search for leads in engineering, for example, type in "engineering associations"; this search would yield a number of associations, including the American Council of Engineering Companies and the National Society of Black Engineers, both of which display their magazines at their websites.) You can also check the *Encyclopedia of Associations*, which is widely available in libraries. After you've identified industry associations, venture online and see if they publish a magazine or newsletter.

Corporate websites. The official website of almost every company—particularly medium and large firms—includes an "employment" or "job seekers" link that's a rich source of information about open positions, pay and benefits, career development, company information, culture, and education and training opportunities. Many sites also let you submit a résumé directly, as an attachment or via fax.

Saw Your Blog—Want a Job?

A blog is an informal, running commentary on a particular subject—beer brewing, software trends, political analysis, kosher cooking, art news, you name it. The blogger vents his or her spleen—or heart—in posts that run about half the length of an op-ed and may be updated three or four times daily.

If you have expertise in a certain niche, writing a blog of your own may help you land freelance assignments—perhaps even a job offer. Recruiters routinely scout out new talent on the Web. If they spot a blog whose author seems a promising candidate, you may become the target of a recruiting effort.

There's more to blogging than spewing your verbiage into cyberspace. The best blogs feature diligent research, keen aperçus, and an emotional connection to the audience. Blogging software (such as Google's "Blogger" application, available free at www.blogger.com) can teach you the basics—including how to carve out a corner of the Internet where you can post. Here are a few of my own favorite career-focused blogs:

Dilbert.blog http://dilbertblog.typepad.com/the_dilbert_blog/2007/07/career-advice.html

Monster Career Advice http://monster.typepad.com/

The New York Times Shifting Careers Blog http://shiftingcareers.blogs.nytimes.com

How to Launch a Career with Your Blog www.fastcompany.com/articles/2006/10/blog_careers.html

Submitting an application and résumé directly to a company has both pros and cons. The upside: Your information makes its way into the firm's database immediately. The downside: Many companies are so inundated with online applications that your chances of being singled out can become a game of "keyword roulette." After all, a company's search is only as good as the person searching for the particular terms she opts to enter. (For recommendations on how to use keywords, see pages 268–269 and 276–277.)

Executive search firms. For certain positions, particularly managerial-level jobs at medium and large firms, an executive-search strategy can produce winning results. However, as a rule, recruiters don't specialize in career-changers. Instead they actively seek out professionals with loads of experience, then try to put them on the fast track to a new job—for which the recruiter earns a hefty fee. Keep in mind, too, that search firms work for employers and typically have specific job "orders" or "contracts" they are trying to fill. (For more on search firms, see page 281.)

As a result, it's wise to send your résumé to dozens of these companies and look for boutique firms that specialize in your area of expertise. This might include Shelton Associates in science and engineering, for example, the Howard-Sloan-Koller Group for publishing, and the Esquire Group for the legal field. Meanwhile, larger recruiting firms such as Korn/Ferry International and Robert Half now specialize in multiple areas, among them medicine, technology, and finance and accounting.

You can find numerous executive-search resources and guides online, including at RileyGuide.com, Bluesteps.com, and RecruiterRedbook.com, which invite you to view directories, listings, and advertisements for hundreds of search firms. In addition, many industry groups include a roster of members who work as recruiters. If you're interested in a particular field—accounting, engineering, medicine, or any other—consider checking with the appropriate association (you can find these online, or look them up in the *Encyclopedia of Associations* at your local library).

Alumni networks. Alumni groups have exploded in popularity in recent years for good reason: The Internet has made it easier than ever to marshal and leverage the power of the human network. Check past employers to see if they operate an alumni network. If so, create a profile and reconnect with former colleagues. Other professionals often have the inside scoop on top recruiters and employment opportunities.

Job Fairs

As noted in Chapter 7, job fairs represent an excellent opportunity for older workers. If you attend a fair, bring a hefty stack of résumés: It's better to toss a few in the recycling bin than miss a golden opportunity. Also be aware that some job fairs focus heavily on service jobs, such as retail, customer support, or medical. So check each job fair's list of corporate participants before you hit the road.

Social-Networking Sites

In times gone by, job seekers had to knock out a seemingly endless stream of résumés and pound the pavement in search of work. Today, enterprising individuals have learned that the right information in the right place online can bring recruiters and employers calling. Social-networking sites attract their fair share of students and dilettantes, it's true, but don't let that scare you off. There's almost nothing to lose—and everything to gain—by creating a profile, linking to friends and colleagues, and using the networking capabilities these sites make available to boost your exposure.

Keep in mind, however, that whatever you post on a social-networking site may be visible to the world. In fact, many job seekers have squandered valuable opportunities because of inappropriate material (or simply rude or lewd comments) they've posted online; you should assume that a prospective employer will go looking for—and spot—any and all dirt you may have dished in the digital space. Make sure your profile and photos exude nothing but professionalism. Avoid references to alcohol, drugs,

Virtually Connected

Here are some of the leading social-networking sites that might land you an interview, or a job offer:

LinkedIn. www.linkedin.com

LinkedIn is like having a nuclear-powered Rolodex at your fingertips. It promotes the concept that work relationships are key to professional success. With 20 million members in 150 industries circling the globe, it has rapidly emerged as a valuable and heavily used resource. When you join, you create a profile that summarizes your education, accomplishments, and work history. You then invite colleagues, clients, partners, and others of your choosing to "link in" to your network (and, conversely, they invite you). Once a person accepts, you can view his or her profile and other connections—as well as the additional people those connections know. Think of it as "six degrees of professional separation."

LinkedIn offers a basic service that is free. For $20 to $200 per month, it also provides premium business accounts with more powerful features. No matter which service level you select, you're likely to find LinkedIn ideal for any number of work- and career-related tasks. Members can search for jobs, look for candidates, find potential clients and customers, reconnect with colleagues and former co-workers, and discover subject-matter experts and partners. The site also features profiles of more than 130,000 recruiters. Many troll the LinkedIn network for job prospects on a regular basis.

Facebook www.facebook.com

This social-networking site describes itself as a "social utility that connects people with friends and others who work, study, and live around them." Members share photos, videos, links, and other content with the larger Facebook community, which numbers in the millions. Although the emphasis here is on the social aspect, the service is increasingly popular among job seekers and employers. Even the CIA is getting into the act: In January 2007, the Agency reported that it had created an ad for potential recruits and posted it within Facebook. (The Agency remained more characteristically mum, however, about how many new hires may have resulted.) And as with LinkedIn, there's no way to predict when your personal circle may overlap a professional one, paying unexpected dividends in the form of job leads or opportunities.

MySpace www.myspace.com

Although this site targets young people craving fun and games, some serious business goes on beneath the surface: Job seekers and recruiters are increasingly using the site to connect with one another. MySpace also maintains a classified-ad section with job postings. You set up a profile and create a network of friends and business partners. Recruiters can then find you by searching for keywords or other criteria such as organizations you've worked for and your interests.

Second Life www.secondlife.com

It sounds like something straight out of a science-fiction film. But this online social community, replete with the avatars (screen doubles) and virtual-reality environments that made it famous, has become a hotbed of job-related activity. In May 2007, recruiting firm TMP Worldwide hosted the world's first virtual job fair at Second Life. More than 1,800 candidates registered for the expo—and over 200 interviews took place as a result. Several people even landed jobs.

The concept may seem odd—if not downright bizarre—but some human-resource experts and futurists predict that virtual interviews signal the shape of tomorrow's employment landscape. In addition, some companies—among them Hewlett-Packard, Microsoft, and Verizon—have created spaces within Second Life to show off their products, services, and employment opportunities. If you're looking for a job at one of these companies and you're reasonably tech savvy, you can always try to impress a hiring manager by dropping in and showing you've got a rich second life.

sex, and other activities that might raise questions about your character —and thus undermine or scuttle a job offer.

Also be aware that certain companies now routinely pull up a candidate's profile and posts on social-networking sites *during an interview*. The idea is to find common interests and passions—thus easing nerves during an interview and creating a bond that may spill over into a working environment. That's the happy payoff. The tragic pitfall, conversely, could be an employer accessing your MySpace profile during your first face-to-face meeting only to discover that your main hobby is instigating boycotts of the company's products!

Minding Your
Business
Not all career swappers aspire to work at a large corporation—or even a small not-for-profit organization. The growing ranks of small-business owners prove that there's life after retirement, downsizing, or downshifting. Opening your own business can prove remarkably fulfilling, but it can also demand a great deal of time and effort. Getting things off the ground requires a clear business plan, sufficient capital, and in most cases strong interpersonal skills (essential for interacting with customers and business partners). And if you're buying a franchise, there will be rules, policies, and procedures to follow.

Of course, ideas are everywhere. Sometimes it's a simple matter of looking at an old problem—or a stale business model—in a new way.

According to the Association of Bridal Consultants, 43 discrete businesses are now involved in the average wedding, including florists, décor consultants, calligraphers, and bridal-registry managers.

Microbreweries are popping up all over the country, grabbing market share and mindshare. According to the Brewers Association, more than 1,400 craft breweries exist in the United States, and their sales are growing 10 percent a year.

Or consider the design-conscious individuals who have carved out new careers for themselves—and forged a new industry in the bargain—by becoming home stagers. Their job is to make sure a house looks its best so it can fetch top dollar when the owner puts it up for sale.

And finally there is a related new career: that of image consultant, or a person who helps professionals plan or perfect every aspect of their lives, from the look of their office to the look of their websites and wardrobe.

You get the idea. The common thread is that a potential entrepreneur must have a business plan in place—something that will guide strategic planning and focus financial resources. It isn't necessary to develop a long and complex document. A well-conceived plan that runs five to 10 pages should suffice to help secure funding and launch the enterprise.

A business plan should encompass your mission, goals, and objectives. It should spell out how the business will operate, what equipment you will need, whether you will require employees, how you will market your product or service, and who your customer base will be. And don't forget to attach supporting documents such as tax returns, any contracts that exist, and copies of licenses and other documents.

A business plan is only one step on the journey to becoming an entrepreneur. A new business also demands capital. If you need financing, any number of options are available. (See also Chapter 8, "Money Matters.") You may also require consulting expertise to help you refine a product or service, develop a marketing and advertising strategy, or find the right employees or services—notably bookkeeping and legal. If you're going to work out of a home office, you will likely need a computer, a separate phone line, a separate checking account and credit card, and ergonomic furniture, including a desk. You may also need to set up a website with e-commerce capabilities.

If your ambition is to start your own business, it's wise to consult a financial planner or tax advisor at the start of your entrepreneurial odyssey. How you choose to structure your business (see sidebar, page 254) can

Crafting a Business Plan

It's tough to build a house with no blueprint. If you're serious about starting a business, you will need a solid business plan. Though you needn't produce a 125-page dissertation spelling out every detail of the venture you have in mind, a sound business plan does need to outline key points, provide direction, and identify your marketplace and competition. In most cases, you should be able to document everything in five to 10 pages.

Here are the key elements of a business plan:

Executive summary: This section lists the highlights of the entire business plan. It must grab the attention of readers—that is, lenders or investors—and give a quick overview of what the business is and how it will work. *Hint:* Wait to write the executive summary until after you have completed the bulk of the business plan.

Business description: This section should clearly spell out the product or service you're selling, how it works, and how your proposed business will produce the item.

Management team: Who will run the company? What experience do they have? This section should include capsule biographies of key players, including their education, professional background, skills, and accomplishments. The strength of the management team—and what it looks like on paper—can go a long way toward securing funding.

Industry background: Provide detailed information about the state of the industry—overarching trends, which direction it's headed, and where your business fits in. Observations and opinions won't do; you should include market research, demographic data, and even barriers to entry.

Competitive analysis: A good plan surveys the competition and explains how your business will grab market share. It discusses your competitors' strengths and weaknesses, detailing how you will position your firm. The plan must answer this: Why should someone buy from me but not my competitors?

Marketing and sales strategy: How will you price the product? How will you distribute it? How will you garner publicity? And what type of advertising, if any, will you use? Finally, do you have any other promotional plans or possibilities?

Operations plan: This section describes how the business will operate on an ongoing basis. It outlines the responsibilities of the management team, key tasks and business processes, and financial considerations such as capital requirements and the cost of goods.

Long-term goals: Indicate whether you seek to hold the business for the long term or sell it within a certain time. If you anticipate cashing in for $5 million at the end of seven years, say so in the plan. (Of course, the plan must corroborate the soundness of such a long-term strategy.)

Conclusion/Appendix: Summarize your plan, if it's unusually long, and provide the documentation needed to support your quest. This includes references, banking information (including net worth), the name of your attorney and accountant, and any contracts, orders, or related business items.

Remember, the work you do up front can pay dividends down the line. A good business plan will keep you focused and show you at your professional best.

have a disproportionate effect on its success—and on how much you pay in taxes. You may also want to check with an attorney to ensure that all your paperwork and agreements are in order. If you're buying a franchise, legal advice and review is imperative.

That said, starting a business has never been within closer reach—thanks to the Internet and today's freelance economy. Alfred Bertke, a 73-year-old resident of Minneapolis, spent more than a quarter-century working as a member of the clergy—after earning both a bachelor's degree and a master's degree in theology from Concordia University in

St. Louis. Then, in 1985, Bertke and the Lutheran Church parted ways. For the next 17 years, he held a number of jobs—including selling insurance and working as a senior secretary at a university—but never felt satisfied. "In retrospect," says Father Bertke, "I was just drifting."

Over the years, Bertke and his wife, Darlene, attended seminars held by various motivational speakers. He struck up an e-mail dialogue with one of them, Shad Helmstedder, who encouraged Bertke to pursue certification as a career coach. In 2002, after attending an intensive three-day workshop at the Career Coach Institute in San Diego, Bertke did just that, and he has worked as a life coach ever since. Bertke runs his own business, Riptide Rescue, which enables him to combine the interpersonal skills he gained as a minister with new knowledge he is picking up along the way. "I've worked with a wide range of people," he notes, "and that includes artists, entrepreneurs, executives, and others looking to recareer. I'm at the point where I'm earning a steady income."

A few demons bit the dust along the way. "I was so concerned about age discrimination when I started out," Bertke admits, "that I wondered if it was wise to post my picture on the website I launched in 2002. Would people see the gray hair and want somebody younger? Not at all. In fact my age has turned out to be a positive: My last three clients told me they wanted someone older—someone with more experience and wisdom."

Buying into a Franchise

The advantages of operating a franchise business are fairly evident. For one, you needn't do all the heavy lifting. A financial investment buys you a recognizable trademark and a proven recipe for success—and you get to run the show. For career-changers (particularly those who have toiled in a corporate environment), a franchise may represent opportunity with a more acceptable level of risk. Failure rates are lower (and profits higher) for franchises than for mom-and-pop start-ups.

NURSING A PASSION FOR CHANGE
SYD WHALLEY, *from pediatric nurse
to foundation lawyer*

WHEN I WENT TO RUTGERS UNIVERSITY, in 1971, I planned to study forestry, but the wife of a high-school teacher planted the idea of becoming a nurse. She thought it was a great career. So I went to nursing school. Lucky for me, I liked it.

I got married at 24. A year later we moved from New Jersey to Los Angeles so I could attend the master's program at UCLA. My husband was a teacher in New Jersey at the time, but he loved music, so when we got to L.A. he took a job in the mailroom at Warner Brothers Records. (Now he's the chairman and CEO, so the move worked out well for him, too!) Attending school on weekdays and working on weekends, it took me about two years to earn my master's degree.

We thought we would live in L.A. for two years and then go back to New Jersey, but it didn't work out that way. There weren't a lot of jobs in my specialty [pediatric oncology] at the time, so I stayed at UCLA for a year and worked as an oncology-care nurse. Then Cedar's Sinai Hospital offered me a position as a pediatric oncology clinical-care nurse-specialist. I was overseeing patient care and teaching the nurses. Later I went back to UCLA as an assistant nurse manager in charge of the pediatric oncology wing. Then I worked at Children's Hospital, where I got to open up a bone-marrow-transplant program.

I worked there for seven years during the 1980s—one of the most incredible experiences of my life. It was rewarding to play a key role in laying out the unit and designing the program. I was working with everyone from the board of directors to housekeeping. We had to hire the nurses, teach the doctors, and ensure that the needs of patients and families were addressed.

During that time, I developed a reputation as a nursing expert in bone transplantation. I got to speak about the subject all over the country. I also developed an extensive professional network and wrote for professional journals.

By then it was the early 1990s. My kids were four and eight, and my husband got a promotion that entailed a lot of travel. One day, I discovered that my second grader had a line to read in a school play and couldn't do it. Until then I hadn't known it was a problem, because the teachers loved him. I had to make some kind of change, so I stopped working.

The first year I was a stay-at-home mom, I got involved with the California Nurses Association as a volunteer lobbyist. A weeklong program called the Nurse in Washington Internship changed my life: I became aware of how to lobby effectively, how to influence public policy. In 1992 I got involved in a PAC called Women in Politics, and by 1996 I was co-chair of the group. This new role brought a sense of empowerment I'd never experienced before. I had always felt that if I worked hard I could change things, but here was a vehicle for making things happen a lot faster and more effectively.

If I truly wanted to influence public policy in a major way, I realized, I would have to learn more. I also realized that most elected officials don't listen to nurses, teachers, or social workers. As a result, I decided to attend law school.

I had separated from my husband in 1992—we later divorced—and I spent the next six years taking care of the children. Finally, in 1998 I started law school at UCLA. I didn't want to become a trial lawyer; I wanted to make laws. It was crazy trying to balance everything; the kids and I would sit home every night, each one doing their homework. It amounted to four hours per week-day and 16 hours on weekends for me.

Only a few law students were over 40. On the day we introduced our-selves I said, "I can't believe I'm leaving my kids at home." A young girl turned to me and said, "Honey, they don't *want* you at home!" It was very funny.

I never worried that things wouldn't work out. I tried to keep events in perspective by asking myself, "What's the worst that could happen?" After I graduated in 2001, one of my professors told me about a fellowship at the Western Center for Law and Poverty, an organization that helps shape public policy through education, advocacy, and—when necessary—litigation. The position paid $40,000 a year. I had to dip into my savings to make the job work out. After I had been there about nine months, the executive director announced her resignation. She had children in high school and found the job too demanding. I told her I understood her situation; I had gone through the same process. She suggested that I apply for the position.

They hired me—not because I was some hotshot lawyer, but because of my experience as a nurse. They liked my people skills and my organizational ability. Today I feel very fortunate to have followed this path through life. I feel that I'm really making a difference.

Interest in franchising has exploded since 1983. More than 760,000 franchises exist in the United States, reports consulting firm Pricewater-houseCoopers, and these outlets account for 18 million jobs and $1.5 trillion in economic impact. Franchise expos and trade shows fill convention halls from Seattle to Miami, offering new and emerging business opportunities that neatly transcend the already ubiquitous Subway Sandwiches, Mail Boxes Etc., and Jiffy Lubes. One franchise show in Los Angeles, for example, drew more than 150 exhibitors, ranging from a historically accurate men's fitness gym modeled after those popular in the 1930s to an ice-shaving shop, complete with root beer, green tea, and bubble-gum flavors. More than 10,000 visitors of all ages wandered the aisles, weighing business opportunities that ranged from the retro to the modern.

5 Myths of Entrepreneurial Success

Hard work guarantees success. No one in his right mind would argue that hard work isn't necessary to get a start-up off the ground. But without a solid product or service, a well-crafted business plan and effective marketing, it's impossible to become a high flyer. In fact, too many fledgling businesses fail because owners mistake time and effort for business savvy. You can't think strategically and make good decisions if you're stressed out and overwhelmed. Likewise, it's vital to know when to pull the plug on an unsuccessful venture. Pouring in more hours or dollars won't turn a lemon into a peach.

Deep pockets guarantee success. Consider this: An estimated 30,000 *new* packaged-goods products streamed into the marketplace in 2003. Nearly 90 percent of these products failed, despite the average cost of $20 to $50 million for a product launch, writes Nirmalya Kumar in *Marketing as Strategy: Understanding the CEO's Agenda for Driving Growth and Innovation.* You can't market or buy your way to success. You must spot an opportunity and execute on it effectively.

A great product translates into strong sales. In reality, the business world is littered with the debris of great ideas and promising products. Think Betamax, New Coke, and the Edsel.) In fact, inferior products often prevail in the marketplace due to a complex array of factors, including public perception, marketing effectiveness, and a company's ability to manufacture, distribute, and service a product efficiently.

A new wrinkle or nuance will win over customers. Maybe. Fewer than 10 percent of all new products are truly innovative or "new to the world," Kumar notes. Yet even if you've created the Next Great Thing, you must differentiate yourself and convince skeptical consumers that you offer a clear value proposition.

It's worth it only if you can sell the business for a windfall a few years down the line. We all hear the incredible stories about multibillion corporations such as Apple and Hewlett-Packard starting in garages or dorm rooms. We read about Google topping $100 billion in net worth. Yet the sobering reality is that most small businesses stay small—and it's possible to earn a nice income and enjoy life as an entrepreneur. While it's always good to aim for the stars, it's also wise to remain grounded in business reality.

Owning or operating a franchise may exert a powerful pull on your imagination. But stay that urge (initially, at any rate), for success demands far more than your signature on the dotted line. Before you can open a franchise, you will almost certainly have to generate a business plan, legal agreements, loan applications, and a dizzying array of other documents.

More important, it's vital to make sure you're doing something that adds significance to your life. If baking hot bagels leaves you cold, take a pass; otherwise you could find yourself bored beyond your *mildest* dreams!

First, make sure you're undertaking a franchise operation that will engage and stimulate you over the long run. (Chasing only money will likely lead to dissatisfaction and burnout.) Second, make sure that the business matches your abilities and steers clear of your weaknesses. If your interpersonal skills do not predispose you to deal with irate customers, for example, you shouldn't be interacting with them. Third, be aware that once you open the franchise you will largely be stuck in that location for the term of the contract—usually at least 10 years (unless you sell). This means that if a spouse lands a new job in a different locale, marital turbulence could ensue. Or if you get the urge to move at some future point, you could find yourself legally constrained to stay put.

Understanding the terms of the franchise agreement is paramount. It's crucial to read the fine print: Are you buying exclusive rights to a territory? Or will you wind up competing for customers with other franchises—perhaps even with the company itself? Your up-front contract scrutiny can also reveal whether any hidden costs exist, including security deposits, travel expenses, and additional franchise fees. Don't neglect to factor in the cost of property insurance, retirement plans, and—if you're planning

Before You Buy a Franchise

Buying a franchise should never be taken lightly. Researching it up-front—known as "performing due diligence"—can save you a heap of trouble later on. So before you sign on any dotted line, make sure you take these important steps:

Know what you're buying. Make sure you understand what various franchisors offer—and expect. Go to franchise expos to learn about different companies, then spend some time looking over the literature, studying the numbers, and making sure there's a good fit.

Check references. Ask the company for references but also step into one or two existing franchise operations and check them out. Talk to the owners informally to gain a realistic perspective of the business and the work. Make sure the comments you hear jibe with the company's literature.

Crunch the numbers. Request a financials package from the franchisor, including your projected operating income and expenses, and what other franchisees are earning. Make sure everything is in writing.

Review documents with your accountant and lawyer. Don't fall into the trap of trying to save a few hundred dollars at the outset or thinking you're equipped to understand the nuances of the contracts and financials. Rely on professionals to provide the expert counsel you need to make a wise decision.

Don't fall in love. Keep your options open. If the numbers don't add up or you have a gnawing sense that a particular franchisor isn't right, continue your search. You may want to check with a competitor or think about an entirely different line of business. It's far better to spend time sifting your options now than to make a mistake and wind up trapped in a new but undesirable career.

to take out a loan—bank interest. Finally, conduct extensive "due diligence" (a.k.a. research) on the franchiser, either online or by interviewing established (or newly minted) franchisees. These vetting steps should give you a sense of how well the business works—and, critically, whether the management team is competent and responsive.

So, to recap: Investigate at length—now—or repent at leisure later on. Know exactly what you're buying into—and understand precisely how it is likely to affect your life outside the business. After all, this is a much more substantive commitment than "merely" changing jobs. Once you decide to invest in a franchise, you can't jump at the next tantalizing employment offer that comes along.

On the other hand, you may have finally found your niche, enabling your work to fulfill you in a way you never thought possible.

Basic Business Structures

Starting a business requires more than a good idea and a willingness to work hard. You must address legal issues—including how you structure the business. Consult an attorney or an accountant to learn the range of options, basically these:

Sole proprietorship. This is the most common way to start out. You're the owner, and you have total control. You report income on Schedule C of a personal tax return, and you must pay federal, state, and Social Security taxes quarterly.

Pros: No barriers to entry; anything you earn is yours.
Cons: You're responsible for business debts and have full legal liability. You may need to use personal assets, such as your house, for loan collateral.

Partnership. You share ownership with one or more people. You report income on personal tax returns. Each partner must pay taxes due.

Pros: Easy to set up. The firm's principals retain full ownership of ideas and intellectual property. With more than one person in a leadership position, bank funding may be easier to obtain.
Cons: Disagreements can spell doom. Each partner is liable for the actions of other partners; this puts personal assets at risk.

Corporation. An individual or group creates a legal entity with owners who serve as shareholders. The corporation pays taxes using forms separate from those for personal returns.

Pros: Owners are not personally liable for the company's actions or debt. It's generally easier to obtain funding and financing.
Cons: Creates a costly structure. The corporation must follow complex rules regarding accounting and compliance.

Limited liability company. This business structure combines elements of proprietorship and partnership with corporations. Each owner pays taxes on personal returns, and each partner in the company must pay self-employment taxes quarterly.

Pros: Owners are not personally liable for debt or legal matters.
Cons: Tax forms and legal issues are more complex than for sole proprietorships and basic partnerships.

Books

The Art of the Start: The Time-Tested, Battle-Hardened Guide for Anyone Starting Anything, by Guy Kawasaki, Portfolio Hardcover, 2004. Offers information, tips, and strategies for getting a new business off the ground.

Business Plans For Dummies, by Paul Tiffany, Steven D. Peterson, For Dummies, 2004. A guide to developing and writing business plans.

The Business Start-Up Kit, by Stephen D. Strauss, Kaplan Business, 2002. Provides all the information you need to start your own business.

Franchise Bible: How to Buy a Franchise, by Erwin J. Keup, Entrepreneur Press, 2007. Covers almost every aspect of starting a franchise and getting it running effectively.

Franchising Dreams: The Lure of Entrepreneurship in America, by Peter M. Birkeland, University of Chicago Press, 2002. A straightforward look at the risks and rewards, the pitfalls and challenges of operating a franchise.

Franchising for Dummies, by Michael Seid and Dave Thomas, For Dummies, 2006. The scoop on franchising from A to Z.

Guerrilla Marketing for Job Hunters: 400 Unconventional Tips, Tricks, and Tactics for Landing Your Dream Job, by Jay Conrad Levinson and David Perry, Wiley, 2005.

The Job Search Solution: The Ultimate System for Finding a Great Job Now!, by Tony Bashara, AMACOM, 2005.

The McGraw-Hill Guide to Starting Your Own Business: A Step-By-Step Blueprint for the First-Time Entrepreneur, by Stephen A. Harper, McGraw-Hill, 2003. Covers every aspect of starting a new business, including writing a business plan, advertising, financing, and franchising.

Small Business for Dummies, by Eric Tyson and Jim Schell, For Dummies, 2003. Looks at opportunities as well as action steps for starting a business.

Start Your Own Business, by Rieva Lesonsky, Entrepreneur Press, 2007. *Entrepreneur* magazine's comprehensive guide to starting your own business.

The Successful Business Plan, Secrets and Strategies, by Rhonda Abrams, The Planning Shop, 2003. Advice and detailed examples of how to write a business plan.

The Unwritten Rules of the Highly Effective Job Search: The Proven Program Used by the World's Leading Career Services Company, by Orville Pierson, McGraw Hill, 2005.

Whoops! I'm in Business: A Crash Course in Business Basics, by Richard Stim and Lisa Guerin. Nolo Press, 2005. (Also available in eBook format from Nolo.com). Offers a wealth of information about starting a small business and running it effectively.

More Resources

PUTTING TOGETHER A BUSINESS PLAN

America's Small Business Development Centers Network
www.asbdc-us.org

Offers mostly free information, guidance, and assistance on starting a business and developing a business plan.

Entrepreneur.com
www.entrepreneur.com/businessplan

Furnishes a thorough overview of what's required to build a successful business plan.

Microsoft Sartup Center
www.microsoft.com/startupcenter

Provides information and tips on starting a business.

JOB-HUNTING RESOURCES

CareerHub
http://careerhub.typepad.com

Leading career experts offer their advice and perspectives on a wide array of job-seeking strategies and other career matters.

Guerrilla Job Hunting
www.guerrillajobhunting.typepad.com

Author David Perry provides unconventional but effective tips and resources to help you land your next job.

MySpace News Careers
http://news.myspace.com/business/careers

This site links to news, blogs, and information on career matters, including job-hunting techniques and career strategies.

GETTING DOWN TO BUSINESS

IRS Small Business and Self-Employed One_Stop Resource
www.irs.ustreas.gov/businesses/
small/index.html

Offers comprehensive information about starting and operating a small business.

**Nolo Business
& Human Resources Center**
www.nolo.com

Addresses issues related to business structure and operations.

SBA Small Business Planner
www.sba.gov/smallbusinessplanner/
index.html

Provides information about business structures, licenses, taxes, and more.

BUSINESS-STARTUP RESOURCES

Federal Trade Commission
www.ftc.gov/bcp/edu/pubs/
consumer/invest/inv05.shtm

Offers "Buying a Franchise: A Consumer," an outstanding overview of what's required to avoid problems and raise the odds for success.

SBA Franchise Registry
www.franchiseregistry.com

Lists names of franchise companies whose franchisees enjoy the benefits of a streamlined review process for SBA loan applications.

SBA Small Business Planner
www.sba.gov/smallbusinessplanner/
start/buyafranchise/index.html

Offers documents and publications on an array of topics related to franchises, including an overview of the industry, franchising strategies, associations and forums, buying FAQs, and more.

Score, Counselors to America's Small Business
www.score.org

Provides comprehensive resources for starting and managing a business, including franchise operations.

FRANCHISING RESOURCES

FranchiseGator.com

This website provides information about dozens of franchise industries—from automotive to travel, from food to computers. Click on a field and you can view listings for individual companies. These describe what the business is and how it operates; they also detail the level of investment required. If you find a certain franchise opportunity appealing, you click a box and furnish your contact information. Franchise Gator then forwards the request to the franchisor, which sends you free information.

FranchiseHelp.com

Offers a franchise directory, news and resources, financing information, and more. The company also publishes a newsletter and a combination of free and for-fee research.

International Franchise Association (IFA)

www.franchise.org

This membership organization, consisting of franchisors, franchisees, and suppliers, provides detailed profiles of more than 1,200 franchisors. Like Franchise Gator, it gives you an option to receive more information.

NEW-BUSINESS RESOURCES

About.com: Small Business Information

http://sbinformation.about.com

A comprehensive guide for almost every conceivable aspect of operating a small business, including developing a business plan, a marketing plan, employee benefits, taxes, and accounting and government regulations.

Bplans.com

www.bplans.com

This site lets you view a wide array of sample business plans for free. Categories range from fitness centers to event planning, from automotive services to B&Bs.

Business.gov

www.business.gov

Offers links to other information sources, which range from human resources to franchise and business opportunities. It also features specialized guides designed for small businesses and for those owned by minorities, women, veterans, and the self-employed.

IRS Small Business and Self-Employed One-Stop Resource

http://www.irs.ustreas.gov/businesses/small/index.html

Provides deduction information and tax guides, forms, and publications focused specifically on the needs of small businesses and the self-employed.

National Association of Women Business Owners

www.nawbo.org   800-556-2926

Represents the needs and interests of 10.4 million women-owned businesses. Offers resources, contact info about local chapters, and news of national events.

National Business Incubation Association (NBIA)

www.nbia.org   740-593-4331

Promotes business incubation and entrepreneurship. The site offers a resource center and numerous resources and a bookstore with NBIA publications.

National Small Business Association (NSBA)

www.nsba.biz   800-345-6728

Serves as an advocate for small businesses. Provides resources to members, including publications, group health insurance, referrals, and discounts with major product and service providers.

Nolo

www.nolo.com

The publisher and online-content provider offers a "Starting a Business" center that includes articles, Q&As, resources, and links to relevant products.

U.S. Chamber of Commerce Small Business Center

www.uschamber.com/sb/default

Offers small-business tool kits focused on finance, government contracting, hiring, insurance, office management, sales and marketing, security, taxes, and trade. A home office portal, available at www.uschamber.com/sb/ business/p04/p04_0750.asp, offers tools for deciding whether you're suited to working in a home office, how to set one up, and how to sort through various legal restrictions.

U.S. Small Business Administration (SBA) Small Business Planner

www.sba.gov/smallbusinessplanner/index.html

The federal agency serves as a clearinghouse for information about starting a small business and transforming a business concept into reality. Its website offers a wealth of information and resources to help you start a small business and run it effectively.

LEADING JOB SITES FOR OLDER WORKERS

CareerBuilder.com

www.careerbuilder.com

In addition to job listings, Career-Builder provides career-assessment tests, business-franchise information, tips on preparing for interviews, steps for setting up a home office, coaching and training resources, and advice on how to use relocation services. The site will e-mail you timely news and information if you register. It features a Job Machine that scans your résumé and makes job recommendations.

Craigslist

www.craigslist.com

This no-frills site offers extensive job listings, which you can view by region, city, or county (as well as by other categories). Although Craigslist doesn't cater specifically to older workers, it's a goldmine for leads. In fact, it has been rated among the most effective job sites on the Web.

DiversityWorking.com

www.diversityworking.com

This site offers nearly 50 career channels, ranging from advertising to transportation logistics. It also lets you search open jobs by state and post your résumé at no charge. A Career Expo area offers articles and information on career and job fairs, including virtual fairs.

Employment Network for Retired Government Experts

www.enrge.us

Helps connect retired government workers with jobs and new careers. Focuses on numerous fields, including executive, professional, administrative, technical, clerical, construction, destruction, maintenance, operations, and many other blue- and white-collar positions.

ExecSearches.com

www.execsearches.com

The site is a premier job board that helps nonprofit, education, healthcare, and public organizations recruit fund-raising, mid-level, and executive professionals and connect them to meaningful work.

ExecuNet

www.execunet.com

The fee-based site (memberships run from $39 to $399, depending on the term) connects executives, recruiters, and other business leaders. It also provides instant alerts when new opportunities arise, as well as a personalized job-search function.

Jobs4.0

www.Jobs4point0.com

With an emphasis on the 40-and-older set, Jobs4.0 helps you find open positions by region, job category, or keyword search. The site emphasizes "diversity of experience" and all job listings come directly from employers.

Jobster

www.jobster.com

Jobster lets you post a résumé online (including a video résumé, if you're so inclined), promote your skills and experience, and otherwise make yourself highly visible to employers. The service taps into thousands of employers, including Fortune 100 companies.

Monster.com
www.monster.com

Monster is an apt description for this behemoth of a job-search site. It boasts more than 1.8 million employment listings and over 70,000 résumés. You can search by job or career category, or by geographic region; an advanced feature lets you narrow your search to jobs near your zip code (you determine the acceptable radius). The section labeled "Careers at 50+" offers tips and advice targeting older workers. The website also publishes monthly e-newsletters for those 50 and above; related message boards connect employers with workers in this age range.

Quintessential Careers
www.quintcareers.com

Although this site provides thousands of job listings and job leads for workers of every age range, it also features a content section devoted to older job seekers. Quintessential Careers includes articles on how to get ready for a career change, how to prepare a résumé, and what's required to work beyond retirement.

RetiredBrains
www.retiredbrains.com

The site focuses on job and work opportunities for older boomers, seniors, retirees, and those on the threshold of retirement. It makes available other resources as well, including news, articles, job descriptions, and personality tests.

RetireeWorkForce.com
www.retireeworkforce.com

This site offers job postings and résumé services as well as virtual job fairs, a career center with assessment tests, and a franchise finder.

RetirementJobs.com
www.retirementjobs.com

One of the leading career sites for boomers and workers over age 50, RetirementJobs.com lets you search by keyword or geographic location to find positions of interest. It also lets you set up search alerts on topics or fields of interest and listen to podcasts on a variety of career-related topics.

Seniors4Hire
www.seniors4hire.org

This is a nationwide career center specializing in job postings for people 50 and older. You can post a résumé, access a "featured employer" section that includes companies such as

Radio Shack, General Nutrition Centers, and Regal Entertainment Group, search through a nationwide jobs database, and avail yourself of a job-notification service based on your criteria.

Workforce50.com

www.workforce50.com

This site, formerly known as SeniorJobBank.org, focuses on career opportunities and jobs for those age 50 and up. In addition to a job board, it features articles, intelligence, marketing tips, and other resources.

Yahoo! HotJobs

http://hotjobs.yahoo.com

HotJobs is another general job site that lets you search listings by specific criteria, including location and categories. It too offers a bevy of features, including alerts, saved searches, career tools, and networking capabilities.

YourEncore

www.yourencore.com

This site serves as a network of retired and veteran scientists and engineers, connecting these older workers to opportunities at major companies such as Procter & Gamble, Eli Lilly, Boeing, and General Mills.

SOFTWARE FOR NEW BUSINESSES

Business Plan Pro, Palo Alto Software. www.paloalto.com/ business_plan_software 800-229-7526

The standard edition ($100) provides more than 500 sample business plans, 9,000 industry profiles, two business books, and the ability to import from QuickBooks. The premier edition ($200) lets you import data from Excel, features collaboration tools and a business-valuation analysis, and lets you view plan-versus-actual financial tools. Runs on a PC with Microsoft Windows 2000, XP, and Vista.

Fundable Plans, Strategic Services Group Inc. www.fundableplans.com. 800-450-2750.

This Web-based software ($39.95) guides you through the process of developing a business plan and obtaining funding. Runs on a PC or a Mac.

PlanWrite Business Plan, Business Resource Software. http://www.brs-inc.com/pwb.asp. 800-423-1228.

This application ($120) provides sample plans, templates, step-by-step instructions, and advice. It also offers advanced tracking, charting, and plan-analysis tools. Runs on a PC with Microsoft Windows XP.

MAKE YOUR
PRESENCE KNOWN

*A focused job search and a righteous résumé
can turn age into an asset*

"DEATH OF A CLOSE FRIEND" ranks high on the "Life Events Scale," better known as the Holmes & Rahe Social Readjustment Rating Scale. But right below it you will find "Changing careers." No surprise there: A professional shift rates as one of life's most traumatic undertakings. Yet one particular part of that process—getting your foot in the door and making an impression on overworked hiring managers—has to be considered the Mother of All Stressors. Not only must you put yourself on the line in a highly unpredictable situation, you're almost guaranteed to face a heaping dose of rejection. Worse, you often have to keep coming back for more.

Rarely is there a tidy detour around this ritualized frustration. You can increase your odds of success, however, by becoming a savvy player of the job-hunt game. This means devoting the time to creating a superior résumé that showcases your unique talents and abilities. It means paying close attention to details, including spelling, jargon, the information you present, and the ways in which you present it. And it means writing a cover letter compelling enough to get you noticed—and land you an interview. In short, an exceptional résumé and cover letter can slingshot you past other applicants and concretize the dream of a new career.

Applying for a Job

Applying for a Job There are myriad ways you can apply for a job, so find out which approach your targeted company prefers. In many cases, more than one approach is acceptable. If so, choose the method you're most comfortable with—but make sure you follow the etiquette that has been established for it.

Online. Hundreds of job boards and company websites allow you— nay, encourage you—to post or submit a résumé online. Some employers ask applicants to fill out online forms. Others provide a button that uploads a file from your hard drive. A few ask you to copy-and-paste text into a space that's provided, or they may use a specialized résumé-building tool to grab your information.

Don't waste everyone's time flooding companies with your résumé. Before you click your mouse, make sure you and the potential employer are likely to click too. Companies are careful to sift out résumés—and candidates— that bear no relation to posted positions. Increasingly, they are using automated filters to spot specific words believed to signal an attractive candidate. More sinisterly, perhaps, the same programs trash submissions containing words or qualities identified as undesirable.

E-mail. If you're applying for a position by e-mail, write a cover letter in the body of the message and send your résumé as an attached file. Keep the cover letter short and include a signature line with your name, mailing address, phone number, e-mail address, and (if relevant) website. Make the subject line of the e-mail message succinct and straightforward. Use a professional-sounding e-mail account, and do not mark the message as "urgent," "high priority," or "return notification requested" (it burdens the recipient).

Mail. It may seem tempting to submit a résumé and cover letter the old-fashioned way—via the United States Postal Service. Although many organizations will scan résumés into their applicant-tracking system, some no longer accept paper. Check an organization's website before

Do I understand the position and how best to apply for the type of work I'm seeking? If you're trying to land a sales job at the local pharmacy, it probably makes sense to stop by the store and fill out an application. If you want to join a law firm, by contrast, protocol dictates that you submit a résumé by mail or electronically. In other words, try to learn the job, the industry, and the hiring environment before you attempt to find work in it.

Do I have my emotions under control? It's perfectly acceptable to confirm that a company has received your résumé, but don't make the mistake of pestering hiring managers or human-resource professionals on a daily or weekly basis: Doing so betrays an anxiety level that can easily derail your job search. Channel your temptation to call or e-mail by sending résumés to other companies instead.

Do my résumé and cover letter present the product—me—in the best light? Try to step outside yourself and view your résumé from the outside in. If possible, ask a friend, colleague, or spouse to scrutinize your résumé to make sure you haven't missed anything—or overstated your case, for that matter. A clean, clear, concise résumé can go a long way toward landing you the job you desire.

Am I transforming age into an advantage? Whether you're looking for a job or starting a new business, you can and should use your experience, expertise, and acumen to your advantage. Be confident; demonstrate how your background has supplied you with a skill set that can help an organization improve its results or get a franchise on its feet. So much of life, after all, is perception: Is the glass half-full or half-empty? Does failing seven times out of ten constitute success or failure? Ironically, your answer to that question may hinge on your choice of career: Are you a designated hitter or a tightrope walker?

submitting anything. Find out its preferences and requirements so your first step is not a stumble.

In person. Applying in person has its advantages: After dropping off your application package, you can leave with the peace of mind that the hiring manager, human-resource specialist, or owner has it in hand. However, if you choose this approach (best for nonprofessional positions), keep in mind that someone may want to interview you on the spot. So, be prepared—mentally and sartorially.

Kiosks. A number of companies have turned to kiosks to accept job

Internship, Not Intern-ment

An unpaid internship may strike you as an outsize invest-ment of time and effort. But more than a few career swap-pers have parlayed that post into success. Working as an intern is a low-risk venture that can leave you highly in-formed about a new career or company. Try these tips to maximize the position:

Take the position seriously. Show up on time every day; take your responsibilities seriously. Excellent performance may translate into a job offer—or, at least, a glowing referral from your manager.

Respect the assignment. Don't wait for someone to tell you what to do. By the same token, don't be content to eternally fetch coffee or run for bagels; instead, look for opportunities to learn, and show your stuff. Seek out projects that seem to hold value for the organization—or simply those that interest you—and don't hesitate to apply your own expertise.

Be realistic. Sure, you have a lot to offer. But understand that an organization—or an individual manager within it—may be reluctant to hand you the keys to the kingdom. Be patient. As you show your value, you will likely command greater respect—and land those coveted assignments.

> **Network, network, network.** An internship is an opportunity to meet successful and sometimes highly accomplished professionals. Make an effort to get to know others. Think about, and suggest, opportunities for working with them. Some of these people may enjoy mentoring you or providing assistance. Be willing to take them out for lunch or meet for a cup of coffee. And don't overlook your fellow interns. They may soon be fast-track professionals looking for employees.
>
> For more information about internships, consider the following books:
>
> *Vault Guide to Top Internships,* by Mark Oldman, Vault, Inc., December 2007. Looks at 750 leading programs and offers insights into landing and managing an internship.
>
> *The Intern Files: How to Get, Keep, and Make the Most of Your Internship,* by Jamie Fedorko, Simon Spotlight Entertainment, 2006.

applications—particularly for clerical, entry-level, or nonprofessional positions. You enter your data (make sure you bring your education, work history, and other information with you) into a dedicated system, which feeds it directly into the company's human-resource database. Some kiosks include personality or skills tests; many allow data entry in Spanish and sometimes other languages. If the questions are unclear or the job descriptions confusing, most kiosks include help functions or a phone.

How to Whip the
Waiting Game One of the toughest aspects of the résumé game

is waiting for responses. Sometimes the process can become downright frustrating—even depressing. The key to success, says career coach Norine Dagliano of EKM Inspirations in Hagerstown, Maryland, is to keep the process moving forward at all times, even in the face of adversity and rejection. "A person must maintain a positive attitude and continue moving forward," she notes. You can't control what other people do or think, Dagliano points out, and overworked hiring managers tend to overlook things until there's a fire under their chair. But you can manage the process in such a way as to increase your odds of success, she says. That means sending out a regular stream of résumés each week. (Some people elevate the task to a part-time or full-time job.) And never stop networking with friends, family, and business associates the entire time.

Nedda Rahme, who oversees hiring for a major research organization based in southern California, says it's fine to phone or e-mail within three to five days to ensure receipt of a résumé. It's also an accepted practice to check back after a few weeks to determine whether the organization has any interest in a phone or face-to-face conversation with you. However, it's crucial that any such inquiries take place in a low-key, nonobtrusive way. "The approach a person takes speaks volumes," Rahme says.

Make Yourself Available

Sometimes even the smallest details can derail a job search. Make sure you use a professional-sounding voicemail or answering-machine message. Too often, says career coach Dagliano, recruiters or human-resource professionals encounter answering-machine messages featuring "talented" grandchildren or a default—and therefore anonymous—greeting. (In the latter case, the potential employer often opts not to leave a message for fear of having reached the wrong applicant.) Some job seekers commit the additional lapse of leaving "call block" in place to deflect unknown numbers. A human-resource staffer may conclude that it's just too hard to reach you, and move on. "Is it any wonder," asks Dagliano, "that some job seekers rarely are called for interviews?"

Résumé Rules

It's tempting to view a résumé as an outdated or ancillary tool, useful only in certain situations. In reality, the résumé is alive and well—though it is evolving to meet the needs of today's job seeker. The more common way of submitting a résumé now is to post it on a career board, where employers may find it via a keyword search. Job aspirants also submit résumés to companies electronically and via fax. Or they may post a résumé at social-networking sites such as LinkedIn or Razumé.com (the latter allows others to provide feedback and attracts recruiters), as well as at other online spaces.

Many electronically submitted résumés wind up in one applicant-tracking database or another. Then, when an organization goes searching for someone with, say, electrical-engineering skills and an ability to speak German, or a degree in art and at least five years' museum experience, the qualified applicants pop up.

Though crafting a résumé falls somewhere between art and science, particularly for older workers, the basics of this job-search tool are essentially the same as they've always been. At its heart, your résumé is an advertisement for yourself and your life experience. It typically contains several sections, including a summary or a statement of your objective, a section that lists your work experience (both paid work and volunteer positions), a section covering your educational background, and a section enumerating any other skills, abilities, or selling points that enhance your marketability. Depending on the job you're hoping to land, you may need to fine-tune the content and presentation.

It's best to update your résumé on a regular basis. After all, you're out to land a new job or a new career—not the same one you held in the past. You may also want to consider keeping multiple versions of your résumé on hand, with each one tailored to the various employment situations you know you're likely to encounter in your field. For a publishing professional, for example, this could mean designing one résumé that "packages" you as a writer, a second that presents you as an editor, and a third vaunting your talents as an online content producer. Fortunately, a personal computer and word-processing program can simplify this exercise in multiplicity.

Older workers should pay attention to a few key issues. It's important to:

Downplay dates. It's generally best to list the most significant jobs or experience on a résumé. Anything previous to that is probably overkill—unless a certain position or sequence of jobs is particularly relevant. By the same token, you may want to deemphasize dates, including your birthdate, year of college graduation, and first few jobs. The sad reality is that it's often best not to give a human-resource manager any potential ammo to discriminate on the basis of age. Instead, emphasize skills, knowledge, and experience. If you feel that you must include dates, focus on skills and showcase your talents. In other words, direct attention to your capabilities, not your chronology. In addition, Dagliano suggests that you "youthanize" your résumé. "Don't write an obituary of your career," she cautions. "Instead, concentrate on the most recent 10 to 15 years."

List all relevant skills, abilities, and accomplishments. "Employers have concerns that people 45+ may be set in their ways, have difficulty with change, are not comfortable with technology, and are biding their time until retirement," Dagliano points out. "Squelch those concerns up front. Include explicit examples in your résumé of changes you have managed and/or led, technology you have introduced and/or implemented, and innovative ideas you have championed." If, over the last decade, you have attended any job-related courses or earned any professional or trade certifications, mention those. If you're strong on writing skills or have specialized technical knowledge, point that out. It's not unusual for older workers to have accumulated a wealth of experience that younger workers cannot match. Be proud of your accomplishments and don't shy away from mentioning them. Most important, be specific. Stating that you helped boost sales or added clients will not suffice. You need to provide specific information, such as "Increased sales by 10 percent" or "Added 50 customers." Likewise, list specific computer or information-technology skills you've acquired and the software applications you've mastered.

Confront gaps. It's tempting to gloss over gaps in employment or year-long stretches outside the workplace when you may have been raising young children or caring for an elderly family member. The problem with leaving such employment gaps on a résumé is that they may raise doubts in the mind of a front-line HR screener or hiring manager. Because you're not immediately available to answer these questions in person, the gate-keeper is apt to draw his or her own conclusions. To stave off questions about short-term gaps, consider displaying your work history in years rather than months. If you were out of work for several years, do your best to explain the circumstances: "From 1988 to 2002, raised family and pro-vided eldercare for a family member." Or, "From 1995 to 1996, temporarily unemployed when spouse relocated to accept position in Seattle." You can explain these circumstances further in a job interview. At this early stage, you simply want to keep a potential employer from concluding that you were fired for cause, or that you made no effort to find work.

10 Steps to a
Winning Résumé
Try employing some of the following résumé-writing strategies to get noticed—and get hired:

Avoid jargon. It's a modern epidemic: Incomprehensible acronyms and jargon plague almost every profession. To set yourself apart, steer clear of the gobbledygook. If a prospective employer can't understand what you're talking about, your chances of landing an interview are next to nil. Even if the targeted job is in a profession similar to the one you worked in previously, clear English will always win the day.

Offer work highlights, not history. Just as the biography of a celebrity showcases the high points of his or her life, so should your résumé touch on only the best moments of your work life. While shunning hype, it should present you in the most favorable light possible. Too many details and too much information—let alone details that are too personal—are a guaranteed turnoff. They are also an imposition: Busy line managers and human-resource executives lack the time to venture into a forest of facts.

Tell the truth. In an era when embroidering the truth seems to have become a national indulgence, it's easy to be enticed by the prospect of stretching facts and figures. Such fabrication is a formula for career flame-out: Should a hiring manager get one whiff of dishonesty, your résumé will be on its way to the delete button or the "circular file" (trash can). Worse, being found out in a background fib once you're hired will shatter your credibility—and very likely usher you out the door.

Watch your language. Too often, individuals penning a résumé wind up using flowery prose and all the wrong words. As explained earlier in this chapter, the growing emphasis on keywords means you must choose the right words—mostly nouns—in order to register as a see-worthy blip on an employer's radar. Once a human gets around to looking at the résumé, however, it's important that it read well, too. A résumé should feature an action verb at the beginning of each sentence: "Managed," "achieved," "boosted," "maximized," and "pioneered" are all examples of effective action verbs. Similarly, avoid words that sound significant but denote nothing, such as "successfully," "total," or "superior." Instead, back up a statement with appropriate facts and figures. Vague, fuzzy, or confusing language will only short-circuit your ability to command attention. To reduce it to a maxim, buzzwords are a buzzkill.

Don't overwhelm. Consistent with the temptation to provide too many details, some job seekers try to build an overly robust case. The distinction between marketing yourself effectively and coming across as boastful or desperate is subtle but significant. Provide concrete information about your most relevant achievements without painting yourself as the second coming of former GE chairman Jack Welch. An employer is simply looking to match his or her skill-and-knowledge requirements with those of a qualified person.

Anticipate snags. Don't help perpetuate stereotypes of older workers as stodgy or superannuated. These images are being demolished by the realities of the new workplace, where more and more people are choosing to stay on the job past traditional retirement age. Make sure your résumé reveals you to be flexible; amenable to training and learning; willing to confront new challenges; and eager to work in close collaboration with others, especially in a team environment. The best antidote to age bias is a candidate whose accumulated job skills and life experiences make her or him irresistible. Simply listing your supposedly winning qualities won't be enough, of course; you'll have to furnish tangible proof of your past accomplishments, then embrace and embody this philosophy of adaptability from Day 1 of your new job or career.

Think beyond work. Most job applicants focus almost exclusively on the experience, skills, and knowledge they gained in paid positions they held in the past. In doing so, however, they neglect a great deal of the "unofficial" experience they may have amassed through volunteering—at their child's school, perhaps, at a social-service organization, or in a professional or community organization where they may have held a board post or some other position of responsibility. If you've been out of the workforce for an extended stretch, or if this volunteer experience complements the skills you've included in your résumé, be sure to include it. Also, if you're considering changing careers, a volunteer position or internship may provide entrée to the opportunity you're seeking. A circuitous route to your goal does not suffer from its sinuousness: Working for a lower salary—or even pro bono—might ultimately lead to a high-paying permanent position.

Tinker, tailor. Too often, Dagliano says, people "send out the same letter and the same résumé to every employer without paying attention to the required skills and competencies." Consider the job and employer you're seeking, then customize your résumé to fit the circumstances. This may mean slightly shading what you emphasize and how you word things. If you're applying for work as a writer at a high-tech company, for example, it's prudent to stress your technical knowledge and writing skills. If you've targeted a position within a PR firm that represents high-tech

A RECKONING WITH REALITY

STEPHANY HUMENIK, *from library aide to paralegal*

I'M CURRENTLY IN THE PROCESS of making a major career change. For the last few years, I've worked as a library aide in the community and as a substitute aide in a public school. Before that, I held a position as the youth director at a church. And prior still to that, I had lived in Pennsylvania for 46 years, where I worked as a program manager at a state-run institution for the mentally handicapped.

Lacking a college degree, however, I found that I had gone as far as I could: When I moved to Lansing, Michigan 10 years ago to remarry, it was almost impossible to get a similar job. In fact, it was difficult to find anything at all that paid much above minimum wage.

It has been tough because my husband, Gregory, has been diagnosed with non-Hodgkin lymphoma and paraneoplastic pemphigus. We found that out in 1999, about a year after we got married. The cancer, which originally spread to his lungs, is supposed to be 90 percent fatal within a year, but thankfully he is now in remission. It's been nine years, but Gregory is still with me. He can't do any physical work—he is on oxygen all the time—but he is able to hold a position as a computer programmer at Michigan State University.

In summer 2003, with my husband's condition becoming a bigger responsibility, I realized I could no longer work full-time at the church. At that point I decided to go back to school and find something that paid more and provided greater flexibility. I had always been interested in law—the profession is growing and the pay is good—so I decided to attend Lansing Community College and earn an associate of business degree with a paralegal specialty. I've been going mostly part-time, though I did attend full-time for one year. To gain experience, I also worked as an intern for a year.

It was tough getting through school and managing the 25-mile commute. There were other curveballs along the way as well: My mother got ill and died, and my husband's stepfather suffered a stroke—he eventually died too. Because of these family issues, I had to skip one semester entirely. But as soon as I got away from school, I felt an overwhelming desire to return. I knew I wanted to finish my studies and earn my degree.

I graduated in May 2008. Now I'm looking for a position. The pay at the larger law firms is in the $40,000 range, but that wasn't my sole reason for becoming a paralegal. I have an interest in elder law—particularly wills, trusts, and probates. I also hope to help people with Medicare. Some states now allow legal assistants to represent clients at Social Security hearings and in other situations.

I'm working with a career counselor from one of the online sites. When I first e-mailed him my résumé, he suggested that I organize it in a different fashion. So I went back and tweaked it to emphasize my skills, experience, and knowledge. He is also helping me to get my résumé out there and conduct an effective job search. The counselor is also helping me locate preferred employers and develop a job-search plan. We meet once a week over the phone. I'm hoping to land a position soon.

One of the things that came out of the coaching and résumé-preparation process is a better appreciation for what I have done. I'd never thought about some of the jobs and positions I had held in terms of the skills they imparted or the knowledge they required, but the career counselor helped me see all that I have done in the past. Those weren't just jobs I held, I realize now—they were much more.

I'm excited and nervous. I haven't been in a full-time job for quite a while, so this is something completely new. I'm 57 and in good health, and my husband has been extremely supportive. Because of his poor health, however, I acknowledge that I could wind up single again, and his income and retirement could be gone. That means I'm in no position to retire, and I feel it's important to be able to support myself. Despite the obstacles, I feel blessed that I have been able to set a goal and achieve it.

clients, you will want to make your prospective employer aware that you're comfortable with technology but also possess the verbal and written communication skills needed for the job. Think about how an advertiser targets a particular audience; in like fashion, you must figure out what your selling points are and how to best package them.

Make age passé. It bears repeating: Age tends to become immaterial when a candidate offers a tantalizing set of skills and knowledge. Make sure you're up-to-date with the minimum level of professional training required, then portray your experience as an asset. As you assemble your résumé, don't make your age obvious—but likewise don't try to conceal the fact that you're an experienced individual with a great deal to offer. You can identify an enlightened employer today by the extent to which he or she recognizes that older workers are loyal, committed, and energetic. So don't be afraid to exude confidence in what you will bring to an organization.

Revisit your résumé. If you're between jobs or careers, review your résumé on a regular basis. It's not a graven tablet—it's a living, breathing document that you should feel free to update as you gain additional knowledge or training via university extension programs, certification programs, and the like. Don't forget to add any recent volunteer or community activities that might be relevant and help you land the job you want.

When Keywords Matter

A few years ago, it was common practice for personnel departments to comb through stacks of résumés and sort them based on how they looked and what they said. Today's trend, by contrast, is toward a screening process that eliminates the human factor. Instead, a computer scans thousands of résumés for keywords and flags those that match an established set of criteria. Only then will a live person read the résumé and decide to proceed to the interview stage. According to the National Résumé Writers Association, virtually all of the Fortune 1000 firms (and many others throughout the corporate and nonprofit worlds) now use keyword searches. Overall, approximately 80 percent of professional organizations rely on this approach to spot promising candidates.

The consequences are stark: If your résumé doesn't contain the keywords that an employer is using for a particular position, you're going to be persona non grata. Trying to divine which keywords to list, on the other hand, may seem better suited to a tarot-card reader. Adding to the challenge, says writer Katharine Hansen, is the fact that most job seekers are conditioned to use action verbs; rarely do they think about nouns, notes the author of the e-book *Words to Get Hired By: The Jobseeker's Quintessential Lexicon of Powerful Words and Phrases for Résumés and Cover Letters*.

The solution? Include words that distinguish you from others. According to Hansen, these words describe "hard skills" such as: "…job-specific/ profession-specific/industry-specific skills, technological terms and descriptions of technical expertise (including hardware and software in which you are proficient), job titles, certifications, names of products and services, industry buzzwords and jargon, types of degrees, names of colleges, company names, terms that tend to impress, such as 'Fortune 500,' and even area codes, for narrowing down searches geographically. Awards you've won and names of professional organizations to which you belong can even be used as keywords."

One way to gain an advantage with keywords is to scan some sample job descriptions provided in books, within software, or by the company you're considering. Other clues may be available through recruiters, career coaches, trade publications or websites, annual reports, or good old-fashioned deductive reasoning (simply think about which keywords make the most sense in your situation). Finally, make sure you put the word "résumé" somewhere on the document itself so that it doesn't get snared in an e-mail spam filter. The idea is not to game the system, but to make sure you're getting the attention you deserve.

Résumé Realities: Making Your Mark

There's no single way to put together an effective résumé. Overleaf you'll find an example of a skill-focused résumé that often works well for older workers and those aspiring to change careers. In this case, a fictional Ms. Lasseter is seeking a new career as a teacher after having worked for more than 15 years as a paralegal and then raised her children. Ms. Lasseter is eager not to draw attention to

Celine Lasseter

15467 Maple Lane
Sacramento, California 94001
Phone: 916-555-5555
Mobile: 916-555-5556
E-mail: celinel@papernapkin.net

PROFILE

A conscientious and detail-oriented professional with extensive experience managing people and projects. An acknowledged leader who is flexible but also able to follow strict standards and coordinate staff to handle wide-ranging activities and responsibilities. Possesses excellent written and verbal communication skills and an ability to work with teams and diverse groups. Returning to the workplace after raising children and volunteering for community organizations. Seeks a teaching position in grades K-5.

KNOWLEDGE AND SKILLS

- Project management
- Public speaking
- Word, PowerPoint, Excel, and other desktop applications
- Internet research
- Interpersonal communication
- Managing disparate groups with conflicting interests and goals
- Group learning

WORK EXPERIENCE

Abrams, David & Karl, LLP, Sacramento, California
Paralegal Manager

Managed a staff of 12 paralegals and legal assistants, coordinating projects and activities to ensure that all work was handled promptly and accurately. Responsible for accuracy of paperwork and records. Developed a system for tracking files electronically that resulted in a 30 percent productivity gain among support staff. Supervised training program and worked directly with partners to develop talent internally and identify recruiting requirements.

- Recognized as the firm's paralegal of the year in 1994.
Left company in 1996 to raise children (worked at firm 1989-1996)

Gibbons and Clark, LLP, Ashland, Oregon
Paralegal

Managed cases for three partners. Responsible for coordinating client meetings, coordinating research, checking legal forms and contracts for accuracy, preparing correspondence, generating reports, summarizing legal documents, and overseeing records searches.

- Advised partners on workflow improvements and software acquisitions.
- Created templates for letters sent by attorneys.

Left company in 1989 to accept position as Paralegal Manager at Abrams, David & Karl, LLP (worked at firm 1981-1989)

OTHER EXPERIENCE

Worked as a part-time volunteer at The Family Literacy Center, Sacramento, California (2004 to present).

Served as a volunteer parent assistant at Adams Primary School, Sacramento, California (2001-2006).

EDUCATION

B.A., English, magna cum laude, University of California, Los Angeles, 1980.
Associate's Degree, Paralegal, American Legal College, 1981.
Teaching Credential, State of California, 2007

PROFESSIONAL AFFILIATIONS

Member, Sacramento Paralegal Association (1989-1996)
Board of Directors, California Literacy Council (2004-2006)

the fact that she has been out of the workforce for several years. Instead, she delivers an impressive list of skills and abilities, including volunteer work and continuing education.

Some Dos, Some Don'ts
An examination of this résumé shows that Ms. Lasseter is playing up her strengths—and accomplishments—while making no attempt to hide her gap in employment from 1996 to the present. The bottom line? It's essential to be completely honest, though what you don't include—and how you present your background and career information— is just as important as what you choose to provide. It's also wise to tailor the information about your experience and knowledge to fit the position you're seeking—though subtlety is always better than blatant horn-blowing. (It may help to think of a résumé as a marketing tool that helps educate prospective employers.)

It's vital to draw parallels between your past skills and knowledge and whatever position you desire in the present. If you once worked as a restaurant manager and you're now seeking a career in nursing, for example, the skills required to order food and supplies apply directly to nursing. So do those of managing a staff and working with other employees and customers. The two jobs differ fundamentally, yes—but a top-notch restaurant manager is likely to transfer many of her management skills to the new profession. The key to landing the job you want is to make sure that prospective employers recognize your abilities and consider you a prime candidate.

Finally (and as previously noted), don't use the "shotgun approach," peppering every firm in the land with your résumé. Try to determine if there's a solid match, for in this case more is less. And given your time and energy constraints, it's probably wise to focus on, say, half a dozen companies. Approach the task the way a career coach might counsel you to: Consider yourself a brand—then market that brand strategically.

Understanding Search Firms

If you're unsure how various recruiters work, you could be in for some unwelcome surprises. According to David Martin, managing partner at Sterling Martin Associates in Washington, D.C., search firms fall into two basic categories: retained executive-search firms and contingency search firms.

"Retained executive-search firms provide a specialized service to the organizations that hire them," Martin notes in his newsletter, "and the organizations are their clients. Contingency firms earn a fee that is contingent upon successful placement of a candidate with an organization." It may behoove you to cultivate a relationship with either—or both—types of organizations, says Martin, but executive recruiters should be viewed as part of a "long-term career-management strategy that may unfold over months or years."

Many job seekers don't realize that a retained search firm is under an exclusive contract to the client organization. Its mission: to seek out qualified candidates for a specific position, usually at an executive level of the organization. If you don't fit that narrow definition, you may feel shunted aside.

A contingency firm, on the other hand, works on a freelance basis: If it fills a position, it receives a fee. In most instances, contingency firms handle mid-level and entry-level job openings. That's why they typically target professional candidates with strong credentials, then "shop them around" to various employers.

Executive recruiters search for top performers in their respective fields, says Martin, so "it's important to make yourself visible in other ways." Those ways include networking events, association committees, and public-speaking opportunities. "In your current organization," he counsels career-change aspirants, "take new assignments to broaden your experience and add to your résumé. By building a strong résumé and developing expertise in your field, executive recruiters will be searching to find you rather than you contacting them."

You on the Tube?

Beyond the electronic résumé is the next trend in futuristic job hunting: the video résumé. More and more job candidates, searching for a way to stand out from the crowd, are posting their résumés online at sites such as YouTube and RecruiTV. If you're looking for a job where image is everything (a political consultant, for example, or the

6 Steps to an Effective Cover Letter

In today's crowded job market, your cover letter must elevate you above the pack. Here's how to make sure you show up on an employer's radar (and computer) screen:

Make it easy to read. Use high-quality paper (20-weight or above) and standard fonts such as Times Roman or Arial. Print the letter in a block format, and sign it with blue or black ink. Don't use Wite-out® or handmade insertions to correct errors; instead, print a new copy. If you're submitting the cover letter by e-mail, type your message in the body of the e-mail and avoid capital letters, abbreviations, and odd spelling or punctuation, such as the shorthand used for today's text messaging on phones (THER 2 TUF 2 RD!).

Show you're a careful reviewer of your own work. Proofread the entire cover letter (which should start with a greeting and close with a signature line). Although a computer spell-checker or grammar-checker can flag many errors, it can't spot typos that are real words, such as "chef" instead of "chief" or "manger" rather than "manager." Nor can software (the machine variety, at any rate) detect "there," "they're," and "their" used incorrectly. Additionally, check to make sure your proper nouns are capitalized and that your quotation marks are of the "smart" (or curved) variety; "non-smart" quote marks (like these) are dead giveaways that you've cut and pasted the text from another source.

Stand out from the crowd. Just as your clothing and demeanor shape the image of you that others form, a cover letter creates a first—and leaves a lasting—impression. Mention your most important qualities and attributes, taking care to spotlight any skills, knowledge, or experience you suspect will particularly benefit the prospective employer. Emphasize words such as "flexible" and "adaptable." This is not an environment that rewards modesty, but at the same time you don't want to come across as egotistical or rigid.

Keep it short. Don't forget you're sending along a résumé as well, so there's no need for the cover letter to relate your entire life story. A cover letter should be no longer than one page. Rather than duplicating facts from the résumé, it should round out that information by conveying additional context or depth.

Emphasize experience over age. Employers look for candidates with the right mix of knowledge, skills, and experience. The fact that you have spent 30 years working in sales or accounting is far less impressive than your specific expertise and accomplishments. Use words such as "significant" or "extensive" to bolster your claims. Words such as "experienced" or "proven" can likewise establish that you have what it takes to handle the job.

Make the right first impression. If you're submitting a package online, advises career coach Norine Dagliano, "Make sure your e-mail address reflects the professional you are." Use a professional sounding e-mail name (raydelgado1) rather than one that undermines your credibility (topdog99). Also, create your own e-mail account, or a special separate account dedicated to your job search alone. Dagliano discovered one male client using his wife's e-mail address for his job correspondence, inviting potential employers to send their responses to "LisaW." "Such clueless behavior," she notes, "is far more common than you might imagine."

creative director of a public-relations agency, this approach might get you in the door for a more serious look—provided the video is compelling and professionally produced. Be aware, however, that a video résumé isn't a replacement for the conventional résumé or a job interview.

A Cover Letter to
Cover Your Bases
With the exception of online job sites, it's wise to send a cover letter with your résumé. Think of the cover letter as the emcee who introduces the headliner of the show: The letter provides a short introduction and gives the audience—that is, your potential next employer—a taste of what you have to offer. It outlines why you want the job and addresses potential liabilities up front, including employment gaps, being forced to go back to work (as a result of death or divorce), or the need to make a geographic move.

A good cover letter helps reduce or eliminate questions that a potential employer may have—but it does so in a deft and seamless manner. For example, you might not want to divulge that you recently divorced and must now return to work. Instead of stating this fact outright—a motivation an employer may understandably find less than compelling—your cover letter can explain that you're seeking work because of "changing family circumstances." A cover letter also lets you make it clear that you're open to relocating or that you're seeking new challenges and growth opportunities.

The quality of your cover letter has a disproportionately large bearing on whether you will be considered for a job. For starters, it must be written in a businesslike manner. This means discussing only what's germane to the job (no personal issues) and writing the letter in a clear, concise, direct style. Second, the cover letter should specifically address the employer in question; dispatching a "form letter" defeats the purpose and is unlikely to produce positive results.

It may help to think of the cover letter as your "elevator speech"—the

June 14, 2007

Ms. Cynthia Geightkepr
Oakmont School District
1780 Constitution Way
Sacramento, California 94205

Dear Ms. Geightkepr:

The demand for dedicated teachers has never been greater. America's future depends on enthusiastic and committed individuals to step into teaching, bringing their expertise, experience, and knowledge with them.

I am interested in becoming a primary-school teacher in your district. My experience in the legal profession—I worked for more than 15 years as a paralegal and office manager—has helped me hone my interpersonal and communication skills and become adept at managing people and tasks. In addition, I am proficient with computers and technology and have an intuitive understanding of children and learning. I served as a board member for the California Literacy Council and volunteered with my children's parent-teacher association and other school events. At this point, I have an intense passion to give back to society, and I believe teaching would enable me to do so.

I have a B.A. in English and recently obtained my teaching credential. I am highly motivated and flexible. Please review the enclosed résumé and feel free to contact me at any time. May I call you in early July to discuss an interview?

Thank you for your consideration.

              Sincerely,

              Celine Lasseter
              15467 Maple Lane
              Sacramento, California 94001
              Phone: 916-555-5555
              Mobile: 916-555-5556
              E-mail: celinel@papernapkin.net

key positive points you could make about yourself if you were riding an elevator to the 12th floor with the head of the company. So you'll want to mention the position you're seeking, state your qualifications for it, explain why you want the job, and then point out why you and the company are such a good match. You can tie it up with a bow by mentioning that your résumé is attached, and that you hope the recipient doesn't mind if you follow up in two or three weeks. (On page 285 you'll find a cover letter that our mythical Ms. Lasseter might have written to accompany her résumé.)

Not surprisingly, those who devote the time and effort required to develop an outstanding résumé and cover letter will be in a far better position to succeed. But one key hurdle still confronts them: acing the interview. Accomplishing that task is the subject of the next chapter.

Books

500+ Keywords for $100,000+ Jobs, by Wendy S. Enelow, Impact Publications, 1998.

The Career Change Résumé, by Karen Hofferber and Kim Isaacs. The official résumé advisers to Monster.com offer step-by-step instructions on how career changers can reinvent themselves via their résumés. The book offers more than 150 sample résumés and cover letters.

Cover Letters for Dummies, by Joyce Layne Kennedy, Hungry Minds, 2000. Offers tips, strategies, formats, and examples of effective cover letters.

Get the Interview Every Time: Fortune 500 Hiring Professionals' Tips for Writing Winning Résumés and Cover Letters, by Brenda Greene, Kaplan Business, 2004. A comprehensive primer for getting the cover letter right.

Electronic Résumés & Online Networking, by Rebecca Smith, Career Press, Inc., 2000.

The Elements of Résumé Style: Essential Rules and Eye-Opening Advice for Writing Résumés and Cover Letters That Work, by Scott Bennet, AMACOM, 2005. A complete how-to guide on making yourself known through an effective résumé and cover letter.

e-Résumés: Everything You Need to Know About Using Electronic Résumés to Tap into Today's Hot Job Market, by Susan Britton Whitcomb and Pat Kendall, McGraw Hill, 2001. Offers advice and tips on how to construct, post, attach, and send an e-résumé, as well as incorporating hyperlinks, images, and audio or video clips.

The Résumé Handbook: How to Write Outstanding Résumés & Cover Letters for Every Situation, by Arthur D. Rosenberg, Adams Media Corporation, 2003. Tips and examples of how to succeed with a winning résumé.

Résumés for Dummies, by Joyce Lain Kennedy, For Dummies, 2007. All you need to know to market yourself to prospective employers.

More Resources

CoverLetters.com

Offers hundreds of free sample cover letters from a wide array of industries, including accounting, engineering, pharmaceuticals, sales and marketing, teaching, journalism, consulting, and law.

Jobweb.com

Offers information, articles, and tips on how to write a tightly polished résumé.

Monster.com

Head to the career-advice section at content.monster.com/résumé/home.aspx for sample résumés, tips, message boards, and other tools.

Job-hunt.org

Offers detailed information on how to construct a résumé using effective keywords.

QuintCareers.com
www.quintcareers.com/resume_keywords.html

Provides an excellent overview of résumé-keyword strategies.

MASTERING THE ART OF THE INTERVIEW

Pinpoint and personalize your skills, knowledge, and expertise in this pivotal face-to-face forum

IT'S TOUGH ENOUGH TO WEATHER a job interview if you're a confident professional with a spotless résumé. When you're changing careers later in life, however, the mere thought of undergoing an interview—conducted, perhaps, by someone who is 20 years your junior—can seem especially daunting. Depending on the situation and the moment, you may feel insecure or defensive. If you're well prepared, though (possibly having brushed up your interview skills beforehand), you should be able to seize the moment—and with it the job you're seeking.

Almost everyone has endured the job-interview process at some point in the past, so you can be confident that the interviewer feels at least some degree of empathy for your plight. Drawing on memories of past interviews survived—and vanquished—can also help build your self-esteem on the eve of this crucial encounter.

What you may be less prepared for is the different boundaries that tend to govern a person's bid to shift careers later in life. For starters, your "sales pitch" will be more substantive: You will very likely have to convince the interviewer *why* changing careers makes the best sense for you at this point in your life. Second, you may confront a benighted interviewer who require assurance that you can become a seamless part of work teams drawn largely from younger generations. (Ageism, deplorably, is still a socially acceptable bias in some remote corners.)

Acing an interview requires the right mindset and attitude. There's no substitute for adequate preparation and research. But other issues factor into the equation as well: managing your jitters, asking the right questions, dressing appropriately, and learning from your mistakes and triumphs. An interview is a dynamic situation—no two sessions are alike—so you'll need to rely on your intuition and adapt on the fly. But if all goes right, it may well lead to a job offer—at which point, despite your eagerness to accept, you must be ready to negotiate your terms of employment.

Channel
Your Energies
In the interview process as in so many other business endeavors, coping with stage fright is fundamental to success. Your personality and expertise can't shine through if you're tied up in knots. The fact that you're nervous isn't a problem. It shows that you care—and, channeled properly, it can help you focus. If a five-mile run helps take the edge off, go for it. If listening to Enya on your iPod does the trick, by all means plug in.

Finding a way to confront and conquer your nervousness, such as establishing a mantra or using mental imagery, can help, says career counselor and coach Helen Harkness. If it fits your personal style, it's also possible to candidly—and humorously—acknowledge your nervousness at the outset of an interview. This can help break the ice and relieve some of the situation's built-in tension—for both parties. Despite any such concession, though, it's paramount to stay calm, poised, and confident. Anything less threatens to undermine months or years of hard work and preparation.

It's also important to step into an interview with an open mind and a positive attitude. Yes, you may desperately want the job and see it as the ticket to your new future. But if you get a sense that things aren't right or that you're not a good fit, trust your instincts and intuition. The last thing you want to do is accept a job and then, weeks or months later, decide that it isn't working out.

"The biggest mistake people make," says Harkness, "is treating an interview as a one-way proposition [in which] the employer asks questions and the candidate answers them." Instead, she suggests, be prepared to ask questions of your own—and to make it clear that you want to find out whether the organization meets your qualifications as well.

Build a Business Case—for You

A good job interview is a conversation. There's no hard sell—and no sense of desperation. An interviewee should never feel obligated to pander to the interviewer by telling that person what he imagines she wants to hear. Instead, he presents his skills, knowledge, and accomplishments in such a way as to demonstrate his value—and show what he's capable of achieving in the real world. In short, he builds a business case for himself, clarifying for the employer how and why he will add value to the organization.

But no longer is it enough to report that you're a "problem solver" or a "team player." Rather, you must provide specific examples of how you resolved certain challenging situations. For example, you might say: "In my last job we saw service costs rise so fast that they began to erode our margins. By assigning dedicated service representatives to individual accounts, I was able to get those costs back under control—and improve our customer-satisfaction rates as well." It doesn't matter whether you're seeking work in an entirely unrelated field. This sort of anecdote proves that you possess the critical-thinking skills required to view a problem differently—and therefore creatively. And that's an asset to any employer.

Likewise, if you've been out of the workforce for a few years, you can shore up the business case for yourself with examples drawn from your volunteer efforts or community involvement. You may have led a fund-raising drive and managed a dozen other people along the way, meeting your goal of raising $5,000. Or you may have volunteered to serve as president of your homeowners' association, overseeing an annual budget of $1 million and working with a disparate group of people to untangle a contentious neighborhood issue. Again, you're showing that you already have the management and teamwork skills you'll need in your new career.

That's not as big a leap as you might think, for many high-level skills transfer surprisingly readily across a wide swath of industries and companies. Someone who is an outstanding sales rep in the medical-device field, for example, can put her persuasive skills to work in convincing potential donors to contribute to a charitable organization.

Part of your task in building the business case for your candidacy is to show that you're bright, capable, and qualified—and that you have

6 Questions to Ask in Any Interview

What can the XYZ Corporation offer me in terms of opportunities for advancement and personal/professional development?

How would you describe the corporate culture at XYZ Corporation?

What are the biggest challenges I'm likely to face in this position?

How would this position play out in terms of a daily routine? Or is there no such thing as a daily routine at XYZ Corporation?

How does XYZ Corporation expect (or hope) its market position to change over the next five years?

Do you envision that the job will evolve or change? If so, how might that affect me?

a winning attitude. "Companies want to hire the best people and develop workers to their full potential," says Gabriel Goncalves, the founder and CEO of Texas assessment firm PeopleAnswers, Inc. "The thinking is: You can train someone who already has the right attitude and values, but even the brightest or most knowledgeable person won't succeed in the wrong environment."

Know Thy Target Long before they first set foot in a potential employer's offices, savvy candidates will have conducted extensive "due diligence" about the organization and its methods of operation. This makes it P.I. (Professionally Incorrect) during a job interview to ask questions about the company's products, services, or employee benefits that could easily have been answered by a visit to its website beforehand. Most company websites include tabs or links for products, services, background papers, and more. In addition, an "About" or "Company Information" tab usually supplies basic information, including a mission statement or business philosophy.

But don't stop there. Sites such as Hoovers.com and Finance.yahoo.com also serve up information about thousands of publicly owned and private firms. (In addition, Hoover's offers a fee-based service that offers more comprehensive descriptions.) Finally, an online search in Google or another search engine may turn up articles, blogs, postings at consumer sites, and analysts' comments about the organization and its products or services. These sites can help you put all the pieces of the puzzle together and step into an interview fully informed. Also, if possible, arrange to have lunch with a current employee or someone else who knows the organization and its culture. Having a sense of what the company does (and what it wants to do) will make you sound more informed during the interview process—primarily because you will be more informed. Such foreknowledge will also help you decide which questions to ask—and, ultimately, whether you want to work at that company.

Make Every
Word Count
Interviews typically revolve around three major issues: what you offer an organization; why you want to work there; and how deep is your knowledge of the company and its products. Doing your homework ahead of time and rehearsing a range of potential answers goes a long way toward making an impact and eliciting a job offer. Not surprisingly, if you can demonstrate your command of the company's business, you're far more likely to relax and impress the interviewer.

Throughout an interview, it's vital to be honest and straightforward. Don't try to gloss over any gaps in your employment history—simply present in the best light possible the reasons why they occurred. If you're looking to downshift, for example, make it clear that you want meaningful work—not a position that will manacle you to a PDA around the clock. Finally, never disparage a former manager or employer.

Many human-resource managers identify "conversational drift" as a major mid-interview turnoff. It's therefore best not to volunteer too much information during an interview or wander too far off the topic of the question. Steer clear of personal discussions. Don't reveal anything that lacks a direct bearing on the position you're seeking.

Admitting that computers intimidate you or that you had problems getting along with co-workers in a previous job or career is a major turn-off—even if you've been prompted to identify your weaknesses or past problems. Instead, think of how you can spin the question in a positive way. For example, if an interviewer asks, "What's the biggest challenge or obstacle you faced in your last job?", you might reply, "I'm probably too much of a perfectionist. I'm just not satisfied until the job is done right." In other words, transform a potential weakness into a selling point.

Holly K. La Vine, director of human resources for SEKO, an international manufacturer of industrial applications, says it's critical to demonstrate you have the right stuff in a compressed time frame. "You have to illustrate how you bring knowledge and expertise to the table. You have

Key Questions

Am I prepared for a face-to-face interview? Success hinges on more than showing up and talking up a storm. Even the most confident job applicant often must deliver valuable information and examples in an abbreviated time frame. The best interviewees spend time polishing their message and preparing for a broadside of questions. They know their story line cold—and they tell it well enough that the interviewer warms to it.

Do I know the company? Everyone has his or her own idea of what it would be like to work for a certain company. A well-known high-tech company or outdoor-gear manufacturer may score high on your Relative Coolness Scale, yet rarely does that mental image overlap the reality of work life at those firms. It's therefore in your best interest to conduct the background research required to uncover your target employer's culture and work ethic before you invest a great deal of time trying to land a job there. The converse holds true as well: Your odds of landing a job are going to be slim if you know nothing about a firm—and that ignorance betrays itself during an interview.

Do I know what I really want? The prospect of a career change can be abstract; working day in, day out in a job at a company is very real. Before accepting a job offer, make sure your expectations match those of the company regarding hours, pay, working conditions, and other practical matters. If your instincts say a job does not feel right for some reason, wait for a better opportunity.

Do I learn from my mistakes? Because it's true that no job seeker is perfect, even those who typically excel in interviews should conduct a self-evaluation afterward. You will find it a worthwhile exercise to identify the strengths and weaknesses you evinced during the session. The more honest you are with yourself, the more you will succeed in honing your interview technique. Use the worksheet on page 299 to rate your performance.

Dealing with Tough Questions

Here are some curveballs you might encounter in a typical interview, followed by a suggested response and its intended effect. When in doubt, take the high moral ground; stressing the positive is a good way to showcase the constructive energy you will bring to the job.

QUESTION: **What was your previous manager's most glaring weakness?**

Response: *She was probably too much of a perfectionist.*
Effect: You use the opportunity to say something good about your former boss.

QUESTION: **What was the least rewarding part of your last job?**

Response: *I didn't get to apply my problem-solving skills enough.*
Effect: Turn a weakness into a strength. Don't discuss negatives that could translate to this next job.

QUESTION: **Do you think you can keep up with the pace of this job?**

Response: *I'm high-energy, flexible, and willing to learn new things.*
Effect: Make your age a nonfactor.

QUESTION: **Do you feel you can make the leap to an entirely new career?**

Response: *Absolutely. I've participated in career counseling, gone back to school to earn another degree, and discussed this line of work extensively with colleagues and associates.*
Effect: You've done the hard work to prepare; now you're ready to transition seamlessly into a new career.

QUESTION: **If we come to terms, you may work with a manager much younger than you. Can you handle this type of situation?**

Response: *I respect a manager's abilities regardless of her age, just as I'm sure she'll respect mine.*
Effect: You make it clear that you're a team player, willing to do what it takes to achieve success.

to convince the interviewer that your skills can bring value to the company." A good interviewer, says La Vine, can detect inconsistencies and outright exaggerations. "A straightforward approach is always the best policy," she notes.

Keep Cool
under Fire Although it's illegal for an interviewer to ask how old you are, you may wind up fielding questions that seem intended to ferret out your age or how long you have been in the workforce. The interviewer may cling to the antiquated notion that older workers lack vitality or commitment. Think of these situations as opportunities to present your experience and wisdom as assets—and to dispel any employer anxieties that might keep you from landing the position. At the same time, though, be careful not to let personal issues tint the atmosphere: Some people have a talent for spotting conspiracies where none exist.

According to Deborah Russell, director of workforce issues at AARP, it's vital to show that "you're 'current' in today's workplace and able to keep up." It's also crucial to stress your willingness to learn new things and back it up with concrete examples from your work history. However, if you encounter direct questions about your age (or the year you graduated from high school, for example), it's wise to report the company to the federal Equal Employment Opportunity Commission (EEOC) or its state-level equivalent. Make sure the company president learns of the incident. A company that flouts age-discrimination laws is effectively removing itself from your list of desirable employers.

If an interview question throws you off balance, don't lose your cool. Stay calm. Deal with the situation "in the moment." The net effect may be that you hurdle this stumbling block and land a great job. If the interviewer appears hostile or adversarial, or if the situation seems to be heading south in a hurry, do your best to answer the questions and ride out the interview anyway. In many interview situations, it's not only what you say that matters, it's how you say it. On the other hand, take care not to jump the gun and pose premature questions about pay, benefits, working hours, job conditions, or other topics. Wait to broach those issues until you have received an actual job offer.

Be Ready for Your Closeup

Interview techniques have undergone a transformation of sorts in recent years. A few companies now request video interviews—especially for candidates who would have to travel far from home for an interview at the head office. If you're asked to conduct a video interview, practice with a camcorder at home, then arrive early at the studio and try to imagine the camera as a friend, not foe. Test makeup and clothes beforehand as a way of avoiding last-minute surprises.

Many companies are turning to "behavioral interviewing" processes. These focus on how you would act in or respond to a specific situation or set of circumstances. For instance, an interviewer might inquire, "How did you react when a co-worker didn't do what you asked?" or "What did you do when you had a customer screaming at you?" It's your task to provide a response that shows you had—and have—the skills and attitude necessary to deal with such situations.

"Organizations are increasingly on the lookout for people who have desired personality traits," says Winfred Arthur, Jr., a professor of psychology and management at Texas A&M University. "They are trying to create the right chemistry." For some employers, that means administering a personality test or a skills-assessment battery before making a job offer. (You might take a test where you're constantly interrupted—the organization's attempt to gauge your multitasking skills.) For others, such as Southwest Airlines and Whole Foods Markets, it means conducting group interviews: The company assembles half a dozen or more applicants in a room, tosses out some questions or problems, then observes the group dynamics. Those who best fit the firm's ideal profile receive an offer.

Worksheet: **Post-Interview Inventory**

After any interview—good, bad, or ugly—conduct your own debriefing. What worked? What didn't? How can you improve in future interviews? Write down your answers to these and any other "post-mortem" queries that occur to you, then sketch out a plan to address problem areas and improve your interview skills.

The chart below is designed to help you evaluate your performance in the handful of domains you can control. Under the "Preparation" category, for example, you might rate yourself a "6," noting something in the "Next Steps" box such as "I need to know more about the company's history and market position in future interviews." Similarly, under "Confidence" you might rate yourself an "8" but note that "I need to rehearse my selling points and anticipate a wider range of questions."

Honesty is crucial—but so is finding the right balance between being too tough on yourself or too easy.

Factor	Rating (1-10)	Next Steps
Preparation		
Confidence		
Poise		
Finesse		
Clarity		
Honesty		

Stay on
Message
Preparing for an interview is half the battle. Thankfully, all sorts of squires are waiting in the wings to help you polish your armor—or conceal its chinks.

A career coach, for example, can put you through a mock interview, using video to analyze your strengths and weaknesses. The technique has been known to reveal an unconscious habit or two as well: Career coach Harkness relates the story of a client who constantly but unwittingly picked his nose. Only upon viewing the video of his mock interview was the shocked client made aware of his career-sabotaging habit. Likewise, a taped mock interview may disclose that you clench your teeth or clasp your hands behind your neck when you get nervous. Eliminating these tics—and replacing them with behaviors designed to project self-confidence—can go a long way toward successfully selling yourself.

If you can't afford a professional coach or video sessions, which may cost several hundred dollars or more, consider recruiting a friend or colleague to help you out. Create a mock-interview scenario that lets you hone your pitch. You don't want your "performance" to seem overly rehearsed, though; the goal is to appear relaxed, engaging, and spontaneous.

Above all, aim to make a mark. According to T. J. Walker, the author of *Media Training A-Z,* "The biggest problem for most of us in job interviews isn't that we made a mistake. It's not that we said something stupid or foolish. It's that a person doesn't leave an impression at all."

A positive first impression, Walker believes, does not necessarily hinge on accomplishments related to your job. You might cite a cross-country bike trip as an example of your tenacity, for example, or mention that volunteer stint in Botswana as an example of your wider worldview. "You have to spend some time thinking about how the examples you decide to give will define yourself," observes Walker. "What's interesting about you? You want to show a prospective employer that you have specific talents that can lead to concrete outcomes for them."

Dress to
Impress Although today's business world has embraced a far more casual sartorial style than the suits-and-boots uniformity of the 1970s, it remains critical to dress appropriately for any interview. As a rule of thumb, it's better to show up overdressed for the role. If you're interviewing for a professional position, this typically translates into a suit and tie for men and a conservative dress or a blouse and skirt for women. Less-formal work environments—those that prevail in a retail outlet or a public relations agency, for example—usually justify wearing a sports shirt or blouse and slacks to an interview. But never dress in anything less than business casual—so leave the open-toed shoes or sandals at home unless the interviewer is hiring lifeguards.

Regardless of your age, the fashion dos and don'ts are the same. Avoid clashing colors and bold statements designed to telegraph your mastery of contemporary couture. Make sure you're well groomed—particularly hands and nails. If you are 55, don't try to come off as 25: Bad toupees, dyed hair, or facelifts cannot forever block an employer from finding out how old you are. (They can, however, make you look silly or deluded.)

Tame
the Time What is your worst "interview nightmare"? For most of us, it's arriving late for the interview itself. Such a lamentable episode can leave an otherwise outstanding candidate feeling deflated. From the interviewer's side of the table, tardiness can pretty much seal the (non) deal.

Obviously it's key to arrive with time to spare. Just make sure it's not *too* much time: Interviewers on a tight timetable will resent your jumping the gun if it forces them to cut a meeting short or leads you to cross paths with other applicants, explains SEKO HR director Holly La Vine. If you do arrive early, bide your time in your car or a nearby coffee shop until the meeting time approaches. Then, about 10 to 15 minutes before the scheduled interview time, feel free to introduce yourself to the receptionist.

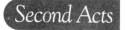

PERM PEAKS AND SILICON VALLEYS

KATHRYN COVERSTON, *from cosmetologist to medical assistant*

I KNOW ALL ABOUT REINVENTING MYSELF. In my early 20s, I became a cosmetologist—a normal thing for a young woman to do in the 1960s. But because of the constant standing, I wound up with a back problem, and I had to find a line of work where I could sit down. In the early 1970s, I began working for the court system of Santa Clara County in California.

During that time, I got divorced. I had two teenage children, so in addition to working for the county full-time I had to work weekends and evenings at a beauty salon. Later, I took a job in a homebuilder's title department, but got laid off in a real estate downturn. At the time, I was making about $50,000 a year without a college degree. "Secretaries won't be around much longer," my own secretary predicted. "You should learn to use a computer." So I took some computer classes through a staffing agency, which led to several assignments at high-tech companies in the Silicon Valley.

I worked as an executive assistant to the president of a major company, then as a contract recruiter. During the 1990s and early 2000s, I worked at Institutional Venture Partners, Hewlett-Packard, and AMD. After the tech bubble broke, however, I was 57 and felt like I was starting to "age out." My contract ran out at AMD and younger people were getting the jobs. Despite all my expertise and experience, companies were suddenly hiring people 20 years younger. It was discrimination, and it was more than subtle.

I took some temp jobs to pay the mortgage and worked as a senior project assistant for an engineering firm in Silicon Valley. In March 2007, that job came to an end during a downsizing. I received a severance package and decided to move to the San Diego area to be closer to my mother. It was a tough decision: I had lived in northern California for 45 years, and I had to leave behind my children, my grandchildren, my church, and my friends.

My mother was thrilled—but she was diagnosed with kidney cancer and died in June of 2007. That really got to me. *I'm going to live the life I want in my sunset years,* I thought to myself. *I'm going to do something that will help society.*

After I finished my initial grieving process, I decided I wanted to work in the medical field. I went to a career counselor, who helped me find a regional occupational program that would train me to become a medical assistant. I started in September 2007 and got my certificate in May 2008. I was fortunate to find out about that program: It would have set me back $12,000 at a vocational school, but I got it for free simply because I knew about it. My sole cost was a few hundred dollars for books.

This educational process was a real eye-opener. I was concerned that I wouldn't be able to learn, that the younger students might resent me, that the teachers would dismiss my ambition. Those turned out to be myths. I was totally focused and devoted to getting the assignments done and graduating. Others could see that—but they did not necessarily possess it themselves. A lot of the younger students were in school only to appease their parents or because they didn't know what else to do.

I worked with a career counselor after I graduated as well. He is making sure I market myself properly, that my résumé looks impeccable, and that I present the right package during interviews. I feel it's important to find the right position in the right place. Because of my circumstances—I lost my house in 2005 after another downturn, and I need both the income and the health insurance—I plan to keep on working.

I feel like I've been to hell and back, but now I'm working to become debt free. I also want to do something meaningful, so all in all it's an exciting time. Thank God age is not an issue in this profession! It's something I should be able to do for many more years.

Staying Balanced During a Job Search

Searching for a new job and making the transition to a new career can be a stomach-churning, emotional roller coaster. You may feel upbeat in the wake of a particularly good interview, only to hear nothing for weeks afterward. Or you may replay an interview in your mind as awkward and tense, then be surprised to find the job offered to you.

Throughout these ups and downs, stay on an even keel. Focus on the big picture, reminding yourself that plenty of employers exist and that finding the right match is essential. Here's one tactic that has proven its worth countless times in the past: Stay busy. You might send a handwritten, snail-mailed thank-you note to each person who has interviewed you, or you might volunteer time for a good cause or conduct research on other potential employers.

If you don't hear back within two or three weeks of an interview, odds are that the employer simply isn't interested. (Unfortunately, this lack of a response is increasingly common today.) If 10 business days elapse with no word, follow up with an e-mail or a phone call—and take pains not to show the slightest hint of impatience or frustration. Once you've made that overture, focus on other opportunities and keep your overall process moving forward.

Equally important: If you receive a job offer or you're invited back for a second or third round of interviews, take it as your cue to think long and hard about whether you truly want to work at the company in question. If the job doesn't seem right, you may be better off waiting until the right situation presents itself.

Blame it on ego, insecurity, or simple insolvency, says career coach Norine Dagliano, but it's hardly unusual—or unnatural—for a person to jump at the first job offer that is tendered. Only later on may they discover that the position is not right for them. In another typical scenario that can leave the hasty applicant dismayed, a better offer unexpectedly filters in just a few days or weeks later.

"Many job seekers refuse to believe that they can have what they truly want," Dagliano observes, "so they give in. There is also a tendency in the over-45 crowd to hear the 'voice' of their parents' generation telling them, 'Beggars can't be choosers' and, 'Any job is better than being unemployed.' Something about this generation fails to equate 'job' with 'happiness,' so they settle for less than what they really want."

Negotiation Is a Walk in the Perks

In the course of agreeing on your terms of engagement, it's often possible to win concessions on perks, flextime, office location, or professional-development opportunities (training, conferences, workshops, and the like). As long as you're reasonable, it does no harm to ask. Perks can also serve as bargaining chips: If a company declines to meet your salary request, for example, you may be able to reach a deal for extra vacation days or a higher signing bonus.

Like buying a car, a bit of up-front knowledge about a company or industry can go a long way. What is the typical salary range? One good place to check that is *The Riley Guide* (www.rileyguide .com/salary.html), which lists a wealth of resources, including government and private wage surveys. You might also consult industry associations and their publications and websites.

Throughout the process, bear in mind that you're involved in a business negotiation. Consider following these ground rules:

Don't take things personally. If you're a blurter—someone subject to impulses—suppress the urge to comment spontaneously on any aspect of an offer.

Be patient. It's impossible to predict when an employer may come through with an offer; it could be days, weeks, or never. Ultimately, you have no option but to wait.

Be polite. By creating a good impression, a little bit of courtesy goes a long way toward maximizing your opportunities.

Although practical considerations—notably how much money you have saved up—are necessarily a big part of the equation, Dagliano says, it's hard for the job seeker to make a sound career decision when feeling anxious about his or her personal worthiness or age, or when feeling desperate because the job search has been so protracted.

Career changers—many of whom lack concrete knowledge or experience in professions besides their own—should heed their intuition. If you receive an offer, no matter how tantalizing, sleep on it before reaching a decision. Review your reasons for changing careers in the first place. (Consulting the self-evaluation worksheets you filled out in Chapter 7 may facilitate this process.) A career change will alter your life, so grab this final opportunity to weigh its pros and cons.

When Mr. Smithers Works for Dagwood

One of the most unnerving aspects of a career change is the ego-challenging prospect of dealing with a younger boss. Taking orders from someone younger than your son or daughter may seem like a journey to the far reaches of hell—especially if he espouses what you deem to be antic notions about the best way to manage a project or market a product. Before you start cursing kismet, however, consider adopting these alternatives:

Keep up with the times. One area in which boomers and other older workers lag is in skill maintenance—particularly in the technology arena. Don't fall into the trap of thinking that the way you have always done something will suffice. Sign up for training sessions, community college classes—whatever it takes to stay proficient rather than grow irrelevant. Stay current with new books, movies, and TV shows—or read a magazine such as *Entertainment Weekly* or *Vanity Fair* that will let you pretend you are. You need not live the "life" of a twentysomething, but with a little bit of cultural literacy you can exert a large amount of cultural leverage.

Lose the 'tude. Don't try to upstage your boss or act as though you know everything. Similarly, avoid lapsing into Disapproving Parent Mode and getting defensive if your ideas are shot down. Finally, fight the temptation to rattle off past accomplishments. Your boss and employer want to know what you can do for them in the here-and-now. Focus on doing your job to the best of your ability—and look for opportunities to excel.

Learn to adapt. Dealing with—that is, accepting—change may be one of the toughest aspects of aging. Over the last quarter-century, computers and technology have radically altered the face of business—and the ways in which bosses and employees interact. If you're over 50, you're probably familiar with a top-down management style—the boss barks commands and everyone scurries to meet them. But in today's workplace, there's less structure and more latitude. You may need to work on teams and learn to take the initiative—without being asked to do so.

Communicate. In many cases, conversation and discussion equal positive results—and a far better understanding of the other person. Ask your boss what he or she would like to see from you; spell out clear performance objectives. Understand how your boss views success, then look for ways to deliver.

Terms of Engagement
Your interview went well enough to elicit a job offer. Now it's time to get down to the nitty-gritty: pay, benefits, perks, work schedule, and advancement opportunities.

Although there are no hard-and-fast rules about compensation, people changing careers or reentering the workforce after an absence of several years should probably gird themselves to accept less than they earned in their previous job. That can be a tactical blow to your self-esteem, but don't let it dilute your focus on strategic goals. If you receive a written offer that's below what you expected, it's perfectly acceptable to ask for more money. However, instead of using a threatening approach ("I'll need $60,000 a year to work for you"), try stating your requirements in a straightforward and businesslike manner ("I really want to work for you, but I'm hoping you can boost the starting salary").

If you're going to ask for more, be prepared to offer reasons why you deserve it. "I have a lot of bills to pay" or "I'm trying to save for a house" don't hold water. Rather, you'll have to objectively assess your value to the organization, then present that information in a dollars-and-sense way. "I am a focused and dedicated employee with a documented history of being productive" is more likely to succeed as a negotiating stance. If you have an offer from another company, you can mention that fact along with a tangible benchmark: "If we can bump up the salary to $75,000, I'll accept the position."

"Salary is just one part of the entire compensation package that should be reviewed before you accept a position," says Atlanta career coach Deborah Brown. "For sales jobs, also take a look at commissions (including typical sales cycles and assigned quotas); bonuses (including what they are based on, how you will be evaluated, and when they will be paid out); any signing bonus; health insurance and other benefits (such as a 401(k) plan or pension plan and life, disability, or long-term care insurance); stock options (and how soon you become vested in them); relocation costs; and vacation and personal days."

If all that sounds like so much window dressing, reconsider the matter. "Something about the compensation package that bothers you before you start the job will bother you even more once you start working with the company," Brown explains. "That's because many people, by nature, tend to focus on what they lack instead of what they have. Also, many people are not clear about the things that are truly important to them, so they don't yet know their ultimate 'deal breakers.' It's important that you be completely happy with the job and compensation in order to start with a positive attitude."

To be certain, the interview is the final hedge to be vaulted in your career-change steeplechase. Clear it cleanly and you're on your way to realizing your dream of finding more fulfilling work. At this point, there's only one major task left: adapting to your new line of work and making the transition to your new life.

Books

101 Salary Secrets: How to Negotiate Like a Pro, by Daniel Porot and Francis Bolles Haynes, Ten Speed Press, 2001. Demonstrates how to use the negotiation process to boost your salary, benefits, and perks.

301 Smart Answers to Tough Interview Questions, by Vicki Oliver, Sourcebooks, Inc., 2005. Offers practical examples of responses with which to arm yourself before a job interview.

Bridging the Generation Gap: How to Get Radio Babies, Boomers, Gen Xers, and Gen Yers to Work Together and Achieve More, by Linda Gravett and Robin Throckmorton, Career Press, 2007. Examines the different generations and what it takes for all of them to function cohesively in the workplace.

Connecting Generations: The Sourcebook for a New Workplace, by Claire Raines, Crisp Learning, 2003. Provides insights into today's intergenerational workplace and the attitudes and values that differentiate groups.

How to Interview Like a Top MBA: Job-Winning Strategies from Headhunters, Fortune 100 Recruiters, and Career Counselors, by Shel Leanne, McGraw Hill, 2003. The complete lowdown on effective job-interview skills.

Negotiating Your Salary: How to Make $1,000 a Minute, by Jack Chapman, Ten Speed Press, 2006. Sorts through the wealth of issues that constitute a total pay-and-compensation package, and offers practical advice on how to make the most of a job offer.

Winning Job Interviews, by Paul Powers, Career Press, Inc., 2004. Tips, information, and concrete instances of how to ace an interview.

More Resources

ekm Inspirations

www.ekminspirations.com

Career coach and job-search strategist Norine Dagliano provides tips and resources for smoothing the transition to the work you love.

GuideStar.org

www.guidestar.org

If you are considering a position at a not-for-profit organization, use this site to obtain salary data for the upper-echelon staff jobs there. You'll be sifting through copies of voluminous tax filings that nonprofits (including AARP) are required to make public. You may need to do some digging (and not every such outfit is eager to promulgate its executives' compensation), but Form 990 gives you the numbers in black and white—and green.

Job-Interview.net

www.job-interview.net

Offers tips, sample questions, etiquette guides, and more.

Jobweb.com

www.jobweb.com

Provides information and articles on how to handle tough questions and otherwise navigate a job interview successfully.

Monster.com

www.monster.com

Discusses all aspects of the interview, including body language, dress, preparation, and warning signs of a bad boss or an incompatible company culture.

Media Training Worldwide

www.mediatrainingworldwide.com

Media training specialist T. J. Walker's site offers news, information, video clips with tips and information, and other materials of value to job seekers.

Salary.com

www.salary.com

This website lets you enter a specific job title and Zip code in order to display detailed data about the pay ranges, bonuses, and benefits typically paid for that position in that location.

SalaryExpert.com

www.salaryexpert.com

After you supply your profession, Zip code, number of years of experience, current salary, and other variables, this website serves up salary ranges and averages for your field and location. A basic report also provides cost-of-living information for the area you select.

CHAPTER

14

You've Changed Careers: Now What?

An annual "career checkup" can heighten your long-term health and financial security

EVEN IF YOU FEEL THAT you've finally found the perfect new career, statistics suggest you will get the itch to switch again at some point in the future: The average person swaps jobs 10 to 15 times over a lifetime and embraces a new career three to five times.

Amid all the tumult and change, there's one constant, and that is personal growth. More and more workers appear to recognize that acceptance of the way things are—some call this "settling"—is not necessarily conducive to long-term happiness and success. What was once new eventually becomes old—unless a person finds fresh challenges and goals. On the other hand, changing careers—perhaps even making a habit of doing so—can help us find fulfillment throughout the various stages and phases of our lives.

Although construction work at age 50 may be inordinately exertive, it's possible to serve as an exhibit designer at a museum—and tap into similar aptitudes and abilities. The rigors of serving as a full-time corporate marketing manager can easily tax the most energetic 60-year-old, yet those same skills, applied on behalf of a nonprofit organization, could dramatically broaden the group's exposure and maximize its impact.

As I've touched upon throughout this book, the richness of the opportunities available may surprise you. But tapping into them will almost certainly require that you achieve self-understanding, assemble the necessary knowledge, and maintain a positive mindset.

It's equally evident that any new career involves an attitude adjustment. Finding your inner compass is only part of the story. You'll also have to adapt to changes in the workplace—and in the world around you. You

---

Key Questions

Am I mentally prepared for a new job and a new career? It's essential to approach a new career with the right mental framework. Don't just show up. If you've spent weeks, months, or years preparing for a new line of work, you can easily spend a few extra hours readying yourself for the new environment.

Am I ready to play the role? Success is more than a collection of knowledge and skills. You must dress the part, apply the right tools, and speak the language. Understand what it takes to fit in up front and you will likely alleviate stress and problems later on.

Have I acknowledged my accomplishment? Once you've successfully changed careers, it's vital to acknowledge the hard work that led to this result. Treat yourself and a loved one to some time off together or dinner in a nice restaurant.

How can I remain open to opportunities? People change. Jobs change. The world changes. No longer is there any such thing as activating cruise control and driving into the sunset. The most successful individuals understand that key ingredients in the recipe for personal and professional growth include a willingness to experiment, an openness to take risks, and an ongoing desire to learn.

may need to upgrade your computer skills, or take a class to "top off" your knowledge of a profession. And you will undoubtedly need to understand the social and practical dynamics of a new job or career: You may find yourself on the low rung of the corporate totem pole, or you may discover that younger workers—younger bosses, for that matter—do not accord you the respect you feel your experience should command.

As anyone who has tried and succeeded—or failed—to change careers can tell you, identifying the path to self-actualization and positive life-long growth demands not just vision but a willingness to foresee and confront tough issues. Your new career may be everything you hoped for, and more—or it may turn out to be nothing like you had imagined. In the latter instance, you may find yourself pondering another dispiriting sequence of "What ifs."

This chapter examines what it takes to manage a new career. It identifies some key factors that you can use as barometers to keep you on track. Ultimately, of course, there's no simple instrument or formula for achieving career success. It's vital to inventory your feelings and stay focused on what's most important—no matter what stage of life you happen to be passing through.

Starting All Over Again Is Gonna Be Rough

A new job is an exciting but nerve-racking experience. Beyond the expected sense of unfamiliarity, you may feel utterly disoriented at first. Learning a tangle of new procedures, processes, and systems can flummox even the most confident individual. Now ratchet that up a few notches by factoring in your recent career change, and you may feel as though you've parachuted into outer Mongolia without a translator. Looking around at your alien new environs, you may even question why you made this change in the first place.

It's also not unusual to switch jobs or careers only to experience a vague sense of letdown afterward. Having weathered all the hard work, anticipation, and excitement involved in accomplishing the career change, you may find yourself thinking, "That's *it?*" Even if you're certain you made the right choice, the reality may not live up to the expectation. Weeks or months may pass before you completely fit in. New people, new work styles, and unfamiliar challenges may leave you feeling dazed and confused, insecure and vulnerable.

One of the biggest sources of psychic pain in a new job, surprisingly, may stem not from any adjustment issues but from the nature of the work itself, says Seattle-based career counselor Robin Ryan, author of *Soaring on Your Strengths: Discover, Use, and Brand Your Best Self for Career Success.* Imagine, for example, that you love arranging flowers as a hobby; you have such an affinity for it that your floral creations bring joy into the lives of family and friends. Naturally enough, you conclude that a career in flower arranging will help you blossom. "But now you have to do it full-time," Ryan points out. "And now you have to work with the flowers that are available in a shop rather than whatever you want, and deal with the financial considerations so that the business is profitable."
If you've done the requisite research up front, you will have prepared yourself for these on-the-job realities.

Another major snag for midlife career changers: Coping with bosses or co-workers who don't fully respect your abilities. If your new colleagues are 20 or 30 years your junior, you may become enmeshed in an array of status and ego issues—including your own. Some co-workers may ignorantly embrace pernicious stereotypes about older workers—you can't keep up, you can't pull your weight—or assume you lack the skills or knowledge to do the job well. Don't be in a hurry, paradoxically, to prove them wrong; they will almost certainly resent a "newbie" attempting to tell them what to do or how to do it.

As with so many other variables in the recareering equation, success may hinge on approaching a new workplace with the proper mindset. Does that mean modeling a positive attitude and a solid work ethic?

Well, yes, but there are many more pieces to the puzzle than that. To figure out what those fragments are and where they all fit, you may find it instructive to pay attention to the way others act and dress. Analyze the way work gets done in your new place of work (rather than the way it's supposed to get done). And seek out and connect with assistants and support staff; they can point you in the right direction, smoothing the transition into your new work life.

"It's great to make an outstanding first impression," career counselor Ryan points out, "but it's also possible to go too far. Try to avoid coming on too strong and too fast. Otherwise, you may elicit resentment."

Making It All Work

Researching a new career—even taking a test-drive as an intern or a volunteer—is far different from working in a field on a daily basis. As the tangibles of your new means of living take hold, glamour fades to gruntwork. Idealism morphs into realism.

Magazines and television talk shows love to offer tips and tactics on how to deal with dead-end jobs and career ennui. Their prevailing mind-set seems to be that anyone who makes a job change will live happily ever after. Only sporadically do they present such truly useful information as how the average individual can or should go about adapting to a new career.

Although you're likely to find greater satisfaction and purpose in your new calling, there are no guarantees. It's equally possible to come face-to-face with frustration and disillusionment. So plan ahead to give yourself enough time—three to six months minimum—to adjust to a new career. Keep in mind, too, that even though you've finally found the right vocation, the particular job you've landed in may still be a bit wrong for you.

If managing a career is an imprecise science, it should be no surprise that one of its strongest governing factors—feelings—likewise lacks precision. Fewer than half of all Americans are satisfied with their jobs, the New

Navigating a New Workplace

Starting a new career requires more than knowledge, confidence, and enthusiasm. You want to put yourself in a position to succeed—and feel good about your work. Several factors are key to building a foundation:

Prepare. Take a couple of weeks off, if you can manage it, before starting a new job. The mental separation from your previous job—and career—is important, and it's always wise to approach a new job in a fresh state of mind. You can also use this downtime to shop for new work clothes; research your new employer by talking to associates, colleagues, and others in your network; and mentally rehearse greetings or discussion points.

Be conscientious. Arrive on time, attend training sessions, file all required paperwork with the human-resource department, and follow through on requests and assignments. Studies show that the first couple of weeks on a new job mold how others think about you and shape their opinions for months and years afterward. In other words, the impression you make is the image you create.

Dress well. In today's dress-down world, it's tempting to fit right in. This is especially true if younger workers surround you. It's prudent, particularly during the first few weeks, to dress up. Use your best-dressed co-worker (or your immediate boss) as a gauge. You're likely to garner more respect and feel better about yourself.

Remember, while you want to fit in and you don't want to look old, "Young and hip can easily translate to foolish and ridiculous," career counselor Robin Ryan says. If you're 50, dump the miniskirts or jeans and T-shirt look. "Wear clothes that are stylish but classic," she adds. "Look professional and respectable."

Ask questions. Don't be afraid to ask questions that reveal you are not quite omniscient. Locating supplies, understanding computer software, and mastering a brain-bursting array of unfamiliar business processes can prove exhausting. Just be sure to thank those who help you—and offer to reciprocate when they need assistance in turn. A good relationship is a two-way street.

Make friends. If colleagues ask you to go out for a beer after work or join them for lunch, make every effort to tag along. However, it's best to understand up front that you're not part of a twentysomething peer group, and that trying to fit in at all costs may prove awkward or inappropriate. Also be wary of anyone who is overly friendly, Ryan says. "It may be authentic, but it also could be a troublemaker who doesn't have any friends for a reason." She suggests being quieter and more observant in the beginning. However, be unflinchingly polite to co-workers, including support staff—even if someone is less than polite to you. A few helpful "friends" can ease the transition and reduce the stress.

Take notes. The first few weeks in any new job can seem overwhelming. A job or training manual may provide "official" answers but lack the practical information you need to navigate the workplace. Keep a notebook on hand: There's no shame—and much to be gained—in taking notes and writing down tidbits of information. Similarly, keep mental notes about who has the power. The person with the most impressive job title does not necessarily wield the most influence around the office.

Show your stuff. Yes, you're new. And no, you don't want to ring the doorbell with a cannon that first day. But it's also likely that you've been hired to bring new energy and perspective to the workplace. So don't be afraid to introduce new ideas; don't refrain from transcending the business-as-usual mindset. Your goal should be to stand out as a "thought leader" among your new colleagues. Your creativity and your willingness to tackle tough assignments will not go unremarked—or unrewarded.

York–based Conference Board reported in 2007, and that was down from 61 percent in 1987.

Let's say you've changed careers and concluded it was a mistake. To begin mitigating the damage, consider revisiting the self-analysis exercises in chapter 5. It's far better to cut your losses early and recoup what you can from the experience. You may need to fine-tune your career ambitions. Rather than aspiring to become a museum curator, you might work as a docent for the time being, or sell art at an upscale gallery. Instead of targeting a position as an auditor at a major corporation, you might become a math teacher or start your own accounting practice.

If you can accept the view that career change is evolutionary—an ongoing process, not an isolated event—it will be easier to maintain your equilibrium and stay focused on your goals. Some measure of anxiety and self-doubt is normal, of course. The key is to keep the negative stuff to yourself—at least while you're at work and in the company of colleagues. If you need some positive reinforcement or additional support, talk to friends, a career counselor, or a therapist. And periodically remind yourself that the distinction between self-assuredness and a willingness to ask questions is a fine line—and that learning to walk it is a fine art. "Without a humble but reasonable confidence in your own powers," as that ultimate positive thinker Norman Vincent Peale once put it, "you cannot be successful or happy."

Getting Down to Business

If you're starting a home-based business or opening a shop, office, or franchise operation, get ready to devote a major chunk of time and energy to managing the start-up. For the first year or two, it's not unusual for fledgling business owners to dedicate 75 or more hours a week to transforming their brilliant idea into a viable, money-making operation.

During this start-up phase, you must be prepared to wear many hats— and balance them adroitly. If you're unwilling to make the commitment—

Exit Strategy: Walk, Do Not Run

A career switch may seem like a new beginning, yet it also represents an ending. If you're parting ways with an employer, you face the task of developing an exit strategy. It's not as simple as picking up your last paycheck, dropping your personal items in a shopping bag, speaking your mind, and heading off to greener pastures. Although you may feel tempted to bolt or let your true feelings be known about a certain boss or group of co-workers, it's best to follow etiquette (provide the required notice) and quell a barbed tongue. A few savory seconds of "payback bliss" is almost guaranteed to boomerang months or years later—and compromise a golden opportunity.

The reality is that you're very likely to encounter these people at some point in the future. And even if you don't cross their paths directly, you may find that lopping off certain once-thorny branches of your professional network can stunt your opportunities for future growth—whether that means finding other positions, gaining access to business leads, or landing a prized account. "It is much better to have former colleagues remember you for your many wonderful contributions," writes executive coach and organizational consultant Gail E. Aldrich, "than to recall that you left abruptly—and that they had to pick up the pieces." Another reason to cultivate your friends and adversaries: You may need a reference at some point in the future.

According to Aldrich, who previously worked as a chief membership officer at the Society for Human Resources Management (SHRM), any exit process has three distinct elements: the announcement, wrapping up, and leaving.

The announcement of your impending departure should come as no shock to your boss, says Alrdrich; instead, you want to keep her informed as you prepare to leave. When it's appropriate, submit a letter of resignation and, if you are met by anger at any point, stay calm and on track. Also, make sure that key people, such as an assistant or partner, find out before the entire office does.

Wrapping up involves developing a work plan so that colleagues can handle your outstanding assignments and you can pass the torch. It also means working with the human-resource department to process paperwork and, in some instances, find a suitable replacement.

Leaving covers saying goodbye and thanking people who provided mentoring or inspiration. If there's a last-day party, be gracious and smile. Utter positive sentiments only.

But burning no bridges does not mean neglecting what you're owed. If you have unclaimed pay, bonuses, or benefits, make sure you collect them. If, on the other hand, you're exiting a partnership or other business venture, you should have devised an exit strategy when you formalized the relationship or started the business. If so, it's now as simple as checking items off a list and taking care of business.

Aldrich likens the exit process to the final episode of *The Mary Tyler Moore Show*. "Mary picks up her few remaining personal items, walks to the door, turns and looks fondly around at the place she has spent so much of her career, shuts off the lights, and then very gently closes the door. It's a good, professional way to leave, and over the long term you will be very happy you made the effort to do it right."

or if you have competing heavy time demands, such as childcare or elder-care—the odds of business success diminish. Also keep in mind that your life partner, family members, and friends may find the adjustment even more disruptive than you. Discuss your new career with them: Try to surface the inevitable conflicts before they become land mines.

Home Is Where
the Office Is
No commute. No dress code. Best of all, no office politics! Sounds like nirvana, right? Perhaps—but let's call it "nirvana with an asterisk," for adapting to home-based work is hardly a heavenly experience. The home-office environment brings new challenges and

trade-offs. Not only do you require a comfortable space to work, you must cope with potential distractions, which can be legion. You may find it difficult to stay motivated. Depending on your situation and temperament, sensations of loneliness or isolation can become very real work hazards as well. And let's not forget the daily bane of telecommuters worldwide, distractibility: *Wouldn't I be able to focus much better on this project if I took a short break to clean the kitchen? Or to prune that hibiscus bush?*

Home-based business owners have devised a wide range of stratagems to combat such temptations. Some, for example, find that the only way to get started in the morning is to dress in business attire. One graphic designer reports that he must get in his car and drive around the block before he can settle into his home office. A financial planner says she tries to schedule client meetings over breakfast; if none exist, she goes out to breakfast on her own. "It's the only way," she concedes, "that I can make the break between home and the home office."

Practical issues, too, will rear their unsightly heads: Business-tax considerations. Liability-insurance issues. Licensing requirements. To become a legitimate marketplace contender, you may also have to create the illusion of near-universal access, which means answering your cell phone and checking e-mail at all hours of the day, night, and weekend.

Here are some additional battle-tested methods for getting the most out of your home office:

Make space. If you're setting up your first home office, it's easy to overlook the need for a defined work area. A common mistake is to settle for the living-room table, or to attempt pressing into service a hutch that you normally use to pay bills or handle correspondence. Cramped quarters can inhibit productivity and creativity. So it's vital to have your own desk—preferably one that is far removed from the main artery of everyday household activity. Not only will this reduce domestic distractions, it will create a space whose focus is work and nothing but. When you sit down there, you know what you're going to be doing. Additionally, make sure you have room for filing cabinets and the sort of customary office supplies you will need to do your job.

Set boundaries. One of the toughest aspects of working from home may be fending off the well-meaning family member, neighbor, or friend. It's all too common for a spouse, parent, child, or buddy to drop by for small talk. Regrettably, tolerating such chitchat allows others to control your time and productivity, threatening to sabotage your output.

Given these realities, it's vital to let others know that your work area and stipulated work hours are strictly off-limits—unless you choose to schedule a lunch or social hour in advance. In addition, make sure you impose structured working hours upon yourself—and honor them. Otherwise you're apt to wind up juggling laundry, cooking, and errands in the middle of your workday. So budget your time appropriately. (Burnout being the flip side of constant access, know when to turn *off* the mobile phone or PDA, too.) The bottom line: Treat your home office with just as much respect as you would a corporate cubicle. Don't make exceptions at home for conditions you wouldn't permit in a business office.

Think and act like a business. In the business world, image is everything. Although the Internet, personal computers, and laser printers can confer worldwide exposure on a small home-based business, it's up to you to look professional and competent. Nothing is a bigger turnoff for potential clients than encountering a voicemail greeting recorded over a background track by Led Zeppelin, or having to listen to your three-year-old granddaughter recite her ABCs before they can leave a message. Other "biz-kills" include poorly designed or cheap stationery, a slipshod website, inadequate or nonexistent tools (notably software applications), and outdated business licenses or permits. A dedicated phone line, a business checking account and credit card, and your own equipment and supplies will all make it easier to adopt—and maintain—a business mindset. Not coincidentally, they will also help you sidestep problems with authorities (the Internal Revenue Service among them).

Tales from the Far Side—
of Recareering For those still standing on the anticipatory side of career change, it can be highly instructive (and inspiring) to hear the stories of like-minded individuals who have confronted their insecurities to realize their dreams.

One such recareering veteran is Mark Noonan, who grew up in Butte, Montana. After graduating from Arizona's DeVry University in 1973 with a bachelor's degree in electronics, Noonan migrated north to the Silicon Valley. There he worked for such high-tech companies as Intel and Sequent Computer for three decades before resettling in Portland, Oregon. "I saw the world change from vacuum tubes to microchips," Noonan reflects. "I saw high-tech creep into almost every aspect of our lives. It was a wonderful career. I experienced some exciting and rewarding times."

Alas, Noonan's world turned upside down on April 3, 2004. On a three-week business trip to China, he was informed that his wife, Carrie, had fallen at home while working on their condo. She had gashed her head and bled to death. "It was a horribly unfortunate set of circumstances," Noonan recalls. "You wind up thinking: If only I had been there, I could have changed the outcome."

Noonan continued to work and travel for almost two years after Carrie's accident, but he found himself struggling to stay motivated. Amid the grief, he came to an important realization: "I had spent 30 years populating the world with computers, and I had spent a lot of time, in the end, laying people off and downsizing, sending careers offshore. I felt sad that I hadn't spent more time with my wife, and now I felt as though I was tearing apart other people's lives."

Noonan, 52 years old at the time, began a quest for work he could feel passionate about. He decided to exit the tech world and return to school to study gerontology. "When I looked into the field," Noonan recalled, "I realized it was very similar to my career path in high tech. As far as needs, requirements, and services for boomers are concerned, things were just starting to take off. There was a tremendous opportunity to do something meaningful."

While studying at Portland Community College, Noonan took on part-time work as a peer mentor at the school. He also landed a volunteer internship at Elders in Action, a Portland nonprofit that helps seniors secure healthcare and housing. After Noonan earned his associate of applied science degree in September 2007, Elders in Action offered him a paid position as a program specialist. "I jumped at the chance," Noonan explains, "because I knew it would bring me a great deal of personal satisfaction."

Today, instead of pulling down more than $150,000 a year, Mark Noonan earns less than $40,000. But instead of spending 60 hours a week in an office and on the road, shackled all the while to a PDA, he interacts with real people who have fundamental problems and needs. "When I am off work," he reflects, "I can visit family and friends. I can go to a film festival one day and brew beer the next.

"My wife's death made me realize that life is not all about work. It's important to find balance. I want to be a well-rounded person who is not totally driven by a paycheck."

Noonan's recareering voyage has not been without challenges. "It wasn't easy going back to school at age 52," he notes, "then making such a radical change. It also wasn't easy landing at the bottom of the totem pole: Instead of making tough decisions, I had to watch others make them. But not having to make those decisions, I realized, alleviated a great deal of pressure and stress.

"Changing careers entails risk—no question—and ultimately I had to confront a fear of the unknown. But I knew this was something I had to do. I wanted to feel energized again, and I wanted to know I was contributing something positive to society.

"When I go home every night, I now feel deeply satisfied. I love the direct interaction with people who are thankful for my assistance. They're looking for support, and I am able to help them do their problem-solving. At the end of the day, I know I am making a big difference."

"I Needed a Change"
She couldn't know it at the time, but Charlene Solomon began her job-change journey in second grade, when she wrote a play that was selected for her elementary school to perform. In high school she dreamed of earning an English degree and teaching Shakespeare to school-children. After a brief stint as a teacher's aide, however, Solomon realized she wasn't cut out for classroom work. So after graduating from UCLA in 1974, she landed a job as an editorial assistant at *Photographic* magazine.

Over the next three years, Solomon worked her way up to managing editor. Later she accepted a position as editor-in-chief of *The Rangefinder*, only to realize that "I was getting too far away from my writing." So Solomon began freelance writing, placing articles in publications as diverse as *Pool & Spa News* and *Parents* magazine. Then, in the early 1980s, when she and her husband, Alan, decided to have a child, Solomon saw that full-time freelancing might be her ticket to work-life balance.

For the next two decades, Solomon wrote for everything from *Working Mother* and *Black Enterprise* to *Los Angeles* and *Life*. During this period she also wrote four books—and earned six figures.

Though she seemed to be living a dream life, Solomon found herself increasingly restless. "I needed a change. I needed to be in an environment where there were more people. I was starting to burn out. The subjects were still interesting, but I didn't have the same kind of passion. And passion had always been a hallmark of my work."

When an opportunity arose to join a start-up company, Expat Spouse, Solomon decided to go for it. "I felt I had the skills and confidence to succeed. I did not want to become stagnant." So at age 52 Solomon joined the corporate world, working as an executive vice president and overseeing a staff of 15. Unfortunately, "I was shocked and unprepared. Seemingly minor problems had a major impact on my day." In response, Solomon hired a career coach and began exploring how she could adjust. Eventually, she grew more comfortable in the job and began to balance her expectations with the realities of managing people.

Then, one week after 9/11, the parent company of Expat Spouse, GMAC, pulled the plug. In January 2002, Solomon landed at another startup, RW3, likewise dedicated to global expatriate and cultural issues. She has worked there for six years and has grown increasingly comfortable in management. At the same time, she has come full circle and is now writing another book.

"The journey has been about building my self-confidence and discovering who I really am," Solomon remarks. "I wouldn't say that I ever set out to change careers or consciously go in any particular direction. It has always been about fulfilling my personal and professional needs and growing as a person. I couldn't be the person I am today without all the changes. I have followed my instincts and intuitions and it has turned out well."

Assembling the Jigsaw
No one can predict where a career journey will lead, or how it may change your life. Like Charlene Solomon or Mark Noonan, you may wind up exploring paths you could not have conceived in your 20s or 30s. But if the unexamined life is not worth living, then perhaps it also holds that the unexamined career is not worth considering.

Especially for those in midlife and beyond, changing careers can transform an existence. Actively sought out or not, a professional upheaval can reshape your world in myriad ways, taking you on a roller-coaster of self-discovery. Amid the chaos, one thing is clear: Pursuing our dreams can create a social impact whose outward ripples are both positive and profound. And, on a more personal level, it may deliver us to a place where reality finally dovetails with imagination.

Books

The Boomer Century, 1946-2046: How America's Most Influential Generation Changed Everything, by Richard Croker, Springboard Press, 2007.

Generation Ageless: How Baby Boomers Are Changing the Way We Live Today... And They're Just Getting Started, by J. Walker Smith and Ann Clurman, Collins, 2007. Offers a glimpse into the lives and thinking of today's boomers.

Passages: Predictable Crises of Adult Life, by Gail Sheehy. Ballantine Books, 2006. The classic work on the stages of life we pass through and how they affect our thinking and feelings, *Passages* remains relevant and useful for potential career changers today.

The Power Years: A User's Guide to the Rest of Your Life, by Ken Dychtwald and Daniel J. Kadlec, Wiley, 2006. Provides a step-by-step guide to empowerment and personal reinvention after 40.

Retire Retirement: Career Strategies for the Boomer Generation, by Tamara J. Erickson, Harvard Business School Press, 2008. Examines today's postretirement workplace and how to navigate it to maximum advantage.

To Be of Use: The Seven Seeds of Meaningful Work, by Dave Smith, New World Library, 2005. The founder of gardening and lifestyle company Smith and Hawken examines how it's possible to bring compassion and decency to the business world and the workplace.

More Resources

**AARP Foundation
Senior Community Service
Employment Program (SCSEP)**
www.aarp.org/money/careers/
findingajob/jobseekers/a2005-01-03-
job_training_placement.html

Helps job seekers 55 and older improve their skills, obtain training, and find a job.

AgeWave
www.agewave.com

Serves as a resource on aging and boomers, with news, research, and publications.

Aging Hipsters: The Baby Boomer Generation
www.aginghipsters.com

This popular website and blog features news, information, and commentary on boomers.

ACKNOWLEDGMENTS

WRITING A BOOK IS A CONVOLUTED ENDEAVOR, and this one could never have come to life without the aid, support, and critical-thinking skills of many people. First I'd like to express my sincere appreciation to Allan Fallow, Managing Editor of AARP Books, whose deft editing, open mind, and unfailing wit made the project so enjoyable. Smoothing rough edges and exorcising more than a few devilish words and expressions from the text, Allan saved me from myself on numerous occasions. It would be an understatement to say that his work dynamically improved the book.

The AARP Crash Course in Finding the Work You Love had its genesis in an article I wrote for the November & December 2006 edition of *AARP The Magazine*. For that my thanks go to the magazine's editor, Steve Slon, and to feature editor Ed Dwyer. Ed's "old-school" approach to journalism—in which he maintains a rigorous focus on crafting the best story possible—helped build a solid foundation for this book. Others at AARP who played a key role in getting the project off the ground include Publications Editor-in-Chief Hugh Delehanty and Senior Vice President Cathy Ventura-Merkel. George Blooston, Julie Preis, Deborah Russell, and Mike Schuster all lent a hand in vetting the text.

AARP's Creative Director, Carl Lehmann-Haupt, designed the cover and oversaw the page design, which was conceived and brought to fruition with flair by freelance designer Dorrit Green.

At Sterling Publishing, I am grateful to Editor-in-Chief Steve Magnuson and former CEO Charlie Nurnberg for their enthusiastic support of the concept throughout its development. Leigh Ann Ambrosi, Sue Levitt, Rebecca Maines, Elizabeth Mihaltse, Jason Prince, Sandra Ribicic, and Erin Stadnik played crucial parts in the book's design, production, and publicity.

A special thanks to all those individuals in the throes of changing careers who carved time out of hectic days to tell their work and life stories for the interviews and profiles that fill these pages. Without them this Crash Course would have crashed on takeoff.

A trio of other individuals helped transform this project into a viable entity.

My assistant, Scott Stephenson, tackled tough research, tracked down key sources, transcribed interviews, and provided insightful feedback on portions of the manuscript. Scott is a bright young man with a promising future as a writer. Assistants Ann O'Sullivan and Rachel Seigneur also transcribed numerous interviews, and both helped me stay on schedule.

On a more personal level, I'd like to thank all of my friends, family members, career-changers, and professional colleagues who provided input, ideas, and support along the way. Their numbers are too large to mention each one individually, but I would like to single out Charlene Solomon for her valuable perspective and suggestions. I am likewise indebted to my wife, Susanne, and to my children, Evan and Alec, for their forbearance as I went MIA in my home office for a seemingly endless string of nights and weekends.

Finally, and most important, special appreciation to my mother, Marcia Greengard. As the person who always made me feel I could achieve whatever I wanted in life, she remains my number one cheerleader.

ABOUT THE AUTHOR

SAMUEL GREENGARD has written professionally since 1981. He has authored hundreds of articles, including stories focusing on career and work issues, for *AARP The Magazine*, *American Way*, *Arrive*, *Business Finance*, *Family Circle*, *Hemispheres*, *Los Angeles*, *The Los Angeles Times*, MSNBC/MSN, *Wired*, and *Workforce Management*. A past president of the American Society of Journalists and Authors, Greengard currently serves as an instructor at UCLA's Writer's Program. He lives with his family in West Linn, Oregon.

INDEX